The Elizabethan Theatre IV

The Elizabethan Theatre IV

Papers given at the Fourth International
Conference on Elizabethan Theatre held at the
University of Waterloo, Ontario, in July 1972

Edited and with an introduction by
G. R. HIBBARD
Department of English,
University of Waterloo

Published in collaboration with the
University of Waterloo

Archon Books

© 1974 by the Macmillan Company of Canada Limited.

Published in Canada by the Macmillan Company of Canada Limited
and simultaneously published in the United States of America as an
Archon Book by The Shoe String Press, Inc., Hamden, Connecticut.
Printed in Canada.

Library of Congress Catalogue Card No. 73-92682

Library of Congress Cataloging in Publication Data

International Conference on Elizabethan Theatre, 4th,
University of Waterloo, 1972.
The Elizabethan theatre IV; papers.

Includes bibliographical references.
1. Jonson, Ben, 1573?-1637—Congresses. I. Hibbard,
George Richard, ed. II. Title.
PR2631.15 1972   822'.3   74-1313
ISBN 0-208-01417-9

Acknowledgments

An international conference, even when it is on a modest scale, as the Waterloo Conference of July 1972 was, involves the cooperative effort of many people. I owe a debt of gratitude not only to those actually named below but also to the numerous others, mainly in administrative or service positions at the University of Waterloo, who contributed in countless ways to the success of the Conference.

Without the generous financial aid given by the Canada Council and the University of Waterloo there would have been no conference. It was they who made it possible. The Vice-President, Academic, P. G. Cornell, and the Dean of Arts, J. F. New, provided unobtrusive but effective backing for the project; and J. Gold, the Chairman of the Department of English, could always be relied on for encouragement, shrewd advice and practical assistance. Simon Fraser University generously helped to meet the cost of a tape, most skilfully prepared by Gerald Newman and six actors from the CBC, and thus enabled members of the Conference to hear excerpts from *The Wasp*. An enthusiastic, cheerful and highly efficient team of graduate students – Mike Bridger, Mary Bales, Bill Davey, Mary Dwyer, Margaret Fraser, Saskia Tuyn and Pat Young – took care of the day-to-day running of affairs. A debt of a different kind is due to David Galloway, now Chairman of the Department of English at the University of New Brunswick. The first Waterloo International Conference on Elizabethan Theatre, held in 1968, was his brain-child; and he organized the two subsequent conferences in 1969 and 1970. Moreover, it was he who made the original arrangements with the Macmillan Company of Canada for the publication of the Conference papers.

The continued association of the Macmillan Company with the Conference is indeed something to be grateful for. The friendly, understanding personal interest that Pat Meany and Diane Mew, the Executive Editor, College Division, take in the proceedings of the Conference goes far beyond anything required by a business relationship. They have made this editor's task enjoyable as well as easy.

The two pages from the manuscript of *The Wasp* are reproduced by courtesy of the Malone Society and the Trustees of the Duke of Northumberland.

The index was compiled by David Cavanagh.

G. R. H.

Contents

Introduction – *G. R. Hibbard*   ix

The Humorous Jonson – *S. Schoenbaum*   1

Ben Jonson on his beloved, The Author
    Mr. William Shakespeare – *T. J. B. Spencer*   22

Hamlet and the Pangs of Love – *J. M. Nosworthy*   41

The Wasp: A Trial Flight – *J. W. Lever*   57

Your Majesty is Welcome to a Fair – *William Blissett*   80

Things as They Are and the World of Absolutes in
    Jonson's Plays and Masques – *Eugene M. Waith*   106

The Revenge on Charis – *S. P. Zitner*   127

Jonson's Large and Unique View of Life – *E. B. Partridge*   143

The Contributors   168

Index   170

Introduction

The three previous international conferences on Elizabethan Theatre, held at the University of Waterloo in 1968, 1969 and 1970, all tended to focus their attention, to a greater or lesser degree but with a truly remarkable tenacity, on the Elizabethan theatre in the strict sense of that term. Though they always included some papers dealing with plays as dramatic literature, their main and abiding preoccupation was with the physical structures in which, and on which, those plays were performed. New ideas put forward at one conference were developed, modified or controverted at the next. A tradition of continuing debate was coming into being in the only way that a tradition can, naturally and spontaneously. It is a good tradition, bearing out Bacon's contention that while knowledge "is in aphorisms and observations, it is in growth"; and there is every indication that it will be resumed when the fifth Conference takes place in 1973. But a conference on Elizabethan Theatre meeting in 1972 could not be oblivious of the fact that 1572 saw the birth of the greatest of Shakespeare's contemporaries in the art of writing for the stage. The time had clearly come to honour and celebrate the achievement of Ben Jonson.

The decision to make Jonson's work the central concern of the fourth Conference brought its own consequences with it. Jonson has indeed much to tell us, especially in his very explicit stage directions, about the way in which his plays were produced, and about the places where they were put on. No one who has once read it is ever likely to forget his scornful yet wholly convincing description of the Hope Theatre as it was in 1614: a place "as durty as *Smithfield*, and as stinking every whit."[1] But it was un-

[1] *Bartholomew Fair*, Ind., 159–60. Unless otherwise stated, the text used for all quotations from and references to Jonson's writings, both here and throughout this volume, is that of Herford and Simpson's *Ben Jonson*, 11 vols. (Oxford, 1925–1952). In accordance with modern practice i/j and u/v spellings have been normalized.

thinkable that the Conference should restrict its considerations to the staging of his plays. Jonson lives and still matters to us because he was a writer of genius and a great personality who stamped himself indelibly on the consciousness of his own time and profoundly affected the course that not only the drama but also literature in general was to take in England during the seventeenth century and later. The only way to do him anything like justice – in so far as that could ever be possible in a mere four days – was, therefore, to attempt some assessment, however limited and random it might prove, of his entire *œuvre*. This aim, in turn, made it necessary to move beyond the theatre to the court where the masques were staged and, eventually, leaving dramatic representations behind altogether, to take some account of that rich body of non-dramatic poetry which, quite apart from its own intrinsic worth, is such an invaluable and indispensable commentary on and complement to the plays.

Of the eight papers given at the Conference, six were devoted to Jonson. Their publication now – not, be it noted, in the precise order in which they were read – seems to invite some comment on the direction that the revival of interest in him and in his writings is taking at the present time. That revival began, of course, with T. S. Eliot's essay on him, first published in 1919 and prompted by the appearance of G. Gregory Smith's volume on Jonson in the English Men of Letters Series. Looking back, Eliot remarked, with every justification, that no critic since Dryden had "succeeded in making [Jonson] appear pleasurable or even interesting"; and then, after paying tribute to the useful factual information that Gregory Smith's book contained, he went on to say of it: "it only fails to remodel the image of Jonson which is settled in our minds."[2] Eliot was asking for a great deal – more, perhaps, than he was entitled to ask for. The remodelling he desiderated is the unmistakable sign of an author's continued vitality. Every age since Shakespeare's has remade him in its own image. Indeed, as T. J. B. Spencer points out in the paper printed below, Jonson himself was already busy fabricating a decidedly Jonsonian Shakespeare as early as 1623. The fact that nothing of this kind had happened to Jonson since the publication of William Gifford's edition of his *Works* in 1816 meant simply that

[2]T. S. Eliot, *Selected Essays* (London, 1932), p. 147.

Jonson had failed to speak to the nineteenth and early twentieth centuries. Most remarkably, he had failed to speak to Matthew Arnold. On the face of it, Jonson as classicist, moralist, critic and poet would seem to be, of all English writers, the one with whom Arnold should have felt the closest affinity. In fact, however, Arnold scarcely mentions him. His verse did not and could not satisfy the expectations of ears attuned to the music of romantic poetry, nor was it amenable to the "touchstone" test.

Eliot ultimately succeeded in doing what Gregory Smith had never sought to do rather than failed to do, because he was in tune with the changing temper of the times. He had every reason to be, for both in his critical writings and in his poetry he was actively engaged in promoting a fresh attitude towards the literature of the past and consciously attempting to create a new kind of sensibility. But he did not succeed immediately or single-handedly. When Jonson finally did re-surface as a living force in the thirties, like some miraculous whale that had spent centuries in the depths of neglect and indifference, the image we had of him was by no means that which Eliot's essay suggests. It owed something to the essay, but it owed as much, if not more, to a work of a very different kind, R. H. Tawney's *Religion and the Rise of Capitalism* (1926). Eliot and Tawney seem improbable bedfellows; yet it was Eliot's concern for verbal texture, coupled with Tawney's interest in the social changes of the sixteenth and seventeenth centuries, that lay behind L. C. Knights's *Drama and Society in the Age of Jonson* (1937). Here at last was an image of the playwright to which those of us who were then in our formative years could indeed respond, for what Knights had done was to set Jonson firmly in our England by relating his work closely to the world out of which it came. The voice we heard speaking to us from the Jacobean Age was that of a great artist using his command of the resources of the English language to protest, in the name of a traditional morality, against the in-humanities of the acquisitive society that was just coming into existence at the time when he was writing. Living, as we were doing, in a time of depression and conflict when the capitalist system seemed to be staggering to a disastrous end, we hailed Jonson as the poet-moralist who had diagnosed the ills of our society when it was still in its infancy. Moreover, in a world where so many of the younger poets wrote out of the conviction that poetry could only justify itself if it helped to change society, Jonson had all the appearance of an ally.

In the pages that follow, that image of Jonson, so dominant in the late thirties and forties, is not to be found, though it still continues to affect our thinking about him and our reactions to what he wrote. It has received the tribute that later times so often pay to pioneering studies: the enduring elements in it have been so thoroughly absorbed into the critical consciousness of the age that they are now largely taken for granted. Over the last twenty years or so students of Jonson have seen their main task as one of rediscovery and consolidation. The emphasis has been very decidedly on his art, which we are now beginning to understand and to appreciate, as we never did before, as a result of the work (to mention only two) of E. B. Partridge in *The Broken Compass* (1958) and Jonas A. Barish in *Ben Jonson and the Language of Prose Comedy* (1960). These critics, and others like them, have been engaged in giving depth, shadowing and solidity to that image of the poet-playwright which Eliot sketched so incisively more than fifty years ago. Seen in retrospect, his essay now appears to be quite as much a program of work to be done as an evaluation of its subject's peculiar qualities and achievements.

Eliot placed Jonson's poetry as poetry "of the surface," and then went on to say:

> Poetry of the surface cannot be understood without study; for to deal with the surface of life, as Jonson dealt with it, is to deal so deliberately that we too must be deliberate, in order to understand.[3]

The kind of study Eliot had in mind is well exemplified by two of the papers that follow. T. J. B. Spencer asks us to reconsider the significance of those familiar lines on Shakespeare prefixed to the First Folio, which seem so pellucid in expression and so warm in admiration that many of us have long taken them at their face value as a heart-felt eulogy. Deploying a Jonsonian knowledge of the Ancients with a lighter touch than Jonson generally used, Spencer leaves us with the conviction that the lines are more conventional than we had thought, and with the suspicion, to put it no higher, that they may well be less

3*Ibid.*, p. 148.

laudatory than we had taken them to be. S. P. Zitner examines an even shorter poem – "Her Triumph" in the Charis sequence – addressing himself to the problem of how and in what sense this celebration of female beauty can be the revenge on the lady that Jonson, in the previous poem in the sequence, promised that it would be. His solution to the puzzle is arrived at primarily through a close reading of the text, but it also owes much to his consideration of the context in which two stanzas from the poem appear in *The Devil is an Ass*.

At this point yet another of the demands Eliot makes on the student of Jonson is being met: "intelligent saturation in his work as a whole"; and in that whole Eliot recognized the masques, so badly neglected at the time when he was writing, as "an important part."[4] They are neglected no longer. Eugene M. Waith puts forward a fascinating hypothesis, both about what Jonson was trying to do in *The Devil is an Ass* and in *The Staple of News*, and about why he did not altogether succeed in the attempt, by making an illuminating connection between the two plays and two of the masques, *The Vision of Delight* and *Time Vindicated*. All four works are, he thinks, concerned with the relationship between the actual and the ideal. But, he goes on to suggest, the conventions and the machinery of the masque lent themselves more readily to the working out of this theme in satisfactory dramatic terms than did the conventions and acting conditions of the public theatre. William Blissett, too, resorts to the masques in his consideration of certain aspects of *Bartholomew Fair*. Taking up the problem of how Jonson managed to make this play of low life, with its comic exposure and dismissal of "the wise magistrate," acceptable to King James and his court, he goes for assistance to *Love Restored* and *The Gypsies Metamorphosed*, a procedure which leads him to the conclusion that at the court performance the entire play could well have been seen as a gigantic antimasque to which the audience of King and courtiers served, by their mere presence, as the masque proper.

In the course of his paper Waith pays particular attention to the way in which the plays he deals with were staged; so does Blissett. Jonson the man of the theatre, the showman ready to exploit every trick of the trade, is very much a part of the com-

4*Ibid.*, pp. 148 and 160.

plex image of the artist that is now being built up. But the percipient Eliot was also alive to this side of Jonson's genius, stressing "the theatrical qualities" of his dramatic *œuvre* and describing it as "a titanic show."[5] Furthermore, he was in no doubt that the plays, properly performed, were capable of giving enjoyment in abundant measure. It is precisely this quality in them that Samuel Schoenbaum brings out and delights in, aerating learning with a Rabelaisian gusto in his presentation of Jonson the entertainer who, much as he may have slighted laughter in his critical pronouncements, certainly knew how to incite it in a theatre audience.

Informing all the papers discussed so far there is a sense of the essential unity that exists within the apparent diversity of Jonson's massive output. Whence does this unity arise? E. B. Partridge provides as good an answer to this difficult yet necessary question as we are ever likely to get. Ranging with consummate ease over Jonson's life as well as his writings, he notices, as many have noticed before him, that in some rather special way there is an intimate and inextricable connection between what Jonson wrote and what Jonson did and was. Then, singling out Jonson's "faith in things," his deep respect for the facts both of history and of nature, as his most marked characteristic, he shows how Jonson, nevertheless, imposes his own personality on these facts. He was able to do this, Partridge thinks, because he had deliberately chosen to take up a dramatic and heroic attitude to life, to cast himself in the role of "the first great professional man of letters England had produced," with the result that the greatest of all his creations was himself. Perhaps we have here an explanation of why Jonson and Shakespeare impress themselves on us as polar opposites. If Shakespeare's capacity to keep his own personality out of the experience he is exploring and defining is best described in Keats's famous phrase as "negative capability," then we need some such term as "positive capability" to describe Jonson's characteristic mode of vision and manner of going to work.

So all is well with Jonson at last; he is receiving, however belatedly, the interest, the understanding and the recognition that he so amply deserves. But is he? Schoenbaum returns an

[5]*Ibid.*, p. 160.

emphatic no. It is not enough for a great dramatist to be appreciated in the study. His plays cry out for production; but, with a few notable exceptions, our theatres remain deaf to that cry.

The two remaining papers are not about Jonson. They illustrate, in diametrically opposed ways, how much we still have to learn about Elizabethan drama. J. M. Nosworthy bravely takes another look at *Hamlet*, the most written about of all plays, and, by fixing his attention on the Hamlet-Ophelia relationship and viewing it as a whole, succeeds in saying something fresh and worthwhile about the play as a whole. J. W. Lever, as he himself remarked, found himself in the happy position of being reasonably secure in the belief that he knew more about his topic than anyone in his audience. Having just completed an edition of the manuscript play *The Wasp* for the Malone Society, he had every reason to be, though the discussion that followed the paper revealed that one member of that audience had, in fact, read the play and read it with considerable care. Lever's full, scholarly and consistently entertaining introduction to this play and of this play left the Conference eagerly looking forward to the appearance of his edition in print. This was a preview that whetted the appetite.

G. R. Hibbard
Department of English
University of Waterloo

The Humorous Jonson

S. SCHOENBAUM

I hope my gracious hosts, who have invited me back for a return engagement at this select conference in pleasant Waterloo, won't account me ungrateful or, worse, discourteous, if I preface my remarks with a few frank comments on anniversary rites for the renowned dead. I expect I am not alone in being of two minds about such occasions. We all know what an orgy of celebration – a weariness to the Gordon Ross Smiths of this world – 1964 produced. Such rifling of bottom desk-drawers! Such laborious efforts to restate for the occasion what one had already said, more freshly, without artificial pressure. Suddenly, for a year, Shakespearian scholarship became, as it were, one massive *Festschrift*. "Much of the book is fluffed out with the author's comments on all the individual plays," remarked the *Times Literary Supplement* reviewer of an anniversary biography. "He has to say something, but he has nothing to say." Now, it seems, in 1972 we are confronted with the same phenomenon on a smaller scale. But fortunately there is another side to the picture; I am not thinking merely of the small rewards of conferences – the renewals of friendships, the chance to meet colleagues for the first time, the transitory pleasures of a booze-up. The commemorative urge, of which literary biography is an eloquent expression, is not ignoble. If, after 1964, Jonson were to be ignored this year, we would deservedly feel some shame. More significant for criticism, a conference such as this allows for a certain stock-taking. We can pause to examine ideas and attitudes that have a general interest rather than confining ourselves exclusively to the specialized contributions which are the usual staple of learned gatherings.

At least that is how I have interpreted my commission today. There are dangers, however, which I cannot claim to have successfully avoided. I am afraid that my theme, when in my circuitous fashion I have finally got round to it, will impress you as having an obviousness which is positively blinding. Moreover, some of you may feel that, in addition to being simplistic and platitudinous, I have taken an anti-intellectual position, or at least one that is unappreciative of the accomplishments of academic investigation. That I would regret, for such is not my intention. About my obviousness I am unrepentant.

I

After these preliminaries let us turn to goose-turds in Jonson. In Act IV, Scene iv of *The Alchemist*, Dame Pliant is hustled before Subtle by her brother the angry boy, and Face. Together they urge upon her the desirability of being a Spanish Countess. "Why? is that better than an *English Countesse?*", the pliant heiress asks, and they explain why it is, by enumerating all the advantages that will be hers: pages, ushers, footmen, coaches. "Yes," interjects Face,

> and have
> The citizens gape at her, and praise her tyres!
> And my-lords goose-turd bands, that rides with her! (IV.iv.48–50)

Goose-turd bands. "Yellowish green" is Herford and Simpson's gloss for *goose-turd*. A more recent commentator, F. H. Mares, in his text for the Revels Plays, is not satisfied:

> goose-turd bands] collars in the fashionable colour of goose-turd green, usually described as a yellowish green. However, to my observation, goose turds are a very dark green.[1]

This interesting intelligence has inspired a poem. By Jeannie Robison, and entitled "On Editing Jonson," the verses (somewhat defectious in the rhyme) go like this:

> What stares you must have caused
> When armed with spectrum and glass,

[1]*The Alchemist*, ed. F. H. Mares (Revels Plays; London, 1967), p. 145n.

You searched the English countryside
For what the geese had passed.

Perhaps you only shoe'd the pile,
Convinced of its darker green.
Or bending down, gently turned
And checked the side unseen.

For judgments must be closely wrought;
Knowledge's end is truth.
And even Jonson must be taught:
Give turds their proper hue.[2]

Much ado about goose-turds. No dramatist in English, surely
(always excepting Shakespeare), comes to us labouring under so
heavy a freight of learned exegesis. Such a burden must have
interesting consequences for criticism.

I am afraid I cannot resist one or two more examples from
commentaries on *The Alchemist*. In Act II, Scene ii, Sir Epicure
Mammon luxuriates in a vision of voluptuous rewards that make,
for him, actual possession of the Philosophers' Stone almost
superfluous. "My mere fooles," he foresees,

Eloquent burgesses, and then my poets,
The same that writ so subtly of the *fart*. (II.ii.61–63)

For which the obliging Mares furnishes this annotation:

the fart] In *Musarum Deliciae or The Muses Recreation* (1656)
are several poems on this subject. One – "The Fart Censured in
the Parliament House" – refers to an event of 1607, was written
before 1610, and is to be found in the Harleian MS. 5191, f.17, so
that it cannot be original to Sir John Mennis and James Smith, who
put out the 1656 volume. That this poem is referred to seems more
probable if we take *burgesses* (62) in its old sense of members of
parliament, since it contains "about forty stanzas of the most
wretched doggerel, conveying the opinion of as many members of
parliament, on the subject" (G[ifford]).[3]

[2]Jeannie Robison, "On Editing Jonson," *Satire Newsletter*, IX (1971), 75.
I am obliged to my colleague, Professor Alan Dessen, for bringing this poem
to my notice.
[3]*Alchemist*, ed. Mares, p. 55. Herford and Simpson gloss "I fart at thee"
(I.i.1) "like the Latin *oppedo* and the Greek καταπέρδω" (*Ben Jonson*, ed.
C. H. Herford and Percy and Evelyn Simpson, 11 vols. [Oxford, 1925–
1952]), X, 54.

What other English dramatist can have inspired learned dissertations on so unprepossessing a subject?

But my favourite is the note on *chiaus* in the magisterial Clarendon edition. "What doe you thinke of me," protests Dapper, "That I am a *Chiause?*" "What's that?", asks Face, to which Herford and Simpson obligingly reply:

> *Chiause.* The word is an imperfect adaptation of the Turkish *chāush*, "messenger," "herald." On 13 October 1611 the King gave £30 to "Two Chiaus or Messengers from yᵉ Turke" (Exchequer accounts, E 403/2731, f.9). W. R. Chetwood, whom Gifford took over without acknowledgement, first traced its English origin in *Memoirs of the Life and Times of Ben. Jonson, Esq.*, 1756, p.15n., but he blundered over the facts and the date. The true story was given for the first time in Sir William Foster's edition of *The Travels of John Sanderson*, a Levantine merchant, published by the Hakluyt Society in 1930, pages xxiii–xxxv.
>
> A Turk named Mustafa reached England towards the end of July 1607, announcing that he was an ambassador from the Sultan, though he took no higher title than that of *Chāush*. He had left Constantinople in 1605 as a courier in attendance on the French ambassador, but he had procured from the Sultan letters to the kings of France and England. The secretary of the Levant Company warned the authorities about him. But he had been received by the French king, and they were nervous about offending the Sultan. The Levant merchants had to entertain him at a cost of £5 a day, and paid all his expenses; he made them even find the thread to mend his clothes. In September 1607 he was received at Windsor, and presented a letter complaining of the depredations in the Mediterranean of pirates sailing under English colours. He departed in November 1607.
>
> He added a new word to the English language, "to chouse," to cheat, because of the way he had fooled the Levant merchants. Chetwood's form of the story that Sir Robert Sherley had sent Mustafa as his agent from the Grand Signior and that he had decamped after having "chiaused" the Turkish and Persian merchants of £4,000 is untrue.[4]

From its exposition learned to put-down supercilious, with side-thrust dismissive along the way, I know of no more masterly

[4]*Ben Jonson*, ed. Herford and Simpson, X, 61.

exemplar of the one-upmanship of footnoting. It is to be recommended to all thesis writers.

Erudite exegesis is one manifestation, and an important one,
of the academic way with Jonson. There are many others. We
study his sources, his verse imagery and prose style, his classical
ideal of form and how he succeeds in living up to it or fails to
live up to it. We are at pains to place him in his proper historical
context as creator of comical satire after Archbishop Whitgift's
prohibition of verse-satire, as purveyor of masques to the Stuart
court, and as burly literary dictator at the Mermaid Tavern. We
use him as a whipping-boy to demonstrate the incalculable
superiority of Shakespeare. My aim today is not to belittle the
fruits of scholarly inquiry into Jonson, although for the last sort
I have little patience. More often than not, Jonson commands the
full deployment of the critical intelligence. One may say of him
what his namesake said of the race of metaphysical poets: to
write on Jonson, it is at least necessary to read and think. Anybody can write on Shakespeare, and everybody does.

The vice of erudition is pedantry, and it is by their pedantries
that Jonson's commentators make themselves fair game for the
wits. Now the pedantry that lurks in the footnotes may be
symptomatic of the more dangerous vice of over-solemnity, which
will surface in the critical introductions and have a baleful effect
on readers, and perhaps ultimately on producers. Yet if Jonson
is, as I believe, a great dramatist, he is great as a comic master.
His triumph resides not primarily in his comical satires, or in the
two Roman tragedies that were jeered off his own stage, or in
the masques whose temporal glories we cannot recreate without
his scenes and machines; not in these, but in the astonishing series
of comedies to which *Every Man in His Humour* is dazzling
prologue. And central to these plays is laughter: rude, boisterous
laughter, more often derisive than genial, but laughter nonetheless. Jonson can be a very funny writer; that is my simple theme
today. This truism has not had the critical attention it deserves.
In a book promisingly entitled *Jonson and the Comic Truth*, John
J. Enck has a chapter which he calls "The Streame of Humour."
But Enck's stream flows through a narrow and well-worn chan-
nel; he has in mind our old and tiresome friends the humours.
Humour (in the unclinical sense of the term) he would banish
to the suburbs of comedy; "one has no choice," Enck informs us

S. Schoenbaum

in his concluding summation, "but to relegate laughter itself to a
marginal position."[5] I submit that too many of us, as critics and
pedagogues, have submitted to this unnecessary necessity and
relegated laughter to a marginal position in pursuing the humours at the expense of the humour. The former, so long as I
can remember, have made matter for the set questions we put to
our students; we have less frequently asked them to explore
Jonson's comic mode.

The study of Jonson should warn us away from overstressing
a point, lest we become, like one of his *dramatis personae*, the
victims of an *idée fixe*. Our ablest critics, the majority of them
anyway, have not sat frozen-faced in the presence of the great
comedies. It is a matter of emphasis, of priorities.[6]

Still I do feel that it is appropriate – even incumbent upon us –
to celebrate Jonson's humour these days when (it seems) criticism has lost all its mirth. In Jonson studies, solemnity takes
varied forms. We do not run the risk of underestimating the
importance of the didactic elements in his art; indeed, we have
a whole treatise on the subject. When the dean of American
literary critics, the late Edmund Wilson, applied his formidable
powers to Jonson, the dramatist emerged as an anal-erotic. This
proctoscopic critique is not one of Wilson's happier efforts. In
Volpone, Mares remarks, "Virtue survives (as in *King Lear*) only
because vice destroys itself. . . ." That vice destroys itself is an
old story, at least as old as the Book of Proverbs, and has
provided a *peripeteia* for innumerable comedies and tragedies.
It should be possible to discuss this phenomenon in *Volpone*
without hauling in *Lear* and thus invoking shades of apocalypse.
Vice and virtue mean different things in different contexts; Volpone is no Edmund, and Celia no Cordelia.

[5]John J. Enck, *Jonson and the Comic Truth* (Madison, Wis., 1957), p. 232.
[6]Rufus Putney in his essay "Jonson's Poetic Comedy," *Poetry Quarterly*,
XLI (1962), 188–204 (brought to my attention by Professor Brian W.
Parker after this paper was written) is fervent in his appreciation of
Volpone and *The Alchemist*, plays which he sees as having "power to charm
us into a state of comic ecstasy." Such enthusiasm is always welcome, but
I am afraid that in *Volpone* Putney sees the comic spirit as disporting itself
more merrily than I can accept. I have also since seen two recent articles by
William Empson on *Volpone and The Alchemist* in *The Hudson Review*
(XXI [1968–9], 651–66; XXII [1969–70], 595–608). These vigorously argued
essays, while protesting against "the pietistic strain in Eng. Lit.," give Jonson
his due as a comic dramatist.

The malaise of criticism has extended to production. Two recent instances. I expect that some in this audience were here in Waterloo in 1969 for the Second Elizabethan Theatre Conference, when the Stratford Festival season included a production of *The Alchemist*. It was reckoned successful enough to go on tour – this play can withstand punishment – and, although there was much bustle and noise, this viewer at least discerned little evidence of directorial conviction that the play was really uproarious. The miscasting of Sir Epicure Mammon was symptomatic. It was rather as though, in an accident of repertory, the actor playing Cassius in *Julius Caesar* mistook Tuesday for Thursday, and wandered into the alchemist's premises. The Stratford Sir Epicure had a lean and hungry look, and we could not for a moment believe that this sensualist – described by his creator as "the fat knight" – would dream of having his bed blown up, not stuffed, down being too hard. The only comic inspiration I recall in the production was the cunning doctor's marvellous machine which, with its pulsations and gyrations, did credit to the memory of Rube Goldberg. This contraption was periodically wheeled out, to the general delight of the spectators, although in Jonson's text it is of course kept off-stage throughout. The most recent production I have seen of Jonson was the National Theatre's *Bartholomew Fair* a few seasons back at the Aldwych in London. The hues – and I am thinking literally of costumes, sets, etcetera – were sombre, and the production as a whole seemed to belong to the Brechtian twilight that for so long kept possession of the British stage, and was at last (none too soon) departing. A reviewer in one posh Sunday paper labelled his notice "Bartholomew Foul." This was an exaggeration – the pig woman is indomitable and the puppet play survives directorial perversity – but I can understand his reaction.

The current state of criticism and performance is one reason for my concern with the humorous Jonson. There is a second. We do well to emphasize Jonson's laughter, which is a manifestation of the popular in his art, because his reputation, at least outside the academy, is precarious, and has been for some time. He has a capacity unique among the classic English writers of arousing the displeasure, sometimes pungently expressed, of his more articulate readers.

As we all know, the Romantic revival of interest in the Eliza-

S. Schoenbaum

bethans, a revival sparked by Lamb's *Specimens* in 1808, brought
back into favour playwrights previously in eclipse. Dekker,
Heywood and Webster benefitted handsomely, I expect in part
because their art is in some respects "Shakespearian." Jonson
fared less well. Lamb included eight specimens from (among
other titles) *The Case Is Altered, Sejanus, The Poetaster,* and
The New Inn: "serious extracts," in Lamb's own phrase, in which
the humorous Jonson is little evident. These the anthologist
followed, for variety, with Sir Epicure Mammon's spectacular
opening dialogue with Surly. Here is exhibited, according to
Lamb, Jonson's "talent for comic humour," but the reader's appreciation of this winning trait is doubtfully enhanced by Lamb's
postscript; for he sees Sir Epicure as "the most determined off-
spring of the author." Mammon's "lying overbearing character"
is "just such a swaggerer as contemporaries have described old
Ben to be."[7] For Lamb's contemporary, Coleridge, Jonson has
become a specimen of another sort: a palaeontological exhibit in
a museum of critical curiosities:

> He [Jonson] could not but be a Species of himself: tho' like the
> Mammoth and Megatherion fitted & destined to live only during a
> given Period, and then to exist a Skeleton, hard, dry, uncouth
> perhaps, yet massive and not to be contemplated without that
> mixture of Wonder and Admiration, or more accurately, that middle
> somewhat between both for which we want a term – not quite even
> with the latter, but far above the mere former.

To Hazlitt this playwright was an acquired taste, like that for
olives, and one which, despite effort, he failed to acquire;
Jonson's power remained for him "of a repulsive and unamiable
kind." To Swinburne he was "as a rule, – a rule which is proved
by the exception . . . one of the singers who could not sing."[8]
So it goes.

[7]Charles Lamb, *Specimens of English Dramatic Poets,* ed. William Mac-
donald (London, 1903), I, 161.
[8]*Coleridge on the Seventeenth Century,* ed. R. F. Brinkley (New York,
1968; reprint of 1955 ed.), pp. 647–48; *The Complete Works of William
Hazlitt,* ed. D. P. Howe (London and Toronto, 1930–34), VI, 39; Algernon
Charles Swinburne, *A Study of Ben Jonson* (Lincoln, Neb., 1969; reprint
of 1889 New York ed.), p. 5. These passages have been conveniently
brought to my notice by Ian Donaldson ("Ben Jonson," *Sphere History of
Literature in the English Language,* vol. 3: *English Drama to 1710,* ed.
Christopher Ricks [London, 1971], pp. 280–81).

This critical heritage was memorably summed up in the next century by T. S. Eliot. "The reputation of Jonson," Eliot begins his essay on the dramatist, "has been of the most deadly kind that can be compelled upon the memory of a great poet. To be universally accepted; to be damned by the praise that quenches all desire to read the book; to be afflicted by the imputation of the virtues which excite the least pleasure; and to be read only by historians and antiquaries – this is the most perfect conspiracy of approval."[9] (The approval, we have seen, is more qualified than Eliot suggests, and it is significant that throughout his essay he refers to Jonson as a writer to be read, not a dramatist to be played.) Twenty years after Eliot wrote, things hadn't changed very much, if we may judge from Harry Levin's introduction to a volume of Jonson's *Selected Writings*: "Ben Jonson's position, three hundred years after his death is more than secure; it might almost be called impregnable. He is still the greatest unread English author. . . . Jonson has always had more attention from antiquarians than from critics, and has too often served as a cadaver over which to read a lecture on the lore of language and custom."[10]

Since 1938, when Levin's edition appeared, the cadaver has evidenced some twitchings of life. In 1952, more than twenty-five years after the appearance of the first volume, the Clarendon edition reached its majestic conclusion; a monument, if not of the new bibliography, then of an older and still valued tradition of humanistic learning. There has been a spate of important books since, among them (to name just a few from which this reader has especially profited) Edward Partridge's *Broken Compass* and Jonas Barish's *Ben Jonson and the Language of Prose Comedy*, more recently Stephen Orgel's *The Jonsonian Masque*, and very lately Alan Dessen's *Jonson's Moral Comedy*, tracing the dramatist's native roots in the early Tudor hybrid moralities. Yale University Press has given us excellently edited texts of individual plays for students. What year does not bring a new edition of *Volpone*? This is no doubt progress, much of it a re-

[9]T. S. Eliot, "Ben Jonson," *Selected Essays 1917–1932* (New York, 1932), p. 127. The essay was first published in 1919.
[10]Jonson, *Selected Works*, ed. Harry Levin (New York, 1938), p. 1. Note that Jonson is referred to here again as a writer for the study rather than for the theatre.

S. Schoenbaum

valuation stimulated by the completion of Herford and Simpson.
Yet I cannot help feeling that the Jonson industry is on the whole
a specialized one, academicians talking to one another; not a
movement that has made any very deep impression on the common understanding. Just a couple of months back the *Times
Literary Supplement* commended as excellent a new edition of
Every Man in His Humour, but described the play itself as
"patently unreadable" (not, please note, patently unactable; performance has not even crossed the mind of this reviewer). In his
recent excellent chapter on Jonson for the Sphere History of
Literature in the English Language, Ian Donaldson is a trifle
stingy in limiting to a handful the excellent studies of the past
half-century, but I am not inclined to question his conclusion
that Eliot's judgment still holds. "For the common reader and
playgoer," Donaldson says, "Jonson still seems to stand as the
most daunting and formidable of English classics, an author one
would gladlier walk round about to avoid than walk in company
with."[11]

II

Perhaps we should not too readily assume that such ought not to
be the case. He became his admirers, Auden says of the dead
Yeats in his great poem. So all writers become their admirers,
and Jonson's reputation may well reflect what he is. Did he ever
actually court the universal audience that Shakespeare has always enjoyed? Does surly Ben really want us to laugh?

It is certainly true that in his criticism Jonson powerfully
espouses the corrective role of comedy as reformer of men and
manners; the comedian no less than the tragedian is, he insists, a
teacher. And, as for laughter, in his *Discoveries* he goes so far
as to declare:

> Nor, is the moving of laughter alwaies the end of *Comedy*, that is
> rather a fowling for the peoples delight, or their fooling. For, as
> *Aristotle* saies rightly, the moving of laughter is a fault in Comedie,
> a kind of turpitude, that depraves some part of a mans nature
> without a disease. (11. 2629–33)

---

[11]Donaldson, "Ben Jonson," p. 280. In his summing up, Donaldson concludes that Jonson deserves remembering as "one of the two great poets of
the English theatre," an estimate with which I am not inclined to take
issue.

This is harsh doctrine, but not without its escape clause (the word *always*); and if laughter depraves, one can only say that it is a form of turpitude to which Jonson in his less austere moments succumbs. So, too, it is well to note that if he plumps strongly for the didactic function of art, he does not ignore the other pillar of the Horatian dictum. His true scope, as he says in his Prologue to *Volpone*,

> if you would know it,
> In all his *poemes*, stil, hath been this measure,
> To mixe profit, with your pleasure. (11. 6–8)

An artist wears more than one mask. To Alfred Harbage, whose *Shakespeare and the Rival Traditions* is, for our period, the most influential work of criticism embodying the moral ideal of democracy, Jonson is the presiding genius of coterie drama. Again and again this dramatist heaps scorn upon that beast, the multitude. "*Expectation* of the *Vulgar* is more drawne, and held with newnesse, then goodnesse," he grumbles in the *Discoveries*;

> wee see it in *Fencers*, in *Players*, in *Poets*, in *Preachers*, in all, where *Fame* promiseth any thing; so it be new, though never so naught, and depraved, they run to it, and are taken. Which shewes, that the only decay, or hurt of the best mens *reputation* with the people, is, their wits have out-liv'd the peoples palats. They have beene too much, or too long a feast. (11. 405–12)

The recurring metaphor of feasting appears also in Macilente's revised conclusion to *Every Man Out*, where Jonson addresses himself to those who can judge:

> The Cates that you have tasted were not season'd
> For every vulgar Pallat, but prepar'd
> To banket pure and apprehensive ears:
> Let then their Voices speake for our desert. (11. 10–13)

He contemns (in the Prologue to *Poetaster*) "base detractors, and illiterate apes." "If it were put to the question of theirs, and mine," he muses in his preface to *The Alchemist*, "the worse would finde more suffrages; because the most favour common errors." Looking about his audience, Jonson casts a disdainful eye on the civet-wits in their new suits, knowing no more than the price of satin and velvet; the mustachioed lisping gallant swearing down all who sit about him; the bottle-headed spectator with a cork brain who squeezes out a pitiful-learned face and is silent. And finally, after the failure of *The New Inn*, we have the bitter "Ode to Himself," in which Jonson heaps abuse on the loathed stage – "They were not made for thee, lesse, thou for them" – and sees himself literally as casting pearls before swine.

In better days he could address the select audiences of the private theatres more amiably. So, in the Prologue to *Cynthia's Revels*, acted by the Children of the Chapel, he is positively flattering:

> If gracious silence, sweet attention,
> Quicke sight, and quicker apprehension,
> (The lights of judgement's throne) shine any where;
> Our doubtfull authour hopes this is their sphere. (11. 1–4)

Whatever Jonson's elitist tendencies, however, it is a fact (as Harbage is well aware) that he wrote almost as much for the popular as for the select playhouses. He furnished Shakespeare's company, the Chamberlain's Men, with *Every Man In* and *Every Man Out*, and then gave *Cynthia's Revels* and *Poetaster* to the Chapel Children. But in June 1602 Henslowe (who had previously paid him for additions to the quintessentially popular *Spanish Tragedy*), was lending Jonson money for a book called *Richard Crookbacke* to be acted by the Admiral's Men, who catered for the masses. With *Sejanus* he was back with Shakespeare's troupe, and the association was continued with *Volpone* and *The Alchemist*. *Bartholomew Fair* is another popular play, produced by the Lady Elizabeth's Men at the Hope Theatre. So it goes. Harbage gets round the problem by suggesting that Jonson's "inclinations and influence" linked him with the coterie.

Elsewhere Harbage acknowledges that, in Jonson's case, genius "complicates the pattern as genius always must." Perhaps we may more properly understand Jonson not so much as an exemplar of either of the rival dramatic traditions, but rather as an archetype of the independent artist; some such fabulous voyager as James Joyce in our own century, embarked on his own creative odyssey, steering his lonely course between the Scylla of applause and Charybdis of derision. Jonson is, like Joyce, an experimenter:

In this alone, his MUSE her sweetnesse hath,
Shee shunnes the print of any beaten path;
And proves new wayes to come to learned eares.
(*Cynthia's Revels*, Prol., 11. 9–11)

But even this attractive view of Jonson must be qualified; for the playwright does not enjoy the same independence as the novelist, and the theatre offers a very different forum from that of the little magazines. The dramatist is forced to please even where he loathes, and the comic dramatist must provoke the laughter of those he seeks to improve. As a professional, Jonson knew as much. "It had another *Catastrophe* or Conclusion, at the first playing," he writes of *Every Man Out*: "which . . . many seem'd not to rellish it; and therefore 'twas since alter'd." And in the remarkably genial Prologue to *Epicoene*, Jonson accepts without protest the unyielding condition of his art: that the drama's laws the drama's patrons give. He writes:

Truth sayes, of old, the art of making plaies
    Was to content the people; & their praise
    Was to the *Poet* money, wine, and bayes.
But in this age, a sect of writers are,
    That, onely, for particular likings care,
    And will taste nothing that is populare.
With such we mingle neither braines, nor brests;
    Our wishes, like to those (make publique feasts)
    Are not to please the cookes tastes, but the guests.
(11. 1–9)

Jonson's theory is not without its contradictions, nor does it uniformly square with his practice. Despite the *Discoveries*, we may seek laughter in his comedy, and despite his scorn for the multitude, his greatest plays may yet find a wider audience than the academy.

III

Of these great plays, in the minutes remaining to me, I can but discuss one or two in any detail. It is only fair that I should confront straightaway the work which exposes my position at its most vulnerable, and so I turn to *Volpone*. For some would not only deny laughter to *Volpone* but also question its proper status as comedy. In his undistinguished but still consulted handbook, *An Introduction to Stuart Drama*, Frederick Boas describes the play as "in its lurid colouring . . . more akin to tragedy than to comedy."[12] This judgment echoes Herford and Simpson:

> . . . in its whole conception and conduct, in the lurid atmosphere which pervades it from beginning to end, in the appalling and menacing character of the principal movers of the plot, it approaches not indeed the profound and human-hearted tragedies of Shakespeare, but, very obviously and significantly, his own grandiose and terrible tragedy of two years before.[13]

These respected authorities can, moreover, appeal to the authority of Jonson himself. Did he not equip his play with a noble dedicatory epistle to the two famous universities; an epistle in which he vows to "raise the despis'd head of *poetrie* againe, and, stripping her out of those rotten and base rags, wherewith the Times have adulterated her form, restore her to her primitive habit, feature, and majesty, and render her worthy to be imbraced, and kist, of all the great and master-*spirits* of our world." (This in 1607, just after *Lear* and *Macbeth*.) In the same preface Jonson admits that his catastrophe may, in "the strict rigour of *comick* law, meet with censure"; but his special aim has always been "to put the snaffle in their mouths, that crie out, we never punish vice in our enterludes, &c." Never mind that elsewhere he insists that comedy should "sport with humane follies, not with crimes" – the corrective mission takes precedence over the niceties of aesthetic criteria. This playwright will instruct and amend licentious spirits; for, after all, "the principall end of *poesie*" is the doctrine, "to informe men, in the best reason of living." Here Jonson sees eye to eye with his sympathetic interpreter, Professor L. C. Knights, who applies to *Volpone* the words of a modern writer not celebrated for his humorous disposition. "The essential function of art is moral," D. H. Lawrence proclaimed. "Not aesthetic, not decorative, not pastime and recreation, but moral."[14] Do we dare, then, turn for pastime and recreation (ignoble

---

[12]Frederick S. Boas, *An Introduction to Stuart Drama* (London, 1946), p. 106.
[13]*Ben Jonson*, ed. Herford and Simpson, II, 49–50.
[14]Quoted by L. C. Knights, *Drama and Society in the Age of Jonson* (London, 1951), p. 206.

pursuits) to this most sardonic of Jonson's masterpieces? There is certainly much to support the view of Herford and Simpson: from the stunningly blasphemous opening scene in which Volpone, an anchorite after the new fashion, invokes the language of Genesis as he makes his obeisance before his altar of dross; to the fierce punishments meted out at the end – Mosca to be whipped and made perpetual prisoner in the galleys, Volpone, his fortune confiscated, to lie cramped with irons until he has experienced the ailments and lameness he feigned. The *dramatis personae* belong not to humanity but to some monstrous zoo, and behave accordingly. For no other reason than greed, a father with one foot already in the grave disinherits and denies the legitimacy of his virtuous son; a husband, known for his morbid jealousy, makes haste to pimp for his wife; a lawyer debases his noble profession, and would for a few small coins plead against his Maker. The protagonist presides over a deformed household of dwarf, eunuch and hermaphrodite. Are they fruit of the fox's loins, or is he as sterile as is his pursuit of gold? The question is raised, glancingly, and left unanswered. Fittingly the word *unnatural* echoes through the play. We may well be tempted to conclude that the comic spirit is allowed to frolic only in the underplot of the Would-be's, she with her voluble vanity, he with his onions and red herrings, their innocent English follies contrasting with (to use the critic's term) lurid Italianate vice; comic relief, if you will. Surely Jonson must have been in a ruthless mood during the five weeks that he burned his way through the composition of *Volpone*.

Yet his Prologue suggests another dimension. Jonson describes his play as "quick comedy":

> All gall, and coppresse, from his inke, he drayneth,
>   Onely, a little salt remayneth;
> Wherewith, he'll rub your cheeks, til (red with laughter)
>   They shall looke fresh, a weeke after. (11. 33–36)

We are meant to laugh after all. And examined closely, with the doctrine for once not uppermost, *Volpone* is rich in mirth-provoking comic invention and detail. There is always the serviceable humour of deafness, with its mistaking of the word. So Corbaccio inquires after Volpone's health:

15

> *Mosca.* His speech is broken, and his eyes are set,
> His face drawne longer, then 't was wont——
> *Corbaccio.* How? How?
> Stronger, then he was wont?
> *Mosca.* No, sir: his face
> Drawne longer, then 't was wont.
> *Corbaccio.* O, good. (I.iv.38–41)

Or:

> *Corbaccio.* How do's he? will he die shortly, think'st thou?
> *Mosca.* I feare,
> He'll out-last *May.*
> *Corbaccio.* To day?
> *Mosca.* No, last-out *May,* sir. (III.ix.12–13)

Take our spruce merchant Corvino. The first comic touch is likely to be missed in the study, for it is merely the direction for his exit, made precipitously, without a word, at the mere mention of his "gallant wife." True, Corvino mistreats the long-suffering Celia barbarously, but cruelty is mitigated by timely double entendre:

> And, now I thinke on't, I will keepe thee backe-wards;
> Thy lodging shall be backe-wards; thy walkes back-wards;
> Thy prospect – all be backe-wards; and no pleasure,
> That thou shalt know, but backe-wards. (II.v.58–61)

This tirade is put in perspective by Corvino's abrupt volte face when informed that Volpone requires a lusty wench, "full of juice, to sleepe by him," a remedy presumably more efficacious than that recommended by the College of Physicians of having a flayed ape clapped to his breast; Corvino is now all husbandly solicitude. Later the third suitor, Voltore, is called upon to perform an about-face of a different kind in the Scrutineo; faced with the necessity for a sudden reversal of tactics, he simply topples over as if possessed (*"Voltore falls,"* reads the stage direction):

> God blesse the man!
> (Stop your wind hard, and swell) see, see, see, see!
> He vomits crooked pinnes. (V.xii.23–25)

This particular bit of business I have seen brilliantly executed by the gaunt John Carradine, who gyrated briefly like a top and was suddenly horizontal. The behaviour to which the legacy-hunters are driven is in all these instances expressive of the author's doctrine, which I shouldn't wish to downgrade; my point is, simply, that we profit through experiencing comic pleasure. Our chief source of such pleasure is the fox himself. We delight in his delicious torments as he is steamed like a bath with Lady Would-be's thick breath. He drops hints, which have an effect opposite to that intended:

> *Volpone.* The Poet,
> As old in time, as PLATO, and as knowing,
> Say's that your highest female grace is silence.
> *Lady.* Which o' your Poets? PETRARCH? or TASSO? or DANTE?
> GUERRINI? ARIOSTO? ARETINE?
> CIECO *di Hadria?* I have read them all. (III.iv.76–81)

Above all, Volpone dazzles us as the quick-change artist. In his mountebank routine, as Scoto of Mantua, he is the ultimate carnival medicine-man, a type that has perennially amused. Disclaiming any kinship with such charlatans – "turdy-facy-nasty-paty-lousy-farticall rogues" – or any mercenary motive ("I have nothing to sell, little, or nothing to sell"), he offers his precious oil, "surnamed *oglio del* SCOTO," for six crowns, but will be pleased to settle for six pence. But Volpone's most stunning (and uproarious) transformations are from the lusty magnifico of Venice to a puling, decrepit old man, shivering in his caps and furs, dripping ointment and coughing out his signature of wheezes: "Uh, uh, uh, uh." The quickest change of all occurs when Celia is left alone with him, and the supposedly impotent invalid (no incantation can raise that spirit, her husband has been assured, a long forgetfulness having seized that part), suddenly leaps upright on his bed and launches into his great seduction speech, a Tamburlaine of the bedchamber. I still remember this scene bringing down the house when I saw it acted, a quarter of a century ago, by José Ferrer in the City Center production. At the end of course Volpone receives his fearsome sentence, but we do well to remember that our emotions are quickly checked; for, after everyone else has departed, the fox remains on stage and, in the traditional fashion of comedy, begs applause – "fare jovially, and clap your hands."

Much of the fun of the play, as my remarks have suggested, requires performance to be appreciated. Moreover, costume, make-up and gesture, by unmistakably identifying the various species comprising Jonson's bestiary, impart to the proceedings an air of grotesquerie which, however unsettling, leaves no doubt that we have not stumbled inadvertently into the precincts of tragedy. Even Knights, who uses such terms as "sombre," "bitterly derisive," and "grim" in his discussion of *Volpone*, must admit in another chapter and context that revivals have provided "some very good fun."

"Of the proper and normal material of comedy, extravagancies and absurdities, there is, in the main plot, nothing," write Herford and Simpson. "Its nearest approach to humour lies in the horrible simulations of the ludicrous effected by the misshapen creatures of Volpone's household."[15] *Extravagancies and absurdities.* It will not, I hope, be taken as disparagement of these learned gentlemen (or of Boas) to suggest that they belonged to a genteel tradition, and that their sensibility was limited accordingly. In recent years we have seen, in the work of a new generation of playwrights and film-makers, an expansion of the domain of comedy into areas formerly regarded by many as off-limits. As audiences we have learned that laughter may coexist, uneasily perhaps, but co-exist nonetheless, with the perverse, the lurid, even the violent. I think of Joe Orton's *Loot* and *Entertaining Mr. Sloane*; I think of Jerzy Skolimowski's film *Deep End*, with its controversial finale of death in the swimming bath. After black comedy we should no longer be surprised that audiences can find amusement in *Volpone*. When in the Prologue we are promised that he will rub our cheeks with laughter, the cunning old master knew what he was about.

Time remains only for a few remarks on one other play. Nobody questions that *The Alchemist* is a comedy, or describes it as sombre, although some critics have worried about the dénouement as if it were somehow puzzling that Jonson's sympathies should go to the Lovewits of this world rather than to a Surly, who is after all a dishonest gamester. Criticism has however tended to preoccupation with Jonson's particularities (alchemy and Jacobean London), and with his classicism, to the neglect of other, no less compelling features. Thus Mares in his Revels introduction devotes a whole section to alchemy and a longish

---

[15]*Ben Jonson*, ed. Herford and Simpson, II, 64.

passage to the unities, while giving only brief mention to "stage funny-business," which he appreciates but is inclined to regard (with other commentators) as beneath the dignity of serious criticism. This to my mind smacks of an aesthetic Puritanism we could well do without. *The Alchemist* pleases not least because of its unabashed use of every mirth-provoking device in the comic dramatist's repertory.

Let me glance with you at a few. Jonson is a master of the art of derogation (did he not, to Drummond, define a schoolmaster as one who sweeps his living from the posteriors of little children?), and nowhere does derogation flourish more happily than in *The Alchemist*. I think of those little thumb-nail sketches of Jonson's gudgeons: Abel Drugger, "A miserable rogue, and lives with cheese, / And has the wormes"; or that child of wrath, Kastril, "come up / To learne to quarrell, and to live by his wits, / And will goe downe againe, and dye i' the countrey"; or Dapper, the lawyer's clerk,

> a speciall gentle,
> That is the heire to fortie markes a yeere,
> Consorts with the small poets of the time,
> Is the sole hope of his old grand-mother,
> That knowes the law, and writes you sixe faire hands,
> Is a fine clarke, and has his cyphring perfect,
> Will take his oath, o' the *greeke* XENOPHON,
> If need be, in his pocket: and can court
> His mistris, out of OVID. (I.ii.50–58)

We are less inclined to associate word-play with Jonson, but it is used in this play to equally deadly effect. So we have Face's mock tribute to Doll –

> at supper, thou shalt sit in triumph,
> And not be stil'd DOL Common, but DOL Proper,
> DOL Singular: the longest cut, at night,
> Shall draw thee for his DOL Particular. (I.i.176–79)

– a passage in which, as Professor Partridge has neatly demonstrated, the wit springs from the terminology of logic as well as of grammar.[16] Doll even becomes the vehicle for a kind of visual pun, as she is briefly seen jump upon Sir Epicure's use of the

[16]Edward B. Partridge, *The Broken Compass: A Study of the Major Comedies of Ben Jonson* (London, 1958), pp. 124–25.

19

word *common*: a device that in English comedy goes back at least as far as John Heywood's *Four P's*, in which the Pedlar hops in a play on *hopes*.[17]

The climax of *The Alchemist*, the great off-stage explosion of the furnace, is justly admired, so it is fitting that we pause also to savour the anticlimax. As Surly temporarily turns the tables on the rogues, and Kastril and Drugger gang up against him, in the midst of general tumult and hubbub, enter the exiled Saint, Ananias: "Peace to the household. . . . Casting of dollers is concluded lawfull." We praise the dramatist's mastery of form – how closely he keeps tabs on the clock while the two hours' traffic of the stage ticks away! – but form is also function, and a primary function is laughter. So in Act III, Scene v, Dapper, having dutifully put vinegar drops in his several orifices and thrice cried "hum" and "buzz" as often, and having cast off his gold half-crown (his leaden heart, a sentimental token, he is touchingly allowed to keep) – having done all this, he is presented with "a dead mouse, / And a piece of ginger-bread, to be merry withall," and bestowed in Fortune's privy lodgings, where "the Fumigation's somewhat strong." Time passes, and much happens. We forget about Dapper, but his creator forgets nothing. The ginger-bread gag crumbles in the gull's mouth, and he emerges dazed from the privy to receive his poignant reward: the honour of kissing the Queen of Fairy's departing part. There are (if you will permit a bad pun) no loose ends in *The Alchemist*. Nor does Jonson pass up any opportunity to invent mirth. When Lovewit suddenly returns to his house, he is surrounded by scandalized neighbours. The merest of bit parts, they appear only in this scene. A lesser playwright would have allowed them to remain ciphers. Not Jonson. And so we have the timorous Sixth Neighbour with a sad tale to relate:

> About
> Some three weekes since, I heard a dolefull cry,
> As I sate up, a mending my wives stockings. (V.i.32–34)

With these two lines, the Sixth Neighbour lives.[18] It is a tribute to Jonson's craft and anything but sullen art.

[17]See T. W. Craik, "Experiment and Variety in John Heywood's Plays," *Renaissance Drama*, VII (1964), 9.

[18]This brief passage was delightfully commented upon years ago in an unpublished lecture by the late F. P. Wilson.

I have once or twice referred captiously to Mares, but let me now, near my close, express gratitude. In his Revels introduction he performs a real service by dwelling on the theatricality of *The Alchemist*, an aspect which, as he remarks, has not been much talked about. The same holds true for Jonson's other plays, and for some more than for this one. The features of his art that I have been stressing today can be adequately expressed and responded to not in the classroom or on the podium, but in the theatre, and only in the theatre. As students we do well to honour Jonson's birthday by conferences such as this, but we honour him best by producing his plays. It is a melancholy fact that while we are engaged in our ritual of scholarship, no complementary ceremony is taking place a few miles away in Stratford. Nor, so far as I know, is a quatercentenary production on the books this year for the Royal Shakespeare Company performing in the other, equally celebrated, Stratford, although they have in recent seasons varied their Shakespearian diet with other Elizabethan cates. While recognizing that amateurs can hardly aspire to the standards of professionals, we can as academics encourage, indeed browbeat, the drama departments of our universities to put Jonson on the boards; that is the serious plea with which I conclude my light-weight offering. This year I have used my best rhetorical powers to attempt to persuade the Northwestern Department of Theatre to revive *Epicoene*, a comparatively neglected play and one that I saw very entertainingly, if toothlessly, performed years ago by students in New York. Well, I didn't succeed. *Epicoene*, I was told, is fare too specialized for a university audience; but next winter Northwestern will do *Volpone*. That is a good deal better than nothing. It is my fervent hope that the great and master spirit we celebrate here this week will in the year ahead be celebrated in many campus theatres, and that a host of spectators will discover through their laughter the humorous Jonson.

Ben Jonson on his beloved, The Author Mr. William Shakespeare

T. J. B. SPENCER

The relationship between Ben Jonson and Shakespeare has already been the subject of a paper at one of the Waterloo conferences on Elizabethan Theatre. In 1969 Samuel Schoenbaum, in "Shakespeare and Jonson: Fact and Myth," gave us a judicious, as well as entertaining, account of the confused, inadequate or unevidenced stories that were current for several centuries, and are not yet dead.[1] He deplored the practice of "Jonson-baiting" and its consequences. Schoenbaum had had several predecessors.[2] You may think it unfortunate that one of the opening papers at a conference which is to be especially concerned with Ben Jonson should have reverted to the inevitable and odious comparison.

Yet it must be admitted that it was Jonson who began it. He, the most articulate literary critic in the early seventeenth century, found Shakespeare a convenient contrast to himself for the purposes of that rough-and-ready synthesis or miscellany of Renaissance literary theorizing which he compiled or "conveyed." He

---

[1] *The Elizabethan Theatre II*, ed. David Galloway (Toronto, 1970), pp. 1–19.
[2] J. Dover Wilson, "Jonson and *Julius Caesar*," *Shakespeare Survey* 2 (1947); G. E. Bentley, *The Swan of Avon and the Bricklayer of Westminster* (Princeton, 1946); L. J. Potts, "Ben Jonson and the Seventeenth Century," in *English Studies* (vol. 2 of the new series of *Essays and Studies*), English Association, 1949; and S. Musgrove, *Shakespeare and Jonson* (The Macmillan Brown Lectures, Auckland, N.Z., 1957).

gave Shakespeare a kind of typological significance: the naturally gifted writer, who fails to discipline himself. He turned Shakespeare into a kind of sparring partner, whom he could make use of in order to justify his own rather solemn and laborious critical position.

Much of the contemporary information about what Jonson thought of Shakespeare is difficult to handle confidently. We ought not to treat jokes in plays and jibes in prologues as evidence of the attitude of Jonson to Shakespeare. Allusions to a "servant-monster," to "tales, tempests, and such like drolleries," to "York and Lancaster's long jars," to the Chorus that "wafts you o'er the seas," to the "mouldy tale" of Pericles, and so on – these belong to a context which prevents our taking them too seriously. The testimony of William Drummond of Hawthornden is after-dinner gossip; delightful and probable, certainly. But could Jonson have suspected that what he said in his cups would be recorded for our cold and puzzled consideration? There remain the opinions Jonson expressed in his notebook, posthumously printed. A balanced eulogy, surely. Shakespeare "redeemed his vices with his virtues. There was ever more in him to be praised than to be pardoned." In each case the circumstances of the statement have to be taken into account. We cannot lump all these varied comments together without careful adjustment.

Ben Jonson did make one clear public utterance about Shakespeare, the eighty-line panegyric printed at the beginning of the 1623 folio: "To the memory of my beloved, The Author Mr. William Shakespeare: And what he hath left us." This has a high reputation. David Nichol Smith, in a moment of uncharacteristic exuberance, described Ben Jonson's poem as "the greatest eulogy that was ever written of a contemporary."[3] He meant, in more sober language, that he thought it to be the greatest verse-eulogy ever made by one poet of another poet his contemporary. This opinion is confirmed by some of our best judges.

Ben's was the noblest tribute, and remains so. For unlike Arnold and Browning, Jonson knew Shakespeare, man as well as book, and his praise is discriminating, and of all the Elizabethan and Jacobean writers he was best qualified by critical bent and creative fire to

[3]*Shakespeare in the Eighteenth Century* (Oxford, 1928), p. 3.

appraise a peerless colleague worthily. He rose superbly to a great
opportunity. The lines . . . are doubly a tribute to Shakespeare,
whose memory evoked the best occasional poem in our language.[4]

For Kenneth Muir, too, the poem "is perhaps the most magnifi-
cent tribute ever paid by one poet to another."[5] "To my mind a
mood of affectionate warmth pervades" the poem, says Schoenbaum; and he goes on to affirm that "we may rest assured that
Heminge and Condell would not have invited Jonson to contribute the principal eulogy of the First Folio if he were not their
fellow's friend, and Jonson would not have penned so noble a
tribute if he did not esteem Shakespeare as an artist and treasure
him as a comrade."[6]

It is, indeed, a remarkable poem. Like *Hamlet*, it is full of
quotations, and perhaps is difficult to judge for that reason.
Jonson was not much given to praising his literary contemporaries. He could turn a compliment elegantly, certainly. He could
issue encomiums upon members of the nobility and gentry who
chose to like him. I would not wish to suggest that Ben Jonson
had a pen for hire, although in his epigram "To Fine Grand" he
gives an amusing picture of himself as providing poems for pay-
ment and afterwards trying to collect his debts.[7] In considering
the poem on Shakespeare, we must, I think, acknowledge its
context. It belongs to the minor genre of "Commendatory Poems,"
the kind of thing assembled by an author (if alive) and by his
publisher to support the sales of a book. The practice was so
familiar that it was possible to have fun at the expense of the
convention, as in the case of the publication of *Coryats Crudities*
(1611). Ben Jonson's poem on Shakespeare belongs firmly in its
place in the front of the Folio. Jonson never took it out of that
context. He did not include it among the poems gathered up in
The Underwood in 1640 (issued posthumously, but apparently
consisting, in great part, of poems arranged by Jonson).

When the folio volume of *Mr. William Shakespeares Comedies,
Histories, & Tragedies. Published according to the True Originall*

[4]Hazelton Spencer, *The Art and Life of William Shakespeare* (New York, 1940), p. 86.
[5]*The Age of Shakespeare*, The Pelican Guide to English Literature, 2 (1955), p. 285.
[6]*The Elizabethan Theatre II*, pp. 3, 18–19.
[7]Herford and Simpson, VIII, 51 (Epigrammes 73).

Copies appeared in 1623, Jonson had rather a prominent place in the preliminary pages. He wrote and signed with his initials the poem which faces and comments on the engraved portrait of Shakespeare – a poem which is elegantly based upon one of the epigrams of Martial:

> This Figure, that thou here seest put,
> It was for gentle Shakespeare cut;
> Wherein the Graver had a strife
> With Nature, to out-doo the life:
> O, could he but have drawne his wit
> As well in brasse, as he hath hit
> His face; the Print would then surpasse
> All, that was ever writ in brasse . . .

And here is Martial on the portrait of a certain Marcus Antonius Primus:

> ars utinam mores animumque effingere posset!
> pulchrior in terris nulla tabella foret. (X.32)

Pride of place is given to Jonson's "To the memory of my beloved, The Author." We can understand how Isaac Jaggard, Edward Blount and the other members of the group who had committed themselves to the publication of the Shakespeare Folio were glad to have Jonson's support. The financial outlay on the venture was heavy, and it was necessary for them to do everything possible to ensure its success. They achieved a kind of social sponsorship of the volume by its dedication "To the most noble and incomparable paire of brethren, William Earle of Pembroke, &c. Lord Chamberlaine to the Kings most Excellent Majesty, and Philip Earle of Montgomery, &c. Gentleman of his Majesties Bed-Chamber. Both Knights of the Most Noble Order of the Garter. . . ." Ben Jonson's intellectual sponsorship was as important. For Jonson was by now the dominant man of letters in England. He had published his own plays in a folio in 1616, and to some people's surprise had dignified them by the title of his *Works* (a name scarcely acceptable for a collection of stage plays). He was on good terms with King James and with members of the court. He had stood up for the dignity of literature, and he had won through. If Jonson had disparaged the publication of Shakespeare's plays, the adverse influence which he and his "sons" exercised might have been serious. It would not be unreasonable to suppose that Ben Jonson's prominence in the preliminary pages of the volume makes it likely that he was granted the privilege of exercising some editorial discretion elsewhere. It is hard to deny that there is a certain amount of misguided pedantry manifest in the Folio. For, example, none of the quartos of Shakespeare's plays published in his lifetime had been honoured by divisions into acts and scenes. But in the Folio the plays had this classical dignity imposed upon them; or at least, upon some of them, for, whoever the redactor was, he soon grew tired of the job and frequently abandoned his act and scene dividing, even in the middle of a play. (Eighteen plays have the divisions in full. Eleven plays are divided into acts, but not into scenes. Six plays have none at all. *Hamlet* has divisions as far as the second act, but thereafter they are abandoned.) Still, the opening page of *The Tempest* looks imposing enough: *Actus primus, Scena prima* appears boldly across the page. Someone is making quite sure that *The Tempest* was not to be taken for one of those "tales, tempests, and such like drolleries" which Jonson had once upon a time castigated or ridiculed.

There was a serious effort to make the volume look intellectually imposing – far more so, even, than the 1616 Folio of Jonson's *Works*. We are given a portrait of the author in socially dignified costume (only Chapman, as translator of the immortal Homer, had hitherto achieved the distinction of engraved portraiture among Elizabethan dramatists).[8] The author is always *Master* William Shakespeare. Along with the commendatory poems is a table of contents, "A Catalogue of the severall Comedies, Histories, and Tragedies" (rather carelessly prepared, for *Troilus and Cressida*, a play difficult to categorize, was omitted). Then there is a curious new heading (above "The Names of the Principall Actors"): "The Workes of William Shakespeare, containing all his Comedies, Histories, and Tragedies. . . ." The plays have now become *Works*, we observe. In addition to the occasional act and scene division, some editorial work has been done to make the plays readable. A few are

[8]There was an engraved portrait of the author prefixed to *Poems: By Michael Drayton Esquire* (Oxford, 1619).

26

provided with "The names of all the Actors" (meaning the *dramatis personae*). Some of the character-descriptions are suspiciously Jonsonian. Poins, Falstaff, Bardolph, Pistol and Peto in *2 Henry IV* are listed as "Irregular Humorists." Roderigo in *Othello* is "a gull'd Gentleman." Lucio in *Measure for Measure* is "a fantastique." Caliban is "a salvage and deformed slave." A location is provided for a few plays; for *The Tempest*, "The Scene, an un-inhabited Island" (not very satisfactory) and for *Measure for Measure*, "The Scene Vienna." Who was responsible for this abortive editorial work on a few plays, especially at the beginning of the volume? Perhaps it was Jonson. Perhaps it was merely an intrusion by that rather Jonsonian scrivener Ralph Crane.

The context of Ben Jonson's poem "To the memory of my beloved, The Author" is, then, that it was an intellectual commendation of a big, expensive, imposing and (dare I say it?) rather pretentiously produced volume. When Dr. Johnson was taxed for praising Shakespeare in the preface to his edition of 1765 more highly than he really believed was deserved, he replied that it was not proper for an editor to disparage the works of his author when the bookseller hoped to profit by the publication. We know nothing of the financial arrangements for the publication of the 1623 Folio. Perhaps all the profits were swallowed up in production costs. But it would be pleasant to suppose that there was a small margin for editorial expenses. I am not making a mean and unevidenced insinuation that Ben Jonson was paid for his great commendatory poem. I do boldly express my opinion, however, that he ought to have been paid for it.

For Jonson had a strong sense of literary *decorum*. He knew exactly the kind of poem which was appropriate to a given context or set of circumstances. There are analogies to the Shakespeare verses in the commendatory poems prefixed to his own plays and collections (including the *Works* of 1616 and 1640). The *Jonsonus Virbius* of 1638 was a remarkable series of such memorial commendations by most of his literary contemporaries and "sons." In such commendatory verses there frequently occur lists of contemporaries who have been surpassed by the poet being praised, and of appropriate Greek and Latin authors whom the poet can be claimed to have equalled or surpassed.[9] Nor did it greatly matter if there was some discrepancy between the genuine literary judgments uttered elsewhere and the panegyric fulsomely expressed in the commendatory poem. "In lapidary inscriptions," said the wise and tolerant Dr. Johnson, "a man is not upon oath."[10] We can grant the same indulgence to the author of a commendatory poem. Even taking into full account the other evidence of Jonson's attitude to Shakespeare – the jests and jibes, the contemptuous judgments expressed to Drummond, the balanced praise and blame in the notebooks – we may well feel that we could have extrapolated (so to speak) the 1623 poem. For the discrepancies need not perplex us. Jonson was remarkably insulting about Donne when talking to Drummond. Donne "for not keeping of accent deserved hanging" and "for not being understood would perish," he said. These are severe censures on Donne's poetic art, alongside contradictory judgments that Donne was "the first poet in the world in some things" and that Jonson had one of Donne's elegies by heart.[11] There is no full-scale verse panegyric of Donne as there is of Shakespeare; but there are two short poems in which the praise is laid on with a trowel.

> Donne, the delight of PHOEBUS, and each *Muse*,
>> Who, to thy one, all other braines refuse;
> Whose every worke, of thy most earely wit,
>> Came forth example, and remaines so, yet:
> Longer a knowing, then most wits doe live.
>> And which no' affection praise enough can give!
> To it, thy language, letters, arts, best life,
>> Which might with halfe mankind maintayne a strife.
> All which I meant to praise, and, yet, I would;
>> But leave, because I cannot as I should!

and

[9]Jonson's commendation of Drayton makes him the rival of Theocritus, Virgil, Ovid, Orpheus, Lucan, Homer and Tyrtaeus. Jonson was praised by Drayton for rivalling Seneca and Plautus in tragedy and comedy ("To my most dearely-loved friend Henry Reynolds Esquire, of Poets and Poesie"; *Works*, ed. J. W. Hebel (Oxford, 1932), 3.229; Herford and Simpson XI.389); by Nathan Field for exceeding Plautus, Horace and Virgil (Herford and Simpson XI.323); and many others, especially in *Jonsonus Virbius* (1638).
[10]Boswell's *Life*, December 1775 (Hill-Powell ed., ii.407).
[11]Herford and Simpson, I.133, 135, 138.

Who shall doubt, DONNE, where I a *Poet* bee,
  When I dare send my *Epigrammes* to thee?
That so alone canst judge, so'alone dost make:
  And, in thy censures, evenly, dost take
As free simplicitie, to dis-avow,
  As thou hast best authoritie, t(o)'allow.
Reade all I send: and, if I find but one
  Mark'd by thy hand, and with the better stone,
My title's seal'd. Those that for claps doe write,
  Let pui'nees, porters, players praise delight,
And, till they burst, their backs, like asses load:
  A man should seeke great glorie, and not broad.[12]

The situation is rather similar with Michael Drayton: "Drayton feared him, and he esteemed not of him," he told Drummond; and "that Michael Drayton's Polyolbion, if he had performed what he promised to write (the deeds of all the worthies) had been excellent: his long verses pleased him not." Yet Jonson's poem "The Vision of Ben. Jonson, on the Muses of his friend M. Drayton" is one of the most vigorous of his verse panegyrics on literary figures; so much so that some critics have suspected an element of satire in it ("sly satire rather than compliment," judged J. W. Hebel).[13]

In suggesting that Ben Jonson's poem ought to be considered without sentimentality, and within its context and within its genre, I am perhaps bringing out into the open, yet again, the opinion of Dryden. In "A Discourse concerning the Original and Progress of Satire" which he addressed to Charles Sackville, Earl of Dorset, in 1693, he says:

an Author of your own Quality [the Earl of Rochester] . . . has given you all the Commendation, which his [Rochester's] self sufficiency cou'd afford to any Man: *The best Good Man, with the worst-Natur'd Muse.* In that Character, methinks I am reading

---

[12]Herford and Simpson, VIII, 34 and 62.
[13]Herford and Simpson, I, 132 and 136; VIII.396 and XI, 147–9; *The Works of Michael Drayton*, ed. Hebel, 3.3; J. W. Hebel, "Drayton's *Sirena*," *P.M.L.A.* 39 (1924), 830; B. H. Newdigate, *Michael Drayton and his Circle* (1941), p. 136, who says that Ben Jonson's language is "too fulsome to be taken seriously. Most of the *Vision* reads like a bit of good-tempered leg-pulling, in which Ben burlesques with deliberate and luxuriously exaggerated pompousness the common run of commendatory verses."

> *Johnson's* Verses to the Memory of *Shakespear*: An Insolent, Spar-
> ing, and Invidious Panegyrick: Where good Nature, the most God-
> like Commendation of a Man, is only attributed to your Person,
> and deny'd to your Writings.

The syntax here is (unusually for Dryden) far from clear. Perhaps the "panegyric" which is "insolent, sparing, and invidious"
refers primarily to Rochester's on Dorset. But even if this is so,
Dryden is certainly saying that Jonson's verses on Shakespeare
are comparable with or similar to such a panegyric. That was
how Pope read it; and he disagreed. "Dryden used to think that
the verses Jonson made on Shakespeare's death had something of
satire at the bottom," he told Spence. "For my part, I can't discover anything like it in them." And Pope firmly rejected this
idea in his preface to his *Shakespeare* in 1725: "I cannot for my
own part find any thing *Invidious* or *Sparing* in those verses, but
wonder *Mr. Dryden* was of that opinion."[14]

But Dryden was not the only seventeenth-century reader who
found Jonson's poem mighty odd. The editor of Richard Brome's
Five New Plays (1659) wrote a preface "To the Reader," and
decided to include Jonson's poem on Brome (who had been his
amanuensis).

> we have here prefixt *Ben Johnson's* own testimony to his Servant
> our *Author*; we grant it is (according to *Ben's* own nature and
> custome) magisterial enough; and who looks for other, since he
> said to *Shakespear – I shall draw envy on thy name* (by writing in
> his praise) and threw in his face – *small Latine and less Greek.*

Dryden in many respects judged Jonson very shrewdly. He
was well aware of Jonson's many adaptations from Latin authors,
his constant literary allusiveness, which is so often lost on the
modern reader. Jonson was, said Dryden, "a learned Plagiary . . .
you track him every where in their Snow. If *Horace, Lucan,
Petronius Arbiter, Seneca,* and *Juvenal* had their own from him,
there are few serious thoughts which are new in him; you will
pardon me therefore if I presume he lov'd their fashion when he
wore their cloathes." But it was not only the "thoughts." It was

[14]Spence's *Anecdotes*, ed. James M. Osborn (2 vols., Oxford, 1966), No.
67 (i.29); *Eighteenth Century Essays on Shakespeare*, ed. D. Nichol Smith
(2nd ed., Oxford, 1963), p. 51.

also the very language itself. "He did a little too much Romanize our Tongue, leaving the words which he translated almost as much Latine as he found them."[15] Jonson's poem on Shakespeare is no exception to this. A closer reading of the poem, paying attention to its numerous Latinisms of thought and phrase, may illuminate something of its tone.

> To draw no envy (*Shakespeare*) on thy name,
>> Am I thus ample to thy Booke, and Fame:
> While I confesse thy writings to be such,
>> As neither *Man*, nor *Muse*, can praise too much.
> 'Tis true, and all mens suffrage.

Here *ample* means, not "adequate," but "copious." In Cicero an *amplus orator* was one who orates richly and with dignity. *I confess*: "make known," or "make a public statement" (not "admit a truth reluctantly").

Jonson then considers the three kinds of false or falsely motivated praise. First, praise can be uttered by those who are ignorant and foolish, and who therefore merely repeat what has been said by others. Secondly, there are those who have a fixed state of mind, and who do not succeed in making any genuine progress towards the truth; they move "without understanding" where they are going. Thirdly, there are the malicious, who cunningly offer (*pretend*) praise but in reality have the intention of damaging the reputation of an author.

> But these wayes
>> Were not the paths I meant unto thy praise:
> For seeliest Ignorance on these may light,
>> Which, when it sounds at best, but eccho's right;
> Or blinde Affection, which doth ne're advance
>> The truth, but gropes, and urgeth all by chance;
> Or crafty Malice, might pretend this praise,
>> And thinke to ruine, where it seem'd to raise.
> These are, as some infamous Baud, or Whore,
>> Should praise a Matron. What could hurt her more?
> But thou art proofe against them, and indeed
>> Above th'ill fortune of them, or the need.

---

[15] *Of Dramatick Poesie. An Essay* (1668).

It must be admitted that these first sixteen lines express Jonson's personal preoccupations with ignorance, prejudice and envy, and that, as he admits, they are not relevant to the commendation of Shakespeare.

> I therefore will begin. Soule of the Age!

Here *soul* means "darling." To a modern reader the ringing phrase "Soul of the Age" sounds like the late eighteenth-century notion of the *Zeit-Geist*, the "Spirit of the Age" – as if Shakespeare were being praised for being the fine flower of the Elizabethan age, the writer in whom the time found its fullest and most characteristic expression, the spokesman of its highest ideals and aspirations. It is probable, however, that Jonson's Latinism here limits the meaning to "darling"; Shakespeare was everybody's favourite.

> The applause! delight! the wonder of our Stage!
> My *Shakespeare*, rise;

that is, come back from the grave: this publication of Shakespeare's works resurrects him.

> I will not lodge thee by
> *Chaucer*, or *Spenser*, or bid *Beaumont* lye
> A little further, to make thee a roome:

It was perhaps a little unkind to make fun of the unpublished poem of William Basse:

> Renowned Spenser, lye a thought more nye
> To learned Chaucer, and rare Beaumont lye
> A little nearer Spenser to make roome
> For Shakespeare in your threefold fowerfold Tombe.

It is possible that it was at one time intended to include the poem by Basse among the testimonies prefixed to the 1623 Folio and that it was later removed as unworthy of the honour. The large number of manuscripts of the poem show that it had a certain amount of popularity.

> Thou art a Moniment, without a tombe,
> And art alive still, while thy Booke doth live,
> And we have wits to read, and praise to give.

Shakespeare's writings are, according to the traditional mode of literary aspiration, a *monumentum aere perennius*. To our ears the couplet here seems to echo the rhyming couplets that conclude some of Shakespeare's sonnets. But it is likely that Jonson was merely dependent upon inherited phraseology from Horace and Ovid.

> That I not mix thee so, my braine excuses;
> I meane with great, but disproportion'd *Muses*:

He refrains from relating Shakespeare to major (but not artistically controlled) geniuses like Chaucer, Spenser and Beaumont, as Basse had done in his poem.

> For, if I thought my judgement were of yeeres,
> I should commit thee surely with thy peeres,

Presumably *of years* means "temporary": "If I supposed that Shakespeare were *of an age*, I should make comparisons (*commit*) between him and his coevals, such as Lyly, Kyd, and Marlowe." These were all Shakespeare's contemporaries, one observes, not Jonson's. No comparisons are made with the living.

> And tell, how farre thou didst our *Lily* out-shine,
> Or sporting *Kid*, or *Marlowes* mighty line.

The pun on the name of Kyd seems to us to be singularly inappropriate. In what sense can the author of *The Spanish Tragedy* be called capricious? But this dreadful word-play makes it certain that *our Lily out-shine* refers to *Matthew* 6.28–9: "Consider the lilies of the field . . . I say unto you that even Solomon in all his glory was not arrayed like one of these." And these puns (as well as Shakespeare's shaking a lance in line 69 below) mean that we must look at *Marlowe's mighty line* a little suspiciously. It is natural for us to take these words as a compliment to Marlowe's dramatic blank verse. But was Jonson really likely to praise the quality of the writing of *Tamburlaine*? Perhaps Jonson is only enjoying linking together the *low* in Marlowe's surname with the rumbustious eloquence of the mighty monarchs in his plays.

> And though thou hadst small *Latine*, and lesse *Greeke*,
> From thence to honour thee, I would not seeke
> For names;

In the case of an unlearned author, the fair comparison would be with his contemporaries, not with the classics of antiquity. But this limitation does not apply to Shakespeare. Although Shakespeare was comparatively unlearned, Jonson does not need, in order to praise him, to turn to such authors as Lyly, Kyd and Marlowe (*From thence*) for a standard of achievement. Shakespeare can stand up to the comparison with the dramatists of Greece and Rome.

> but calls forth thund'ring *Æschilus*,
> *Euripides*, and *Sophocles* to us,
> *Paccuvius*, *Accius*, him of *Cordova* dead,
> To life againe, to heare thy Buskin tread,
> And shake a Stage: Or, when thy Sockes were on,
> Leave thee alone, for the comparison
> Of all, that insolent *Greece*, or haughtie *Rome*
> Sent forth, or since did from their ashes come.
> Triúmph, my *Britaine*, thou hast one to showe,
> To whom all Scenes of *Europe* homage owe.

I once thought it rather absurd of Jonson to *call forth* the Greek tragedians, and Pacuvius and Accius.

Is this the writing of a well-informed person? We can stand for Seneca, of course. But it is hard to include the Greek tragedians, too little known and too little available to make the comparison intelligent; and as for Accius and Pacuvius, there could be few criticisms more pointless than to ask anybody to call forth their meagre fragments, those ghostly writers, mere names in biographical dictionaries. Perhaps it is only Ben Jonson's fun. I would like to think so. But I doubt it. I fear he wants to be impressive. Like a medieval poet, he has licence to mention the names of great authors without their books.[16]

I now know better. In a highly literary panegyric like this poem, erudite Latinisms are part of the accepted procedure. The two early Roman tragedians are praised together by Horace:

[16]*Shakespeare Survey* 10 (1957), 36–37.

> ambigitur quotiens, uter utro sit prior, aufert
> Pacuvius docti famam senis, Accius alti . . .
>
> (*Epistles* II.1.55–56)

And by Quintilian in a famous passage: "virium Attio plus tribuitur, Pacuvium videri doctiorem, qui esse docti adfectant, volunt" (X.1,97). Moreover, *him of Cordova dead* is not a clumsy periphrasis for the name of Seneca (*Cordubiensis*). Ben Jonson's favourite, Martial, had written on the birthplace of so much literary genius:

> duosque Senecas unicumque Lucanum
> facunda loquitur Corduba (I.61)

Nor could Jonson have failed to know the poem written by Seneca himself:

> Corduba, solve comas et tristes indue vultus,
> inlacrimans cineri munera mitte meo.
> Nunc longinqua tuum deplora, Corduba, vatem,
> Corduba non alio tempore maesta magis . . .[17]

> He was not of an age, but for all time!
> And all the *Muses* still were in their prime,
> When like *Apollo* he came forth to warme
> Our eares, or like a *Mercury* to charme!

Jonson continues to emphasize Shakespeare's merits as being greater than those we can usually accord to "moderns" (that is, praise for their distinction in their own age). Shakespeare is great both in comparison with his contemporaries (*of an age*) and with the classics (*for all time*). Indeed, he is a kind of classic; for his writings have the freshness of the great achievements of antiquity (when *all the Muses still were in their prime*); they give the impression of being inspired by Apollo (*Cynthius aurem / vellit et admonuit* is remembered from Virgil, *Eclogue* 6.3–4, combined with a stroke of wit about the Sun God rising

---

[17]*Poetae Latini Minores*, ed. Baehrens (1882), vol. 4, p. 62 (No. 19). Compare also Statius, *Silvae*, ii.7, which celebrates the poet Lucan, born at Corduba, like his uncle Seneca:

> Felix – heu nimis! – et beata tellus . . .
> Lucanum potes imputare terris!
> hoc plus quam Senecam dedisse mundo . . . (24,30–31)

in the morning, dispelling the darkness, and *warming* us) and by Mercury, the god of eloquence.

> Nature her selfe was proud of his designes,
> > And joy'd to weare the dressing of his lines!
> Which were so richly spun, and woven so fit,
> > As, since, she will vouchsafe no other Wit.
> The merry *Greeke*, tart *Aristophanes*,
> > Neat *Terence*, witty *Plautus*, now not please;
> But antiquated, and deserted lye
> > As they were not of Natures family.

The claim that Aristophanes, Plautus and Terence were underrated because of Shakespeare's reputation is hyperbole. It seems unlikely that anyone in the seventeenth century who could read these ancient dramatists felt less admiration for them because of Shakespeare's achievement.

Aristophanes can legitimately be called *tart*, that is, keenly satirical, but the addition of the proverbial phrase "merry Greek" to him is weak and little appropriate.[18] Terence was "neat" because of the pure and undiluted quality of his language: clear, and to the point. *Floures for Latine spekynge. Selected and gathered out of Terence* was a common school book, first published in 1533, and there were many later editions.

> Yet must I not give Nature all: Thy Art,
> > My gentle *Shakespeare*, must enjoy a part.
> For though the *Poets* matter, Nature be,
> > His Art doth give the fashion. And, that he,
> Who casts to write a living line, must sweat,
> > (Such as thine are) and strike the second heat
> Upon the *Muses* anvile: turne the same,
> > (And himselfe with it) that he thinkes to frame;
> Or for the lawrell, he may gaine a scorne,
> > For a good *Poet's* made, as well as borne.
> And such wert thou.

We cannot fail to remember the curt comment to William Drummond in 1619 "that Shakespeare wanted art" and to notice the

[18]T. J. B. Spencer, " 'Greeks' and 'Merrygreeks': A Background to *Timon of Athens* and *Troilus and Cressida*," in *Essays on Shakespeare and Elizabethan Drama in Honor of Hardin Craig*, ed. Richard Hosley (Columbia, Missouri, 1962).

contradiction with the passage in *Discoveries* (written, it seems, between 1623 and 1635): "Would he had blotted a thousand. . . . His wit was in his owne power; would the rule of it had beene so too." But the truth is that Jonson has now ceased to be writing about Shakespeare at all; he has got on to his favourite literary theory, that *poeta nascitur et fit.*

> Looke how the fathers face
> Lives in his issue, even so, the race
> Of *Shakespeares* minde, and manners brightly shines
> In his well torned, and true filed lines:

These are surely some of the most interesting lines in the poem. They are a testimony that Shakespeare was a personal writer; that those who knew him as a man heard his voice and recognized his personality when they read his writings. Whether his lines were, as Jonson here alleges, *well torned and true filed* is another matter. The word *race* is striking. It refers to the characteristic flavour of wine due to the soil where the grapes grow; and so it easily came to be used metaphorically of speech and writing (along with the adjective "racy" and the substantive "raciness"). But Jonson here puns on its meaning "generation" in association with *issue.*

> In each of which, he seemes to shake a Lance,
> As brandish't at the eyes of Ignorance.

In spite of the pun on Shakespeare's name, it is Jonson's own activity that he attributes to Shakespeare.

> Sweet Swan of *Avon!* what a sight it were
> To see thee in our waters yet appeare,
> And make those flights upon the bankes of *Thames,*
> That so did take *Eliza,* and our *James!*

Shakespeare as the "Swan of Avon" has become a byword.[19] The borough of Stratford-upon-Avon encourages this bird; its em-

[19]Leslie Hotson (*The First Night of "Twelfth Night,"* 1954, p. 79) states that, as the servants of the Lord Chamberlain, Baron Hunsdon, the men of Shakespeare's company wore "livery coats of fine blue cloth, bearing below the left shoulder their noble master's cognizance, a silver swan flying – the badge which, as well as being 'the proper ensigne of Poetrie . . . the swanne,' gave their great poet his nickname, the *sweet Swan of Avon.*"

T. J. B. Spencer

blematic use there abounds; and probably many persons suppose
that Shakespeare is symbolized by the local bird. But we have no
reason to suppose that swans were particularly notable on the
Warwickshire Avon, any more so than on the Thames or on other
English rivers.

The swan was, of course, the emblem of poetry, and sacred to
Apollo. Jonson is alluding cleverly to Horace's encomium on
Pindar in his *Odes* IV.2 (*Pindarum quisquis studet aemulari*).

> multa Dircaeum levat aura cycnum,
> tendit, Antoni, quotiens in altos
> nubium tractus . . .

Pindar was born at Thebes, where the river is named Dirce, and
Shakespeare was born at Stratford, where the river is named
Avon. So, as Pindar was the Swan of Thebes-upon-Dirce, Shakespeare was the Swan of Stratford-upon-Avon. And there were
plenty of Latin precedents for the swan as a symbol, including
another ode of Horace (II.20), where the poet prophesies his
immortality: he will change into a snow-white swan. Jonson's use
of the symbol elsewhere helps to amplify his meaning here. In
the *Ode allegorike* of 1603 (prefixed to Hugh Holland's *Pancharis*, a poem about Owen Tudor and dedicated to King James
I), Jonson describes Holland as "a black swan":

> A gentler Bird, then this,
> Did never dint the breast of *Tamisis*.
>
> Marke, marke, but when his wing he takes,
> How faire a flight he makes!
> How upward, and direct! . . .

And he goes on to explain how Apollo

> shew'd him first the hoofe-cleft Spring,
> Neere which, the *Thespiad's* sing;
> The cleare *Dircæan* Fount
> Where *Pindar* swamme.[20]

Ben Jonson was, in due course, himself the Swan of Thames in

[20]Herford and Simpson, VIII.366.

William Hodgson's poem "On the author, *The Poet Laureat*, Ben. Jonson," prefixed to the folio of 1640:

> clearer notes than his
> No Swan e'er sung upon our Thamesis;
> For Lyrick sweetnesse in an Ode, or Sonnet
> To BEN the best of wits might veile their Bonnet.[21]

Later on, Henry Vaughan was the Swan of Usk, *Olor Iscanus*.

> But stay, I see thee in the *Hemisphere*
> Advanc'd, and made a Constellation there!

The stellification of the person memorialized by the poem is conventional enough. But Jonson then, with characteristic wit, uses this situation to turn Shakespeare into an astrological power.

> Shine forth, thou Starre of *Poets*, and with rage,
> Or influence, chide, or cheere the drooping Stage;
> Which, since thy flight from hence, hath mourn'd like night,
> And despaires day, but for thy Volumes light.

This seems merely to express Jonson's dissatisfaction with the London theatre in these years. The death of Shakespeare in 1616 hardly marked a moment of despair for the King's Men; probably the death of Burbage in 1619 was more significant. Many of Shakespeare's plays (along with those of Fletcher) remained a valued part of the repertory. But Jonson's description of the importance of the publication of the volume for the theatre is agreeable hyperbole.

"An insolent, sparing, and invidious panegyric"? Dryden's words are too strong. But he was right, I believe, in discerning a certain lack of sympathy. The poem has something of the flavour of a blurb, designed to sell a book; the panegyric is at times wild, only this side of absurdity. It is not intended to impress us as being well-considered, and in this respect it compares unfavourably with the thoughtful paragraph in Jonson's notebooks. It is primarily a literary composition, entertainingly making use of

---

[21]Herford and Simpson, XI.350–1.

literary conventions. It is full of wit and clever adaptations of Latinate words and thoughts. It lacks sobriety, and is all the better for that. It is a poem and not an *affidavit*.

I do not find Jonson's lack of sympathy with Shakespeare's genius offensive. I do not feel unhappy at being unable to believe (with Samuel Schoenbaum) that "a mood of affectionate warmth pervades" the poem. I find the partial antipathy excusable, when I remember what mutual dislike has been nourished by great literary contemporaries. I am willing cheerfully to allow Ben Jonson to temper his praise of Shakespeare with a certain acerbity, especially when I recall what Dr. Johnson thought of Gray, or what Wordsworth thought of Keats, or what Keats thought of Shelley, or what Byron thought of Wordsworth, or what Coleridge thought of Tennyson – or, for that matter, what we think of one another.

Hamlet and the Pangs of Love

J. M. NOSWORTHY

The action of *Hamlet* arises out of hatred, out of the hero's hatred towards the murderer upon whom he seeks to achieve absolute revenge. Yet one remarkable feature of that hero's character is his capacity for loving and for inspiring love. The "great love which the general gender bear him" in the play has been endorsed by the general gender of both the theatre and the chimney-corner from Shakespeare's day to our own. Hamlet's own love, as is natural, is bestowed mainly upon Ophelia and his mother, and it obviously attaches in like measure to King Hamlet. But we are shown how the love which memory holds for the recently dead father extends, in the appropriate degree, to the long-dead Yorick. He loves, according to their merit and degree, Horatio, Laertes, Marcellus and the strolling players and conjures even Rosencrantz and Guildenstern by "the obligation of our ever-preserved love." It is my purpose to suggest that certain of these relationships are basic to our understanding of the play.

Hamlet's response to the Ghost's initial revelations,

> Haste me to know't, that I, with wings as swift
> As meditation or the thoughts of love,
> May sweep to my revenge

draws together the three dominant aspects of his own destined pattern of behaviour, yet there is potent irony. He does not sweep to his revenge, and the two immediately personal factors which most retard his actions are precisely meditation and love. In the general Shakespearian context, meditation is the differential, since

41

Hamlet stands alone amongst the tragic heroes in making any serious effort to temper emotion with reason.

Revenge and love are, of course, the ever-present ingredients of Shakespearian tragedy; they extend, in varying ratios, from *Romeo and Juliet* through to *Timon of Athens*, where things go awry, so that love degenerates into conspicuous waste and revenge into impotent vituperation. And it is significant that, for Shakespeare as for Aristotle, crime and retribution within the family produce the most effective form of tragedy – a circumstance which gives special relevance to Macbeth's kinship with Duncan and affords a further explanation for the breakdown of *Timon of Athens*, whose hero stands in total, and far from splendid, isolation. *Othello* and *King Lear* are both tragedies which strike a fairly even balance between family ties of love and duty and the opposing force of retribution; but the pattern in *Hamlet* is more close-knit in the sense that, if all had gone well, the two families involved would have been unified by the marriage of Hamlet and Ophelia. Since, however, all goes ill, the theme of vengeance is obviously paramount. Yet there remains the need to consider just how much emphasis the dramatist has placed upon the theme of love.

Shakespeare tends to discount the more obvious aspects of love in certain of the play's relationships. The bond between Claudius and Gertrude, though genuine enough, is subject to the kind of emotional poverty that Claudius reveals in his admonitions to Hamlet and in his speech to Laertes:

> But that I know love is begun by time;
> And that I see, in passages of proof,
> Time qualifies the spark and fire of it.

The mutual ties between Hamlet and his mother do not seem to be conspicuous or significant, and if modern critics assure us that they are both, I suspect they have drawn their conclusions from Freud rather than from Shakespeare. There is little clear evidence that Polonius is deeply attached to his children and they, in their turn, give the impression of being bound to him by feelings of duty rather than of love. To Laertes and his relationship with Ophelia I shall return.

In the event the courtship of Hamlet and Ophelia is very much retrospective and implicit. Perhaps, if Shakespeare had given them a balcony scene, as in *Romeo and Juliet*, the commentators would have been quicker to recognize them as "a pair of star-crossed lovers." As it is, much nonsense has been written about them and several stubborn heresies survive. Most of these are based on the so-called nunnery scene, in which Ophelia, it would seem, appears as a deceitful and more or less loose woman. Shakespeare's portrayal, we have been told, looks back to Belle-forest's story of *Hamlet*, where the usurping king, in order to test Hamlet's apparent madness, arranges for him to be tempted by a harlot. Such an assumption is objectionable on *prima facie* grounds. Shakespeare's immediate source was not Belleforest's story. It is generally accepted that he was indebted to the lost *Hamlet* play, written probably by Thomas Kyd, based probably on Belleforest. Since we have no way of knowing what Kyd did with Belleforest's character, or what Shakespeare did with Kyd's, no conclusions can be drawn. Even so, the theory would have some claim to acceptance if, in fact, Belleforest said anything about a harlot. All that his story supplies is a brief account of what he regards as a rather poor stratagem whereby a beautiful young woman is set in a secret place to allure Hamlet's mind with flattery and crafty means. The plot is disclosed to Hamlet by the friend who accompanies him and then by the damsel who, we are told, loves him more than she loves herself and has done so since childhood. It is true that Belleforest seems to imply that Hamlet has sexual intercourse with the girl, but that does not convict her of harlotry. Nor has it any demonstrable counterpart in the nunnery scene.

Ophelia's wantonness, then, is something contributed either by Shakespeare or by the commentators, and my suspicions rest on the latter. The term "nymph" which Hamlet applies to her may be associated with nymphomania in the mind of a modern reader, but no such association existed in the minds of Shakespeare's audiences. Those familiar with the play and with classical mythology may have detected proleptic irony, since the categories of nymphs include Dryads, the tree-nymphs who died with the trees that they inhabited, and Naiads, the nymphs of rivers and brooks, who were thought to possess those afflicted with madness. The word may therefore anticipate the circumstances of Ophelia's death but, in its immediate context, as Dr. Johnson appears to have recognized, it almost certainly relates to her piety. Since Hamlet finds her at her orisons, it is not entirely surprising that he should soon after commend her to a nunnery. What is surprising is that Professor Dover Wilson should have sought to persuade us that "nunnery" here is synonymous with "brothel." There is more to be said for Professor Harold Jenkins's closely reasoned argument that, in directing Ophelia to a nunnery, Hamlet commits her to virginity. The nunnery scene is the direct consequence of Polonius's plan that

> At such a time I'll loose my daughter to him,

and much has been read into the verb. It is possible that Polonius is playing the pandar and is prepared to hazard his daughter's virtue, but, if so, his attitude is strangely at odds with that assumed in Act I, Scene 3. He has kept her virtually a prisoner, bidding her "lock herself from his resort." If, then, we see him as her jailer, we may, after all, do better to interpret "loose" in its more usual sense.

Even if Ophelia is not the temptress, there is still, it seems, a substantial body of critical opinion which regards her as a deceiver, and much has been made of her alleged lie in the nunnery scene. When Hamlet suddenly interjects, "Where's your father?," she answers, "At home, my lord." The answer is, of course, defensible on merely practical grounds. We must allow that, if her reply had been, "hiding behind the arras with the king," the play would almost certainly have been brought to an abrupt, bloody and wholly unsatisfactory conclusion. We must allow, too, that, in terms of the Elizabethan stage, "At home" is not a precisely localizing phrase and may mean nothing more than "Somewhere in the palace." It is Hamlet, not Ophelia, who narrows the location to "in's own house."

These are relevant considerations, but neither affords a full explanation. The other possibility is that Ophelia believes her answer to be a true one. She knows the reason why Polonius has arranged the meeting with Hamlet, ostensibly at least, but it is by no means certain that she has been made a party to the eavesdropping. The stratagem is presented thus in Act III, Scene 1, 28–49:

> King.   Sweet Gertrude, leave us too;
> For we have closely sent for Hamlet hither,

That he, as 'twere by accident, may here
Affront Ophelia. Her father and myself, lawful espials,
Will so bestow ourselves, that, seeing, unseen,
We may of their encounter frankly judge,
And gather by him, as he is behav'd,
If 't be the affliction of his love or no
That thus he suffers for.

      Queen.   I shall obey you.
And for your part, Ophelia, I do wish
That your good beauties be the happy cause
Of Hamlet's wildness; so shall I hope your virtues
Will bring him to his wonted way again,
To both your honours.

      Ophelia.   Madam, I wish it may.
               [*Exit Queen.*]

      Polonius.   Ophelia, walk you here. Gracious, so please you,
We will bestow ourselves. [*To Ophelia.*] Read on this book;
That show of such an exercise may colour
Your loneliness. We are oft to blame in this,
'Tis too much prov'd, that with devotion's visage
And pious action we do sugar o'er
The devil himself.

It seems to me entirely credible that Claudius's information to
Gertrude is an aside and that so is Polonius's

              Gracious, so please you,
              We will bestow ourselves.

Since no directions are printed at this point in the early editions,
nothing can be either proven or disproven. If I am accused of
having invented two asides it touches me not, for other commentators have invented more ambitious and, I think, less plausible
stage directions in this same scene. In suggesting that Ophelia is
wholly innocent of complicity, I am fortified by Polonius's words
at lines 187–89:

              How now, Ophelia!
        You need not tell us what Lord Hamlet said;
        We heard it all.

45

Why should he tell her this if she already knows that he and Claudius have been eavesdropping?

In general the critics have concentrated too much upon the nunnery scene with the result that many things relevant to the love story of Hamlet and Ophelia have been overlooked. I propose, therefore, to attempt a consecutive narrative, relating the details to attendant circumstances and, once or twice, pausing to comment.

It is clear that, at the outset, Hamlet and Ophelia are deeply in love. He has, she tells Polonius, made many tenders of his affection, importuning her with love in honourable fashion and giving countenance to his speech "with almost all the holy vows of heaven." I do not, of course, suggest that they are practically man and wife, but we should recognize that, by Elizabethan custom, the exchange of holy vows could have made them so since this served as the basis for *sponsalia de praesenti* which amounted to full marriage. Such, it seems, was Shakespeare's own experience with Anne Hathaway and, perhaps for that reason alone, we should acknowledge the deep significance of Hamlet's vows. But the security which those vows imply is threatened by the circumstance of Gertrude's o'erhasty marriage, and the generalization, "Frailty, thy name is woman!" shows him already assailed by fears, if not by doubts. At more or less the same time Ophelia's security is itself being undermined. Laertes discounts the trifling of Hamlet's favours but delivers what is, on the whole, a reasonable warning that, although his love may be genuine, his choice in marriage is subject to "the main voice of Denmark." Polonius, in his turn, disparages Hamlet's advances, assures her (as he later tells Claudius) that

> Lord Hamlet is a prince, out of thy star;
> This must not be

and bids her "lock herself from his resort." There is a subtle distinction to be observed here. Laertes's warning that Hamlet is subject to the will of the people is true but, though disturbing, not prohibitive, since Ophelia may well be the people's choice. Polonius, on the other hand, roundly asserts that she cannot be because of disparity in rank. This, I suggest, is nonsense. Polonius himself is a lord, and is addressed as such not only by his children and Reynaldo but also by Hamlet. He is the product of a convenient piece of dramatic compression which accords him the functions of Master of the Royal Household, Lord Steward, Lord Chamberlain and others. His daughter, who, within the context of the play, is the second lady of Denmark, must surely be at least as eligible as four of Henry VIII's wives had been.

We may assume that, consequent upon the Ghost's revelations, Hamlet's fear of woman's frailty has hardened into doubt, with the result that Gertrude is now seen as a "most pernicious woman," and Ophelia's own reliability is something that needs to be established. The vows which he has made to his father's spirit must necessarily take precedence over those made to her, but only until he has effected a revenge to which he confidently expects to sweep "with wings as swift/As meditation or the thoughts of love." There is certainly no warrant at this stage for supposing that Hamlet has renounced his claim to Ophelia or that his hopes of marriage have in any way diminished.

It is when Hamlet bursts into Ophelia's chamber that tragic misunderstanding becomes operative. The distress and perplexity which the incident arouses in her is sufficiently communicated in her report to Polonius, who interprets Hamlet's behaviour as "the very ecstasy of love," provoked by her refusal to see him or to receive his letters. Some commentators equate it with the assumption of an antic disposition. Others call it plain madness or, like Professor Dover Wilson, subtly detect "the after-effects of some terrible dream or overpowering delirium, such as was known to attack melancholic subjects." Any, or all, of these explanations might serve, but perhaps the truth is at once more simple and more complex. Hamlet fears that Ophelia has rejected him; he has but recently encountered his father's ghost, has been subjected to terrible revelations and commanded to a no less terrible enterprise. It is almost literal truth that he has

> been loosed out of hell,
> To speak of horrors

and we need seek no further explanation for his distracted manner and dishevelled appearance. If he makes perusal of Ophelia's face, it must surely be in the hope of discovering whether she has rejected him, whether she is frail like Gertrude, whether he should inform her of the Ghost's disclosures, whether he should tell her of his "antic disposition" and make her privy to his plans. If, thereafter, he raises a sigh that shatters his whole being, is it not because he is unable to resolve his doubts and because he cannot or must not or dare not confide in her? We may recognize in this the extremity of bewilderment and despair. We know far more of the facts than Polonius does and can therefore proceed to a more comprehensive judgment.

If Hamlet may not confide in Ophelia, we feel that he should at least warn her against misinterpreting his assumed eccentricities. The letter which Polonius laboriously reads to Gertrude and Claudius raises problems. If it was written before Hamlet's meeting with the Ghost, it can scarcely be reckoned more than a heartfelt but florid and conventional effusion. If, on the other hand, it was recent, its purpose must obviously be deeper. What, in effect, its ill numbers would then mean is: You will see strange things and I shall seem strange, but whatever doubts assail you, do not doubt my love for you – an assurance that is given the additional emphasis of "but that I love thee best, O most Best, believe it." This, I would observe, is not the solution of an enigma. It is precisely what the letter says when viewed from one particular and not demonstrably invalid standpoint. To suppose that Ophelia's personal tragedy springs from her failure to discern the purport of the letter is to lean heavily on conjecture when conjecture is perhaps unnecessary. What in general she fails to recognize is the indestructibility of Hamlet's love for her.

In the fishmonger section Hamlet fears that Polonius, like Jephtha, is prepared to sacrifice his daughter and it is now that he first pleads for the preservation of her virginity. His words, in conformity with the "antic disposition," are enigmatic, but their general purport seems clear enough. It is a ready inference that Hamlet still clings to the hope of regaining Ophelia's love, but the famous soliloquy that precedes the nunnery section suggests that that hope is fast disappearing. He there alludes to the pangs of a love that is "despiz'd" according to Q2, "dispriz'd" according to the Folio. Either adjective could apply. In what follows both do.

The antic disposition is clearly in evidence in the encounter between the two lovers, though the eccentricity is of manner rather than of matter. Misunderstandings multiply. Hamlet, believing that Ophelia has rejected him, directs her to a nunnery at least as much in sorrow as in anger. We need not follow Professor Dover Wilson in alleging, against all textual warrant, that anger arises because Hamlet detects Polonius and consequently believes her to be a liar and a decoy. The point is that she has rejected him, without apparent cause, at the time when he most needs her support, and has returned his gifts with words that may not be entirely innocent of provocation. I do not think it wholly fanciful to discern coldness in

> remembrances of yours
> That I have longèd long to re-deliver

or the arrogance and pent-up fury of a woman scorned in

> Take these again, for to the noble mind,
> Rich gifts wax poor when givers prove unkind.

I question whether Ophelia, at this point, is quite the demure and self-effacing creature that critics and producers would often have her be.

The sequence of irony is remarkable. Hamlet supposes that Ophelia has rejected him. She believes that he has rejected, or is rejecting, her, and returns his gifts. This confirms his impression, so that he proceeds to confirm hers and ends by petulantly denying that he ever loved her in terms so vehement and uncharacteristic that she concludes that he is mad and lapses into a state of despair and grief that foreshadows her own madness. Hamlet's speeches are fraught with nuances and by-dependencies, but not, I think, with all the mysteries that commentators have alleged. Claudius is surely right when he remarks

> Nor what he spake, though it lack'd form a little,
> Was not like madness.

What in effect this section yields is a lovers' quarrel which, as Ophelia recognizes, has reached the point of no return.

Whether Hamlet has abandoned all hope is less clear. His concern for the preservation of Ophelia's virginity suggests that perhaps he has not. His subsequent outrageous behaviour in the play scene, however, does nothing to repair the damage. He addresses her throughout as if she were a woman he had just picked up on the street and her responses are at first brief and distant. She unbends a little and ingenuously asks him questions, but his answers are at first detached and then hostile. She recovers with the comment, perhaps sarcastic, perhaps playful, but certainly not neutral, "You are as good as a chorus, my lord," only, when rebuked, to sound the poignancy of "You are keen, my lord, you are keen." There is altogether a curious detachment about these exchanges, with nothing to remind us that there had ever been close ties between the two, save for Hamlet's bitterly pointed comment on the brevity of woman's love. The relationship that should have led to marriage ends here only in those mocking echoes of the marriage service which are virtually the last words they speak one to another.

The circumstances of Ophelia's madness are all bound up with the tragic story of her love. Deprived of her lover, deprived of her father at the hands of that lover, she wanders abroad, like Jephtha's daughter, bewailing her virginity. She is not pregnant, as some commentators have absurdly maintained, but it is quite likely that, in her own deranged mind, there exists the conviction that she is. Her document in madness is charged with obvious sexual fantasy and, as Shakespeare's audience would have known, the Valentine song, in its entirety, is a young woman's complaint against the youth who has seduced her and has gone to sea, leaving her to bear his child. Ophelia's snatches of old tunes imply that that is what Hamlet has done, and we now see how, in her madness, she may strew those "dangerous conjectures in ill-breeding minds" which so much disturb Horatio and the Queen, who now stand alone in the defence of Hamlet's good name.

Shakespeare has shown us the stages through which true love has passed on its way to utter destruction, but it is only at Ophelia's graveside that Hamlet reveals the full quality of that love:

> I loved Ophelia: forty thousand brothers
> Could not, with all their quantity of love,
> Make up my sum.

This, in range and magnitude, goes far beyond anything that Romeo, Troilus and Antony are able to express, and not even

Othello makes a larger claim. Yet there are critics who insist that Hamlet's protestations must not be taken seriously. Professor Dover Wilson would have us believe that Hamlet is roused from "unconcerned surprise" to "rodomontade" and "uncontrolled hysteria" by the "ranting insincerity" and "indecent over-emphasis" of Laertes, and that "it is not love for Ophelia." In general this view seems to me to invoke the stubborn heresy that certain of Shakespeare's tragic heroes (notably Othello) luxuriate in self-dramatization which is, among other things, a form of self-deception. In particular it is open to the objection that it bases a speculative judgment about Hamlet on a no less speculative one about Laertes, and it is to Laertes that I now turn.

Those critics who do not stress his ingrained villainy speak of him as treacherous or uncontrolled or worthless or dissolute or insincere. Bradley voiced one general attitude when he observed that Hamlet "describes Laertes as a 'very noble youth,' which he was far from being," and it was, I believe, Sir Frank Benson who crystallized another attitude in his advertisement: "Wanted: a left-arm slow bowler able to play Laertes." Against these views of him as scoundrel, wastrel or nonentity we can, I believe, oppose a formidable body of evidence drawn directly from the play itself.

Hamlet does describe him as a "very noble youth." He addresses him as "my brother" and speaks of "this brother's wager." He protests, "I loved you ever" and declares, "I'll court his favours." He concedes that Laertes's "definement suffers no perdition" in Osric's

> believe me, an absolute gentleman, full of most excellent differences, of very soft society and great showing: indeed, to speak feelingly of him, he is the card or calendar of gentry, for you shall find in him the continent of what part a gentleman would see.

We may, like Hamlet, deplore Osric's affected manner but that is no reason for rejecting his testimony.

Of the final duel, the question to be asked is not whether it is a fair fight, which it is obviously not, but whether we have the right to expect a fair fight. Laertes's obligation to revenge is no less than Hamlet's and the principle of "may the best man win" simply does not apply. His duty is to destroy his father's slayer and, since he is evidently a less skilled fencer than Hamlet, the stratagem is quite necessary. He is, of course, allied to the forces of evil, but that is due to erroneous judgment which Claudius's guile has made it impossible for him to avoid. What, in effect, the King begins by implying in the final scene of Act IV is that Hamlet is a homicidal maniac. The fight in the graveyard does nothing to dispel this impression, nor does the hero's proclamation of madness immediately before the duel. Queensberry rules are as inapplicable in the context of madness as they are in that of revenge. What, however, merits remark is that Laertes himself has genuine scruples: "And yet 'tis almost 'gainst my conscience." He accepts death as a fitting punishment – "I am justly kill'd with mine own treachery" – and absolves his adversary of all blame, even though he still does not know the facts that establish Hamlet's innocence. This, I suggest, is magnanimity, as the Elizabethans conceived it.

With this in mind we may profitably work backwards. The grief and rage occasioned by the killing of his father, by the madness and pitiful death of his sister, and by the "maimed rites" accorded to her are both natural and intelligible, but they lead to violence in speech and action that may be excessive. It is arguable that, both in Act IV, Scenes 5 and 6, and in the graveyard scene, he indulges in self-dramatization. Hamlet accuses him of ranting – but Hamlet is too angry to weigh his words. I cannot believe that he, in calmer mood, would have endorsed Professor Dover Wilson's charges of "ranting insincerity" and "indecent over-emphasis." Such allegations must stand or fall in the light of what can be inferred about Laertes's relationship with his sister, and this takes us back to the first act.

The relevant scene (I.3) appears on the surface to comprise three lengthy pieces of advice, with Polonius merely repeating to Ophelia what she has already been told by her brother. If so, Shakespeare was being extraordinarily clumsy unless, as some critics affirm, he was trying to show that Laertes is very much his father's son. But, for two reasons, I doubt whether that was his purpose. In the first place, the analogy would be established only if Polonius's counsel to Ophelia preceded that of Laertes and, in the second, there are elsewhere in the play remarkably few signs of any close resemblance between the two men. The truth, I suggest, is that in Act I, Scene 3 Shakespeare drew distinctions which would have emerged clearly on the stage and which are by no means obscure in the received texts. The heavy father is impatient, scornful, untrusting, tyrannical and very much concerned for his own reputation. Laertes, by contrast, begins by imploring Ophelia to write to him and her reply, "Do you doubt that?" immediately conveys the close understanding that exists between them. The advice that he then offers, though mistaken, is perfectly reasonable in a brother who is solicitous only for her welfare. When she retorts with a *tu quoque* it is not, I think, her waspishness which is revealed but the easy give-and-take that informs their relationship. That the whole tone of the exchange is one of affection, sincerity and tenderness is established not only at the beginning but also by the charged and imploring phrase, "Fear it, Ophelia, fear it, my dear sister." The fact that Laertes receives Ophelia's counsel with the assurance, "O, fear me not," disposes of the charge of dissipation which arises from the dialogue between Polonius and Reynaldo in the first half of Act II, Scene 1, and from that alone. Shakespeare does not accuse Laertes of gaming, drinking, swearing, quarrelling and drabbing. Nor does Polonius. We are not told that Polonius believes that he indulges in vice: merely that he fears or suspects that he might. All in all there is little reason for questioning the honesty of Laertes's assurance that he will not tread "the primrose path of dalliance."

What emerges, then, is not the intemperate firebrand of critical belief but a loyal subject of Claudius, whom he innocently believes to be the lawful king, a resolute and dutiful son and, above all, a loving and solicitous brother. Shakespeare, in his own distinctive way, more than once emphasizes his basic gentleness. We may note the predilection for floral imagery which Laertes shares with the noble-natured princes in *Cymbeline*. We may reflect upon how much heartbreak is packed into his anguished apostrophe

O rose of May!
Dear maid, kind sister, sweet Ophelia!

and into his no less anguished entreaty:

Do you see this, O God?

If words such as these mean anything, they must surely mean everything.

The show of stoicism with which Laertes receives the news of his sister's death gives way to tears. There is nothing here to suggest that his grief is anything but overwhelming. And so it is at her obsequies. There is righteous indignation in his protest to the churlish priest, for he is defending her innocence and chastity. There is towering rage against Hamlet, whom he believes to be the author of Ophelia's misfortunes as well as Polonius's slayer. But over and above this, there is profoundest grief. When he leaps into the grave and cries, "Now pile your dust upon the quick and dead," is it not because this alone offers the hope of reunion with all that had been precious to him?

If I have laboured thus in the defence of Laertes's wounded name, it is in the hope of affirming the quality and magnitude of the final conflict. In the graveyard scene his integrity is the yardstick by which we have to measure that of Hamlet. The hero's claim of love for Ophelia means very little if Laertes is the insincere wastrel of critical opinion. But if the bond between brother and sister was as firm as I have suggested, the sum of Hamlet's love must assuredly be accounted as great as that which any man ever bestowed upon any woman. If we refer back to Ophelia's speeches at Act I, Scene 3, 110–14 and Act III, Scene 1, 97–99, we shall find evidence to suggest that it was.

The irony of the graveyard scene is complex almost beyond definition. Ophelia is buried in the grave that had held Yorick, whom Hamlet had also once loved. The two men who prepare to do battle to the death in that grave are her brother and the lover who affirms his eternal love for Laertes and addresses him as brother. For both of them death stands beckoning, with the promise of release and fulfilment. This is ironically accommodated in Claudius's allusion to his own purpose: "This grave shall have a living monument." That monument, as is fitting, will comprise both Hamlet and Laertes.

We move, then, to the catastrophe, and here again the character of Laertes is relevant. Claudius, we observe, has ceased to be an active participant. He has laid his plans and has now merely to sit and watch them taking effect. It is the conflict between Hamlet and Laertes which becomes, in consequence, the clash of "mighty opposites" and it is necessary that the devoted brother should also present himself as the noble avenger. To match Hamlet against a worthless scoundrel would be to proffer a lame conclusion. But Shakespeare, I think, intended that his hero should have a worthy opponent, and it is that intention which renders the final encounter a thing of heroic magnitude.

I have spoken of the balancing of love and revenge and hope that I have shown that the two themes are substantial and ultimately inseparable. To designate *Hamlet* merely a "revenge tragedy" is, I think, to degrade it. The genre was not a particularly exalted one, and *Hamlet*, viewed primarily as a contribution to it, is not conspicuously successful. Action and motivation had been better managed by Kyd in *The Spanish Tragedy* and by Shakespeare himself in *Titus Andronicus*. It is convenient at this point to recall that the catastrophe of the play was not at all to the liking of Dr. Johnson:

> The catastrophe is not very happily produced; the exchange of weapons is rather an expedient of necessity, than a stroke of art. A scheme might easily have been formed, to kill *Hamlet* with the dagger, and *Laertes* with the bowl.
> The poet is accused of having shewn little regard to poetical justice, and may be charged with equal neglect of poetical probability. The apparition left the regions of the dead to little purpose; the revenge which he demands is not obtained but by the death of him that was required to take it; and the gratification which would arise from the destruction of an usurper and a murderer, is abated by the untimely death of *Ophelia*, the young, the beautiful, the harmless, and the pious.

Coleridge, too, protested that Hamlet dies "the victim of mere circumstance and accident," and these strictures are valid in the context of Senecan revenge tragedy. Shakespeare has satisfied Aristotle's demand for the probable but not for the necessary, and there is an appalling waste.

But *Hamlet* is not as Senecan as all that. No ghost, either in armour or nightgown, returns to point the moral or adorn the tale. Instead, it is left to Horatio to pronounce absolution and to Fortinbras to voice the panegyric, and we sense that herein a new tonality has been established. The revenge plot has been extended, enriched and rationalized by what I take to be one of the greatest of love stories, and that with no prompting from either Seneca or his Greek models. It is convenient that we should remind ourselves that, of the thirty-three Hellenic plays that have come down to us, precisely one – the *Antigone* – contains anything remotely resembling a "love interest," and that Aristotle, instancing those tragic situations that involve strong ties of affection, confines himself to brother killing brother, son killing father, mother killing son, son killing mother, but ignores both the husband and wife relationship and that of man and maid. It was with Cinthio and the Italian neo-Senecans that romance came to share the scene with revenge; while it was Denores, faithful to Aristotle but impatient with the restrictive themes of classical tragedy, who demanded that tragedians should concern themselves with matters both more recent and more romantic, giving, as example, his own version of the Thyestes banquet in a scenario based on Boccaccio's tale of Guiglielmo Rossiglione. Shakespearian tragedy, with possible obligations to Thomas Kyd, reflects these developments, though fulfilment was gradual. There is, in a sense, too much romance in *Romeo and Juliet* and, in *Julius Caesar*, too little. In *Hamlet* the two elements of revenge and romance are at last in harmony and a new age of tragedy begins.

The Wasp: A Trial Flight

J. W. LEVER

Who or what is *The Wasp*? To this day the play remains a mystery. Nobody has seen it acted since the closing of the theatres during the English Civil War. Never has it appeared in print. Eminent scholars of the drama have remained in total ignorance of its contents. Anonymous, undated, *The Wasp* survives in a single manuscript on which only the barest comments, and even these of doubtful accuracy, have ever been published. To be able to introduce it in this company is a rare privilege, for occasions are few and topics are scarce on which a speaker nowadays may feel so confident that he is better informed than his hearers. What is more remarkable is that such an introduction should be needed, since indeed the most obscure fact about this play is its continuing obscurity. In an age when the least scrap of information bearing on drama of the Elizabethan age comes up for minute scrutiny, it might be supposed that *The Wasp* was either quite insignificant or quite fabulously arcane. Actually it is a play of uncommon interest and merit; the whereabouts of the manuscript have been known for a full hundred years; and a transcript has been available for the last forty. In this strange case it seems right to preface my account of the play with a brief sketch of the kind of attention, and inattention, it has so far received, if only by way of a cautionary tale for hopeful young research students.

The first published announcement of *The Wasp*'s existence appeared in the third report of the Historical Manuscripts Commission in 1872, which listed among the manuscripts at Alnwick Castle, Northumberland, the following items:

Folio. Temp. Elizabeth. A comicall History in the form of a play

called the Waspe, or Subjects President (imperfect). A play (Friar
Bacon?); also imperfect. In 1 Vol   (page 118 b).

Literary scholarship followed, at a respectful distance of fifty-
nine years, with Sir Walter Greg's eleven-line account in *Dramatic Documents From The Elizabethan Playhouse* (1931),
pages 360–61, under the classification "Manuscript Plays C 6."
Here *The Wasp* was dated about 1630, and the manuscript
described as possibly autograph, containing prompt notes in another hand which gave the names of two actors, "Ellis" and
"Ambros." One of these, thought Greg, might be Ellis Worth or
Ellis Bedowe, the other Ambrose Beeland. An edition was stated
to be in preparation. The shortness of this notice, with its mention of only two names in the prompt notes, strongly suggests
that Greg had not himself consulted the manuscript. It seems
very likely that he took his information from W. L. Renwick,
Professor of English at Armstrong College, Newcastle-upon-Tyne
(now the University of Newcastle), who was engaged at about
this time in editing the other play bound in the same volume,
tentatively named *Friar Bacon*, for the Malone Society under
Greg's general editorship. Renwick may have looked over some
pages of *The Wasp*, without feeling called on to examine it
closely. He certainly knew that an edition of that play was in
preparation, for the editor was a research student of his own
department working for a master's degree. About a year later
Renwick placed inside the cover of the manuscript volume a note
dated September 30, 1932, which stated with regard to *The
Wasp*: "It has been transcribed by Mr. J. J. Gourlay of Armstrong
College, who thinks that the 'Captain Jordan' whose name appears in the Manuscript may be the author – Thomas Jordan
1612?–1685?". This thoughtful insertion was no doubt meant to
ensure that intending investigators might know at the outset of
Gourlay's undertaking. Finally in 1936, when Renwick's own
edition of the other play in the volume, now entitled *John of
Bordeaux*, was published, the introduction mentioned in a foot-
note: "Rotographs, and a transcript of *The Waspe* by J. J.
Gourlay, are in Armstrong College Library, Newcastle-upon-
Tyne."[1]

---

[1]*John of Bordeaux* or *The Second Part of Friar Bacon*, ed. W. L. Renwick,
Malone Society Reprints (1936), Introduction, p. v.

One might suppose that after 1936 serious students of seventeenth-century drama would take the open opportunity of reading and assessing the play. Let us see. In 1941 the first two volumes of G. E. Bentley's authoritative work *The Jacobean and Caroline Stage* appeared, with a number of conjectures in the second volume on the identity of the two actors mentioned, as Greg had pointed out, in the prompt notes to *The Wasp*.[2] "Ellis," wrote Bentley, might possibly be Ellis Bedowe; but, he added, "Ellis Worth, a much better known actor, seems a more likely candidate."[3] Alternatively, "Ellis" might be Ellis Guest, described in 1625 as the leader of a company. As for "Ambros," he was "conceivably" Ambrose Beeland, a royal violinist who had been a member of the King's Company in 1624.[4] The qualifying words "seems" and "conceivably" give to this guesswork an air of scholarly caution which is quite misleading. Had Bentley consulted either the manuscript or the transcript, instead of taking all he knew of the play from Greg, his comments might have been helpful. He would then have seen that the "Ellis" of the prompt note was one of two unnamed attendant lords with a part consisting, according to which of the two lords he played, of either a total of five lines or one. This was clearly no role for the well-known actor Ellis Worth. Nor could "Ambros" have been the adult and accomplished Ambrose Beeland, since this part was that of a small boy. Bentley would also have found in the prompt notes the names of four more actors, three of whom, together with Ellis Bedowe, appeared in the list of members of the King's Revels Company at Norwich in March 1635 – an important document frequently alluded to in *The Jacobean and Caroline Stage*. But to return to the forgotten Gourlay. In a letter to *The Times Literary Supplement* of June 5, 1943, he replied to Bentley's conjectures, putting the case for "Ellis" as Ellis Bedowe and naming the four actors passed over by both Bentley and Greg. Gourlay went on to claim that *The Wasp* was written by Thomas Jordan, and that it was performed about 1638 by the amalgamated King's Revels–Queen Henrietta's players at Salisbury Court. In conclusion he referred to his own transcript and investigations, mentioning that these had not been published.

[2]II, 362, 363, 453, 627.
[3]Ibid., 362.
[4]Ibid., 363.

Bentley's comments came twelve years later. In Volume V of
The Jacobean and Caroline Stage (1954), noting that Gourlay's
work was unpublished, he declared roundly: "I know of no
edition of the play." Gourlay's opinions on authorship "presented
no evidence whatever," and his dating amounted to "reasoning
from conjecture." "If," Bentley added, "the names which Mr.
Gourlay read and Dr. Greg did not" were present, then a date
of c. 1634–36 was most likely.[5] And there the matter has rested.
Gourlay's transcript and commentary is still in the university
library of Newcastle-upon-Tyne. The text contains a number of
inaccuracies, but at least enables an enquirer to form a fair idea
of the play. The claim that Thomas Jordan was the author is not
very convincing, depending as it does upon stylistic habits and
political attitudes common to many other authors of the time,
together with some similarities of imagery and phrasing in
Jordan's writings which might have been suggested by this play
in which he had undoubtedly been assigned a part. On the other
hand Gourlay's views about the probable date of performance,
the company, and the theatre, are quite well grounded. Immature
as it is in some respects, this pioneer study should not have been
ignored. Yet up to now, thirty-six years after Renwick's published
mention of its existence and location, I have found no further
reference to it in any work on seventeenth-century drama.

In this account of *The Wasp*'s long hibernation I have touched
upon matters of authorship, date, performance. These will be
returned to, but our first consideration must be the play itself.
The Wasp, or Subject's Precedent – to give the full title in
modern, unambiguous spelling – is in its main plot a political
thriller disguised as history, in its sub-plot a comedy of disguise.
The setting is an imaginary Britain ruled by the Roman Prorex
Marianus and his obnoxious favourite Varletti. In the opening
scene the native British barons make their bitter protest against
the foreign tyranny. An oath is sworn to rid themselves of the
sycophantic Varletti or else depose the Prorex. Spokesman and
leader of the baronial faction is "plain home spun Archibald,"
"old Tom," the highly vocal champion of castle against court,
Britain against Rome, rustic simplicity against foreign fads. Un-
derstandably Archibald and his fellow-peers feel a deep antipathy

[5]V, 1433–34.

to the "germaine Crochetmonger" Varletti, described as "a skipping Zenny," "a fellow bred, no better then a ffidler." The antipathy is returned in full measure by Varletti, who sees Archibald as "the kersy Lord, the lynsy wollsy gentlem̄," and sneers at the barons as "bull befe eaters." But the alignment is not as simple as it seems. Plain Tom Archibald, who "cannot desemble," is also the Prorex's agent, who throughout the play acts a double part as traitor and true man to either side, now egging on the barons, now advising the Prorex on how to stave off rebellion. Nor is the Prorex as gullible as we are led to think. He humours Varletti to the point where that spoiled minion asks to marry his ruler's sister, then rounds on him suddenly and banishes him from court. Intrigue follows on intrigue in rapid succession. Varletti, posing as the statesman in retirement, plots to murder the Prorex while out hunting; Marianus is rescued by Archibald and his barons; but Varletti cunningly throws the suspicion back on his enemies. Accordingly Archibald is cast into prison, there to grind corn at the mill, while his wife is dispatched to work in the laundry and his young son to serve in the kitchen with the black guard. But Archibald is undaunted. He rejoices in hard toil and takes his bread and water with the relish of hunger. Overheard by the Prorex, who watches him in concealment, he declares his unabated loyalty to his sovereign. Soon enough he escapes, aided by the Keeper, who turns out to be the baron Conon in disguise. Learning of a new conspiracy by Varletti and Gerald, the prodigal son of his fellow-baron Gilbert, Archibald impersonates the great soldier Percy, "rashe, blody, & vain glorious, Blinde of an Eye," and assumes leadership of the revolt. His ultimate aim is meanwhile kept dark. "Leave that to me," he declares. "Heaven prosper my Intent / & call my life the subiects president."

The sub-plot is neatly dovetailed into the main story. Gilbert Earl of Clarydon, one of Archibald's peers, has been affronted by Varletti and "caperd . . . out of an honord offyce." After they have taken their pledge at the beginning of the play, the barons visit Gilbert at his castle, to find him apparently on his deathbed, heartbroken at his misfortunes. He dismisses his old friends, bids his wife a last farewell, and is seen to die. Left alone with his faithful man Howlet, the dead man sits up and makes his arrangements for a mock funeral, then departs. After Gilbert's supposed demise his wastrel son Gerald (or Geraldine) goes to court, where the Prorex enlists him to spy on the now-banished Varletti. He visits the ex-favourite intending to provoke him into treason, but is himself won over by Varletti's forceful wife Katherine and joins them in their plot to kill the Prorex. Meanwhile Gilbert reappears disguised as an eccentric malcontent known as the Wasp because he buzzes angrily against the world's abuses. In his "fantastick & ridiculous habit" he returns to his supposedly widowed Countess in her country retreat at Walthamstow. Though "dayly cloyd wth suitors," she has refused to make a new match, but now finds herself irresistibly drawn to the Wasp. "Hast Any stomach to mary?" she asks him; "Ime most Horibly in Love wth the." Gilbert parries the proposal, but suggests that they keep house together and give out that they have been privately married. This will rid her of the suitors; "besides," he remarks, "we are not the first paire of Barbarie pidgeons, that have brizd & billd togither in the day & flowne to severall Locker holes at night." Accordingly they live together ostensibly as man and wife, and the Wasp manages the estate on the Countess's behalf. But soon there is a rift. The Countess accuses the Wasp of abusing her trust: he has racked her tenants and cut down her trees, committing just such abuses as Archibald had condemned early on in the play. She takes her case up to the Prorex, who summons them both to appear. Gilbert now answers her charges by simply removing his disguise. As the true owner of the estate and no mere factor, he may do as he pleases with his own. The Countess apologizes to her husband and the pair are happily reconciled.

The play builds up to a finale charged with political symbolism. The barons, apparently in league now with Varletti and Gerald, led by Archibald disguised as the warlike Percy, break into the palace of the Prorex to cries of "downe wth the tyrant downe wth the oppresso^{r}." The Prorex is forced to surrender his crown, and Varletti and Gerald become joint kings. A banquet and ladies are brought in for a celebratory orgy. But as the festivities are about to commence the table turns and the cates for the new kings are seen to consist of toads, newts and live snakes. A naked sword descends which hangs by a slender twine above Gerald's head; he sees a Fury armed with shears about to cut it. Such are the horrors that attend usurpers, and to be rid of them they are at last glad to restore the crown to its rightful owner. To an accompaniment of soft music the table turns again, affording "comfortable vyands" to the true king. Archibald expounds the significance of it all in terms of the mystic power exercised by a monarch:

> his Lookes are armd wth such divinitye
> they alter Nature, & drive essences
> out off all Being. strike treason on its knees –
> turne Arrogance into obedience –
> & devills them selvs to Angells, he can vnlock
> yor Caskett royall; & weare all these Iewells
> in there trew Lustres, that crowne the wedding Ring
> ffitts no mans Temples but a royall king. (Fol. 22b)

This is not quite all; some unfinished business may remain in the way of punishments and rewards. We can only guess, since the end of the play is missing. But in terms of theme, Archibald's speech with its apotheosis of kingship strikes a note of finality.

At an obvious level *The Wasp* is lively entertainment, with its blend of pseudo-history, genial comedy, disguises, reversals, discoveries, and political intrigue. This is heightened by the verbal facility, the fluent blank verse and exuberant prose. The dialogue is full of energy, especially when it conveys a certain tongue-in-cheek quality typical of this author. Even the rascally Varletti is given his attractive moments, as when, after a long silence, he replies to the barons' gibes at his musical interests:

> & yet, my lord to showe
> I am sencible, (tho careless) of there envye
> I will vouch safe a slite rebuke vpon em,
> Bean-chaweing Barrons home to yor contry farms –
> dispute the price of Beans & buttermilk
> & cast vp by yor flaile Arithmetick
> how many Barly sheves will cram a barne
> & medle not wth musick tis an Art
> too much above yor swineish Intellects. (Fol. 6)

The author evidently enjoys himself; his pen flows so readily that there are places where the prompter has felt, as Jonson felt with Shakespeare, *sufflaminandus erat*, drawing a line against some over-ebullient effusion. "torture me, teare me, rack me, roast me," cries Archibald, "boil me in scalding Lead bake me in Brimston Ixions whele, sisiphus stone, Prometheus vulture, Phalleris bull"; "& miloes ox stop thy throat," Varletti shouts back. The prompter too feels this should be stopped, and the whole passage comes out (Fol. 8). But in general the author has his way, and in the plot he rides the helter-skelter of intrigue with uninhibited zest. The play is charged with recollections of former stage hits. Gilbert's death-bed scene begins with reminiscences of John of Gaunt's in *Richard II*, shading into suggestions of *Volpone* on his couch. Howlet as the canny servant is in the line of Brainworm in *Every Man in His Humour*. Plain Tom Archibald echoes Woodstock's "I'm Plain Thomas, by th' rood, I'll speak the truth." Varletti's angling for the sister of the Prorex is inspired by the similar scheme of *Sejanus*; while his masterful wife Katherine, who taunts her husband for his lack of manly ambition and arranges an assassination plot, bears a family likeness to Lady Macbeth. A key phrase in *The Spanish Tragedy* – "Thanks, good Horatio" – is parodied, and *Hamlet*, too, gets in. Gerald is enjoined to revenge his father's murder, committed, he is told, by the Prorex, who poisoned him. "Wele kill him at table kneling at his devotion," he replies, but is told that "that were to charitabler [*sic*]." In two scenes finally cut out after the minor parts had already been allotted, Howlet meets a quartet of Middletonian knaves: Grig the hangman, Dampit the Lombard broker (a name picked up from *A Trick to Catch the Old One*), Kenwell the decoy and Huntit the informer, whose shady activities in Roman Britain extend from Gunpowder Alley to Hazards Bridge, Wapping, Croydon and Kingston. *The Wasp* by these tokens would seem to be a lively continuation of the Elizabethan-Jacobean popular tradition by a writer of considerable talent whose head is full of recollections, conscious or unconscious, of the great plays of Shakespeare, Jonson and Middleton.

But *The Wasp* is more than popular entertainment. Closer consideration reveals more sophisticated planning. The play is not, of course, a reconstruction of history, though the barons' condemnation of Roman tyranny in the first scene comes from the speech of Agricola in Tacitus. On the other hand, there are no such popular distractions as clowns, comic foreigners, magic, drum-and-trumpet battles, or romantic episodes. One finds prac-

tically no violence and very little bawdy. The sub-plot is well
tied in with the main action, and even the deleted scenes of city
comedy, though wildly anachronistic, are not completely at
random. The four knaves Grig, Dampit, Huntit and Kenwell are
drawn out of their seedy habitats to woo Gilbert's Countess and
are put to flight by his man Howlet disguised as a constable.[6]
The play is in fact structurally weakened by the deletion of these
scenes, which shrinks Howlet's part as a prankster and leaves
little support for the Countess's complaint that she is "cloyd wth
suitors." The tale of the disguised husband, it is true, belonged
to a well-worn genre and had been frequently dramatized, as in
Marston's *The Malcontent,* Chapman's *The Widow's Tears,* Middleton's *Michaelmas Term,* Beaumont's *The Faithful Friends,* and
Rowley's *A Match at Midnight.* The author of *The Wasp* may
have known all or any of these, but his treatment of the theme is
his own. Gilbert's device of the mock funeral supervised by
Howlet is more deftly managed than other methods of presenting
the husband's disappearance and return. Nor does the play
moralize, as was usual, about the levity of widows. Gilbert's
attitude is amused and detached, unlike the jealousy of Jarvis,
the husband in *A Match at Midnight,* whose contrivances most
nearly resemble those of the Wasp. Unruffled and good-tempered,
Gilbert merely acts in a spirit of curiosity, indulging a whim to
find out how his wife will conduct herself after his death.

The main plot in its stress on intrigue has some affinities with
Dekker's drama of disguises, *The Welsh Embassador,* set in
Anglo-Saxon times. The double-dealing of the Prorex is not unlike the tricksy king Athelstan's handling of sexual politics, and
it is interesting that in both plays the name Conan, to be found
(like Elidure) in Geoffrey of Monmouth, Spenser and elsewhere,
is spelt "Conon." But the political and social themes, as indicated
by *The Wasp's* sub-title, *Subject's Precedent,* belong to a different, more earnest tradition. In this respect the play is closer to
the anonymous *Nobody and Somebody,* set in Geoffrey of Mon-

---

[6]The theme of the rich widow pestered by rascally suitors may perhaps
have been suggested by the lost Red Bull play *Keep The Widow Waking,*
by Dekker and Rowley; according to the ballad thought to have been
inspired by this play, the widow Anne Elsdon was wooed by a broker, a
horse courser, and a comfit-maker. (C. J. Sisson, *Lost Plays of Shakespeare's
Age* [1936], pp. 103–6.)

mouth's Britain, with its tyrant, weak monarch, wise old coun-
sellors, cynical favourite, and joint kings.[7] Both plays descend
from a class of drama which flourished in the early 1590s, including Marlowe's *Edward II*, Shakespeare's *Richard II* and
King John, and most notably *Thomas of Woodstock*. As "tracts
for the times" these explored the unresolved conflict that pre-
vailed until the Civil War between the ideals of the old nobility,
the new standards at court, and the subject's duty of allegiance
to the sovereign.[8] Woodstock as Plain Thomas abhors sycophants
and hates the artificialities and extravagance of court:

> Should the fashion last I must raise new rents,
> Undo my poor tenants, turn away my servants,
> And guard myself with lace. (I, iii)

Similarly Plain Tom Archibald explains why he wears homely
attire:

> because I wonnot were oakes of my Back (as too many doe,) &
> let my parkes go naked. Besides I cannot roast my Beefe in Harvest,
> nor warme my workmen & Tenants at xpmass, wth a few silken
> shredds: no let my Woods growe & make Leavy Tentes to howse
> my dere in . . . poore widowes too, & orphanes, may have some
> comfort of the wind-falls & brushy vnder woods, for thats all there
> vailes. (Fols. 5–5b)

Both Woodstock and Archibald warn their rulers of the danger of
rebellion. Woodstock refuses to join the revolt against King
Richard, declaring:

> His youth is led by flatterers much astray,
> But he's our king, and God's great deputy. (IV, ii)

Nevertheless True Thomas's scruples do not save him from prison
at the instigation of Bagot, and subsequent murder. Archibald
belongs to a wilier strain. At heart as plain as Woodstock, he

---

[7]The names Elidure, Archibald and Marianus in *The Wasp* may have been
taken from Elidure, Archigallo and Martianus in *Nobody and Somebody*,
rather than directly from Geoffrey of Monmouth.
[8]See Michael Manheim, "The Weak King History Play of the Early 1590's,"
Renaissance Drama, n.s. II (1969), 71–80. Manheim notes the shift in
appeal to audience sympathy from rebels to ruler in *Edward II*, *Woodstock*
(though less marked), *Richard II*, and *King John*.

knows how to play a double game. Accordingly he leads the rebellion in order in the end to defeat it and expose the ambitions of the royal favourite, saving in the process his own skin as well as his ruler's. In a regime bolstered by informers and undercover agents he is both traitor and true man, king-breaker and king-maker. The author of *The Wasp* understands the Stuart political world quite well. The disguises and intrigues of his play dramatize the prevailing duplicity, and also the conflict of loyalties, amounting to social schizophrenia, which beset the old landed gentry as it tried to straddle the opposite principles of adherence to the standards of its class and allegiance to the new despotism. All this is skilfully conveyed through the remote, pseudo-historical setting of Roman Britain. While in plays based on English history and affording obvious parallels to the contemporary scene the shifting of sympathy from rebels to ruler was often awkwardly abrupt, it is achieved here through a deft juggling of attitudes which permits Archibald and his barons to evince at one moment their bitter hatred of the Prorex as a foreign tyrant, at another their loyalty to him as the true, divinely appointed king.

So considered, the play appears not as a mere diversion, but as a shrewd comment on Stuart politics disguised, like the Wasp himself, in a "fantastick & ridiculous habit." Historically, the rivalry between royal favourites and landed artistocracy, court and country, had been endemic for centuries; but it mounted to a crisis in the period between the ascendancy of Buckingham and the outbreak of civil war. Over these years the old nobility swung round from vociferous discontent to fanatical royalism. The process is mirrored in the play. One should guard against hasty identifications of type figures with actual persons; but the case is strong for associating Varletti with George Villiers, first Duke of Buckingham. It rests on a number of details, each of which could be claimed as mere coincidence, but which are cumulatively impressive. Varletti is introduced with gibes at his skill in dancing. "Yes he can dance, & do his grownd trickes cleanlye . . . he caperd Clare out of an honord offyce . . . let sincapace looke well vnto his ffooteinge" (Fol. 3). Villiers, we recall, was celebrated as the best dancer at the court of James I. On one memorable occasion, when the King was in a black mood, he had sprung forward "cutting a score of lofty and very minute capers with so much grace and agility that he . . . appeased the ire of his angry lord."[9] Varletti is described by Archibald as "a fellow bred, no better then a ffidler"; Villiers's mother before she married had served almost as a menial in the house of Lady Beaumont. The Prorex in the course of the play makes Varletti "high admirall of our navy royall"; Villiers was appointed to the post of Lord High Admiral. It may be noticed that the name Varletti, besides its overt suggestion of "varlet" and its Italianate ending, is also a near-anagram of Villiers; and that Varletti's wife and the wife of Villiers were both called Katherine. The author, we may think, was quite adept at suggesting parallels to an audience looking for political allusions which he could repudiate as accidental if challenged.

With Buckingham as its concealed villain, *The Wasp* presents the traditional three-cornered contest of king, favourite and nobles with special topicality. This is not to imply that the play offers detailed references to contemporary events. Varletti's plots to assassinate the Prorex and take over the kingdom have no historical basis – though indeed Buckingham's enemies believed him capable of anything, and he and his mother were widely suspected of having poisoned King James. It was enough that behind the fiction of baronial conspiracy, intrigues and counter-intrigues, and the emergence of Archibald as the mainstay of monarchy, might be discerned the realities of the Grand Remonstrance, the attempted impeachment of Buckingham, the rallying of the nobility to the King's side, and the ascendancy of Strafford, ertswhile leader of the parliamentary rebels. *The Wasp*, which begins with an echoing of Agricola's call to revolt, ends with the reconciliation of the barons and the Prorex and Archibald's assertion of the magical powers and prerogatives of kingship. In this final resolution the theme of the subplot reinforces that of the main. Gilbert the Wasp is in fact the rightful husband of the Countess, as the King is the rightful husband of his people. Taking him to be no more than her factor, his wife had accused him of mismanaging her estate and abusing her trust. In his assumed personality Gilbert does indeed violate the very principles laid down by Archibald early in the play, of care for the land and its tenants. But the estate happens to be his own. In the

[9] G. P. V. Akrigg, *Jacobean Pageant* (1962), p. 223; based on *Calendar of State Papers (Venetian)* 1617–19, pp. 113–14.

last resort he may deal with it as he pleases. When therefore Gilbert reveals his true identity, his wife acknowledges his absolute rights. Similarly, in the symbolical *dénouement* that follows, the *Prorex* becomes invested with the mystic prepotency of *Rex*. And in the seemingly mixed metaphor of Archibald's peroration the rights of sovereign and husband are equated through a compounding of regal and matrimonial symbols:

> that crowne the wedding Ring
> ffitts no mans Temples but a royall king.

If, as I believe, *The Wasp* proves to be a play of uncommon merit, the problems of authorship, date, and theatrical provenance will have a more than routine interest. I shall state what facts we have and offer a few conjectures, but I have no hope of making the schools ring with a Faustus-like *sic probo*.

It may be said at the outset that the text of the manuscript is in autograph, written by an author with a normally regular English hand slightly influenced by Italian forms. The writing is generally clear, and through quite long passages few alterations are made. But there are small slips, and occasionally words or phrases are tinkered with. The additions or alterations are usually interlined above, but sometimes these have had to be crowded in to left or right, or even laterally along the margin, resulting in obscurity or even illegibility, though leads are usually added and caret signs marked. Much if not all of the play would seem to be fair copy from a rough earlier draft, which has been gone over yet again, though it is just possible that this was a writer of extraordinary fluency who wrote almost as fast as he thought.[10] However that be, the manuscript ranks technically as "foul papers," for parts of it at any rate could not possibly serve as

[10] A further scrutiny of the manuscript since this paper was read supports the second alternative. Even on the cleaner pages there are minute changes of letter-formations, hesitations in punctuation or syntax, and substitutions in the course of writing. Nearly always these are deliberately stylistic, rather than accidental slips in transcription. The author may have worked from a preliminary sketch, but it seems that much of the dialogue was directly composed, with unusual but not unhalting fluency, and subsequently revised with interlineations reflecting second or yet later thoughts. In their apparently uncorrected state, parts of the manuscript may be analogous to the state of Shakespeare's play scripts as described by members of his company.

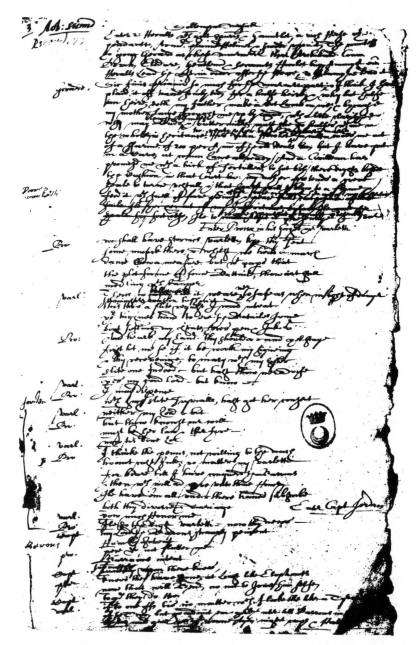

Two pages from the original manuscript of *The Wasp*

prompt copy. The author, however, is certainly used to theatrical usage. He takes care to separate the speeches with short lines, and writes in the speech-prefixes after completing the page. Stage directions are usually clear and concise, with the details left to be worked out in production: "showes a Paper," "Bed discoverd Gilb: in it," "Enter Howlet in som od disguise," "Enter Clarydon, throw of his cloke Apeare disguised as the waspe," etc.[11] Familiarity with stage practice shows even where, as at the beginning of Act II, quite elaborate arrangements are specified:

Sollempne musick
Enter 2: Heralts wth gilt spurrs & Gauntlet, a rich Herse wth pendantes, Armo^r. plumed Helmet & sword vpon it, The countess & yong Gerard as chefe mourners – then Archibald. Conon, Devon, Elidure, Gentlemē & servants Howlet buzy Amongst e'm Heralts Lead the rest in order after the Herce, x fflamyns lead it. (Fol. 7)

In production there might have to be only two or even none of the ten flamens called for, and other trimmings might be cut down; but this would still not upset the main plan for the funeral procession.

Attempts to identify the author's handwriting have so far produced only negative results. A major difficulty is its regularity. Unusual but not unique spellings occur, such as "scylence," "plaes" (place), "lombe" (loom), "cease" (seize). There is some resemblance to Hand E in the short addition to *Sir Thomas More* which Greg assigned to Dekker, and this includes habits of capitalization and punctuation. But both writers followed a style fairly common in the first third of the seventeenth century. Gourlay's claim that the play was by Thomas Jordan would have to be substantiated by an authentic specimen of that author's hand; the instances he cited are very doubtful.

The Wasp is bound together with *John of Bordeaux*; but the binding is Victorian and seems to have been done not long before the report of the Historical Manuscripts Commission in 1872.[12] There is no other connection between the two plays. Nor does

[11]Fols. 3, 3b, 9, 12.
[12]As Renwick pointed out (*John of Bordeaux*, Introduction, p. v), the fly-leaves have 1869 in the watermark; moreover, a letter from J. Duffus Hardy of the Public Record Office, dated 8 July 1870, to a Mr. Martin who was cataloguing manuscripts, mentions his fruitless enquiries concerning *John of Bordeaux* without any reference to *The Wasp*.

The Wasp at all resemble, in style or handwriting, the collection of manuscript plays by William Percy also kept at Alnwick Castle. It seems, however, an odd coincidence that the one extant version of a play whose main character Archibald impersonates a warlike Percy should be found at the Percys' ancestral seat. At one place in Act V, where Varletti calls out "Art thow there percy!" a hand has been drawn in the left margin pointing to the allusion (Fol. 21). Was *The Wasp* ever performed at the castle? Did William Percy in his latter years of seclusion see the manuscript, notice the family name, and decide to acquire it? Or was it bought by Thomas Percy, an eighteenth-century collector and bibliophile? To add to the mystery we may note the appearance in the play of some north-country dialect words – "brewis," "jannick" (jannock), perhaps "scaperloiting," and such usages as "wonnot" and "shonnot."

The appearance of at least one other hand besides the author's shows that the manuscript was prepared for stage production. Warnings for entrances are written in some twelve to twenty lines in advance of the characters' appearance, and connected to the entry directions by leads, as in the manuscripts of *The Welsh Embassador* and *The Lady Mother*, and in the 1634 quarto of *Two Noble Kinsmen*. The author's act headings for Acts III and IV have been struck out and new headings in the other hand inserted later, as a result of the excision of the city comedy episodes. Directions for musical effects have been added: recorders for Gilbert's funeral procession with its "sollempne musick," flourishes at the state entries for the Prorex, horns for the hunting scene, and "soft musike" for the banquet in Act V. In this last act, too, a series of covert references to political affairs in Spain, Italy, France, Holland and Russia have been toned down with an eye to possible censorship. In their original form they allude, though not as specifically as one could desire for dating purposes, to the tyranny of the Spaniards in the Indies, risings in France, shipwrecking and piracy by the Dutch, and a prolonged state of civil war in Russia. Of particular interest is the inclusion in the prompt notes, as has been mentioned, of the names of six actors, given as "Jordan," "Barot," "Ellis," "Ambros," "Morris," and "Noble." The manuscript is not quite complete; but since a transcription would have had to be made to serve as a prompt-book, it is unlikely that the last page, if it had survived, would reveal whether the play received the licence of the Master of Revels.

The names of the six actors provide valuable information. "Jordan" and "Barot" are Thomas Jordan and John Barrett, who appear as thirteenth and fifteenth on the list of members of the King's Revels Company supplied by George Stutfield at Norwich on March 10, 1635. They are also in the printed cast list of Nathanael Richards' *Messalina*, together with Mathias Morris, all three actors taking female parts. *Messalina* was entered in Stationers' Register in October 1639 and printed in 1640 with a statement on the title page that the play had been acted "by the Company of his Majesties Revells." Three "Ellises" were known actors in the late Jacobean and Caroline period: Ellis Worth, Ellis Guest, and Ellis Bedowe. Since this actor has only a minor part, it seems most unlikely that "Ellis" designated either Worth or Guest, who were well established by the 1630s. Ellis Bedowe, however, appears only once, as twenty-first on the Norwich list of 1635. The name "Ellis" is also in the stage directions of Daborne's *The Poor Man's Comfort*, again in a minor part, together with "Sands," i.e. Thomas Sands, who was twelfth on the Norwich list. Thus four of the six named actors in *The Wasp*, Jordan, Barrett, Morris, and Bedowe, belonged to the King's Revels Company before it broke up, owing to an epidemic of plague which led to the closing of the theatres in May 1636. We may note incidentally that the bracketing of Ellis Bedowe with Thomas Jordan in *The Wasp* and with Thomas Sands in *The Poor Man's Comfort* signifies that actors as far down as twenty-first on the Norwich list were connected with the King's Revels Company; a fact which weakens Bentley's repeated claim that the complete list of twenty-eight must have included some other, unidentified company. It seems more likely that the remaining seven names below Bedowe's were of children or hired men.[13]

The other two names of actors in *The Wasp* are "Noble" and "Ambros." Noble appears only once, together with Morris, in a scene later marked for deletion. He has here a silent part as one

---

[13]The King's Revels must have been a large company to perform *Messalina*, which called for a cast of over forty at a time when doubling of parts was no longer customary. The presence at Norwich of twenty-eight men and boys, including wardrobe keepers, hardly seems excessive.

of two supposed officers of the watch, who enter with Howlet, disguised as a constable. Nothing further is known of this shadowy figure. But more can be told of Ambros. He has an interesting and attractive part in the play as Archibald's young son, a fearless little chip of the old block. To the Prorex who calls him a liar he retorts:

> Ile swere thow ner wert solyo^r w^{t}ere thow art by that word. give a trew gent. the lye? so much I am tho but a little one, . . . oh that I were a man for there sakes – Ide ha the combat on him durst but think soe. (Fol. 15)

Sentenced to serve in the "black guard," he escapes and visits his father in prison, bringing him food and drink, defiant as ever. Such a part was calculated to win over any audience, and it was given extra fat after the play had been written, with Ambros brought on again in the revolt of Act V, when he shrilly echoes his seniors' cries of "downe wth the tyrant downe wth the oppresso^r." Again the conjectures of Bentley and Greg, who had not read the play, are groundless. Ambrose Beeland, a noted violinist already associated with the King's Company in 1624, was of course too old to be Archibald's small son. We may turn instead to little Ambrose Matchit, who took the part of Felixina, the beautiful daughter of the usurer Clutch, in Thomas Jordan's comedy *Money Is An Ass.* This play was performed by a cast of eight young actors, five of whom, including Jordan himself, appeared in the Norwich list.[14]

Our main clue to the date of *The Wasp's* performance lies in the approximate ages of the named actors. Barrett, Jordan and Morris, we have seen, played the female parts in *Messalina.* This must be dated after July 1634, when William Cartwright Senior, who acted the Emperor Claudius, was still, according to the information then given by Kendall to Crosfield, at the Fortune Theatre. The terminal date would seem to be May 1636, when the theatres were closed by plague, for after their reopening late in the next year the name of the King's Revels Company had disappeared. Of the actors in *Messalina* who are mentioned in

---

[14]These were Thomas Lovel, Thomas Sands, Thomas Jordan, Walter Williams and Thomas Loveday. Their positions on the Norwich list were respectively 11th, 12th, 13th, 14th, and 16th (Bentley I, 297).

The Wasp, Barrett, the lascivious empress of the title role, became in life the father of a son in November 1637. Jordan, who took the part of Messalina's virtuous old mother Lepida, published his first volume of verse, *Poetical Varieties*, in the same year. It would seem that by the time of the 1636 closing of the theatres both young men were reaching or had reached an age beyond which it was not feasible for them to take women's roles, even allowing, as we must, for the evidence that some of these parts were played by youths right through their teens.[15] At this transitional phase of an actor's career he was compelled to step down from leading feminine roles and start again at the foot of the ladder, understudying his seniors and serving his apprenticeship in walk-on male parts. This is surely the situation that gave rise to Jordan's production of *Money Is An Ass*, as implied in the Prologue introducing the play:

> Tis new, Ime sure, nere Acted, there's none know it
> We never had more Tutor, than the Poet
> Since it is thus, Let us harsh censures scape
> Had every Actor been some others Ape,
> Seen his Part Plaid before him, you might say,
> We had been Children not to Act the play . . .

These lines are often taken to mean that the play was performed by children; but if so, the statement would lose its point. A child actor trained to take a female part was not "some others Ape," and did not see "his Part Plaid before him." It was the actor nearing his majority, too old for most women's parts, too young for an important role as a man, who must often have played the sedulous ape to his seniors. *Money Is An Ass* was designed as a shop-window for such as these, including Jordan himself. It gave an opportunity to young actors to show their talent in their own right. Of the cast of eight, six took male parts, with the two girls' roles of Felixina and Feminia allotted to the younger boys Ambrose Matchit and Will Cherrington.

[15]Ezekiel Fenn was born in 1620. In Glapthorne's *Poems* of 1639 the Prologue was headed "For Ezekiel Fenn at his first Acting in Man's Part." Hugh Clark acted Gratiana in Shirley's *The Wedding* in 1626, a year before his marriage. Theophilus Bird, exceptionally, acted the female part of Massanissa in Nabbes's *Hannibal and Scipio* (1635) at the late age of twenty-six.

It would seem, then, that *Money Is An Ass* was performed later than *Messalina*, when the leading "boy actresses" were growing past their roles and juniors were taking their places. Jordan, instead of playing the mother of the Empress, is now Captain Penniless, an impoverished gallant who woos Clutch's younger daughter. Sands, who sang in Glapthorne's *The Lady Mother* of 1635 "as like the boy at the whitefryers as ever I heard" – who was, in fact, the boy singer at Salisbury Court in the Whitefriars[16] – now appears as Clutch's manservant Calumny. There can be little doubt that Jordan's play was intended for a private playhouse, not for some improvised performance on a provincial tour. The Prologue is spoken "by night"; in Act IV, Scene ii, first Calumny, then Clutch, enters in "the Musique Room," "above." In the next scene Calumny slips "behind the hangings" and overhears "behind Arras" the lovers on the stage. The "Musique Room" cannot have been very high above stage level; Clutch comically hesitates whether to jump down to prevent his daughters eloping with their lovers. "May a man break his neck hear think'st thou," he asks. "His neck?" answers Calumny; "scarce hurt his foot." Such references accord well with the kind of stage shown in the vignette on the title-page of *Messalina*, which as a King's Revels play would have been performed at Salisbury Court. *Money Is An Ass* would probably have been performed either a little before the closing of the theatres in May 1636 or not long after their reopening in October 1637, when part of the King's Revels Company was amalgamated with some of Queen Henrietta's Men and the name King's Revels ceased to be used. The fact that the quarto does not mention any company by name rather suggests the later date.

Returning to *The Wasp*, we note that five of the six named actors have minor adult parts as messengers, attendant lords, constable's aids, and the like. Barrett, who took the title role in *Messalina*, is now the servant to Varletti in Acts II and III, a messenger in Act III, and an unspecified "One" in Act IV, with a total of seven lines to speak in the whole play, including one in a deleted passage. Jordan, who had had the hardly less important part of Lepida, Messalina's mother, is a Captain who enters in

[16]Malone Society Reprints (1958) lines 675–76. Greg, Bentley and Arthur Brown, the editor, concurred that the reference implied a performance by the King's Revels Company at Salisbury Court.

Act II to announce the arrival of the barons in three speeches of four lines in all, and is also one of two attendant lords of the Prorex in Act V, speaking either five lines or two, according to which lord he played. Neither Jordan nor Barrett could have doubled with the two important women's parts of Gilbert's Countess and Varletti's wife Katherine. The only other female part in the play is that of Luce, the Countess's lady-in-waiting; she is addressed as "my girle" and has seven rather precocious lines to speak. It is a part that could well have been taken by Ambrose. Like *Money Is An Ass*, *The Wasp* would seem to belong to a time when the erstwhile "leading ladies" Barrett and Jordan were reduced to the status of small-part actors, while little Ambrose Matchit enjoyed his heyday as winsome maiden or pert boy. If so, the two plays may be dated fairly close to each other.

Like *Messalina* and *Money Is An Ass*, *The Wasp* seems to have been written for a purpose-built theatre. In the first scene the barons, having vowed to overthrow Varletti, visit Gilbert, hoping to recruit him to their plot. On the stage they merely turn in the direction of the tiring house façade. "This is Mount Claridon," says Conon, "lets call him forth." The Countess receives them and tells them of her husband's grave sickness. Some twenty lines before, the prompter's note reads "Bed readye," and in the dialogue Archibald now says "vncurten come come lets se him"; after which comes the authorial stage direction, "Bed discoverd. Gilb: in it." A discovery space concealed by curtains is presumably required. Near the end of the play when Gerald usurps the crown, he finds over his head a sword suspended, while a Fury with shears prepares to cut the thread. Business such as this calls for the use of an "upper stage" or balcony, but only for a few minutes; on the other hand, there is quite frequent need for sound effects – recorders, horns, flourishes of trumpets, etc. – best produced in a "music room" above the main stage. It is thus most likely that *The Wasp* was written for performance at Salisbury Court, by a cast including a number of King's Revels actors, either shortly before the closing of the theatres in May 1636 or soon after their reopening in October 1637. Gourlay's date of about 1638 is perhaps not far from the mark. The extreme terminal limit for the production as planned must be set at March 1640, for on the last day of that month the mortal remains of "John Barrett Player" were laid to rest in St. Giles churchyard.

His elder son William, born in 1637, had already been buried there two months before, and his second son Gustavus was to join them within six weeks of their father's death, when he was not quite eighteen months old. On the world's stage none of the Barretts had been assigned a substantial part.

Life is short, art is long, but the ways of scholarship are sometimes the longest of all. Even an account of this play has been delayed ten years longer than was anticipated. But at last, a century after it was discovered, *The Wasp* is stirring, ready to buzz about our heads and take flight into the polluted atmosphere of our time.

Your Majesty is Welcome to a Fair

WILLIAM BLISSETT

The winter season at court began in 1614 on All Saints' Day with the performance of a new play by Ben Jonson, *Bartholomew Fair*. An audience being assembled, and the King being set in expectation, the Prologue steps forward to speak these words:

> Your Majesty is welcome to a Fair;
> Such place, such men, such language and such ware,
> You must expect: with these, the zealous noise
> Of your land's Faction, scandaliz'd at toys,
> As babies, hobby-horses, puppet-plays,
> And such like rage, whereof the petulant ways
> Yourself have known, and have been vex'd with long.
> These for your sport, without particular wrong
> Or just complaint of any private man
> (Who of himself or shall think well or can),
> The Maker doth present: and hopes tonight
> To give you for a fairing, true delight.[1]

A prologue directly addressed to the King must be especially careful to strike the right note itself, or else its larger purpose, to establish the tone and decorum of the play, will be impaired at the outset. The first line works very well: deference in "your

[1]All quotations from *Bartholomew Fair* are taken from the Revels edition of E. A. Horsman (London, 1960); I am indebted also to the editions of Eugene M. Waith (The Yale Ben Jonson, 1963); Edward B. Partridge, The Regents Series (Nebraska, 1964); and Maurice Hussey, The New Mermaids (London, 1964). All other citations of Ben Jonson are taken from the edition of Herford and Simpson in eleven volumes (Oxford, 1925–52, hereafter cited as *H&S*). For inauguration of court season, see E. K. Chambers, *The Elizabethan Stage*, 4 vols. (Oxford, 1923, corrected 1951), I, 21.

Majesty," pleasantness in "welcome" and piquant incongruity in "a Fair" – since persons of royal estate would never see such places of popular resort and might well be curious, and so might the higher nobility, the ambassadors, the ladies of quality. Of course, it must be understood from the beginning that the language and manners of the Fair will be very different from those of an ideal court or even from the normal ways of the kingdom as the King would like them to be. (For King James was, in theory, strongly opposed to lewd and blasphemous speech and had a quite genuine aversion to noise and crowds and faction.) The poet adroitly establishes noisy faction as the enemy of the Fair and of the ensuing play. If the King is to be above faction, he must also show himself to be above being scandalized at toys; rage and petulance, vexing to the quiet of the kingdom, are to be laughed at for sport. The poet can guarantee there to be nothing libellous of any private man, and so the supreme public man may enjoy it assured, and receive his "fairing."

We happen to know what Ben Jonson privately thought about fairings.

> *What* petty things they are, wee wonder at? like children, that esteeme every trifle; and preferre a *Fairing* before their Fathers: what difference is betweene us, and them? but that we are dearer Fooles, Cockscombes, at a higher rate? They are pleas'd with Cockleshels, Whistles, Hobby-horses, and such like: wee with Statues, marble Pillars, Pictures, guilded Roofes, where under-neath is Lath and Lyme; perhaps Lome. Yet, wee take pleasure in the lye, and are glad, wee can cousen our selves.[2]

There is no inconsistency here, for what Jonson offers the King is not a tinsel fairing from Smithfield, nor yet a gilded fairing of Whitehall, but "true delight" – something to please the understanding.

From the Induction we know that *Bartholomew Fair* was first acted in the Hope Theatre on 31 October, 1614; the performance at court took place on 1 November. This double première[3] is

[2]*H&S* VIII, 607.
[3]In the matter of the "double audience" and in some other points I have been anticipated by Ian Donaldson, *The World Upside-Down* (Oxford, 1970). My lecture was written and delivered before Mr. Donaldson's excellent chapter on *Bartholomew Fair* came to my attention. See especially p. 48 on two audiences and pp. 71–74 on the meaning of the play for the King.

highly unusual and seems to indicate that the play must have been written with two very different audiences in mind, or at least completed so; for it is flatly impossible that preparations for court performance and the writing of a prologue and an epilogue could have been the work of a single day. Records of performances at court do not, in many cases, name the play performed, and so it is not easy to determine whether *Bartholomew Fair* is unique in this regard, but I can find no other clear instance. We know that court officials were usually most careful in the discovery and preparation and "reforming" of plays so that they might be "convenient" for performance at court.[4] It is possible in this case that the play was inspected at a rehearsal, and then that its extraordinary complexity led to a postponement of public production until the last moment before a court production already commanded. However that may be, the officials seem to have taken a chance that there was "no offence in't" – a departure from normal practice and, in the case of Ben Jonson, to judge by his career to this date, a risky one.

Echoing Drummond of Hawthornden, one may say of Ben Jonson that hot water was one of the elements in which he lived. A man of choleric humour, who had as a soldier slain his man in single combat before both armies, who killed a fellow-actor in a duel, who beat Marston and took his pistol from him, who engaged in public quarrels with dramatists and masque-makers, Jonson also fell afoul of the authorities on a number of occasions. As a young playwright he had a hand, perhaps the leading hand, in *The Isle of Dogs*, "a lewd plaie . . . contanynge very seditious and sclandrous matter," suppressed with total effectiveness by official order.[5] Surviving that, he was given opportunity to please the Queen near the end of her reign and the King at the beginning of his, and failed in both. Of *Cynthia's Revels* it has been observed that a mere patronizing denial of her faults after presenting them as the topic of public discussion would scarcely satisfy Queen Elizabeth's appetite for praise.[6] After his small success in entertaining Queen Anne and the Prince at Althorpe in the summer of 1603, Jonson produced *Sejanus*, clearly calcu-

[4]Chambers, I, 223, 224; see also M. S. Steele, *Plays & Masques at Court* . . . (New Haven, 1926).
[5]*H&S* I, 151, 140, 15.
[6]*H&S* I, 396.

lating on a call to present it before the learned King, and clearly miscalculating. It failed with the general public because of its iron weight, but it seems to have run into additional trouble because of its satiric implications: if the court of Augustus in *Poetaster* was alive with recognizable caricatures, why not the court of Tiberius here?[7] Nor would King James (who very soon was seen somewhat to neglect his public duties for the pleasures of the chase) relish being reminded that a legitimate ruler skilled in statecraft could also be both negligent and depraved. *Catiline* some years later also failed, for like reasons: it must have been truly boring in the theatre, and while it has in the person of Cicero a pretty compliment to the dramatist, there is nothing in it for the King's comfort.[8]

Between the two Roman plays Jonson was incarcerated for his part in *Eastward Ho*, in 1605. It is not difficult to ascertain what the offending passages were or (in two instances) how they offended. Captain Seagull descants on the marvels of Virginia as an earthly paradise:

> And then you shal live freely there, without Sergeants, or Courtiers, or Lawyers, or Intelligencers, onely a few industrious Scots perhaps, who indeed are disperst over the face of the whole earth. But as for them, there are no greater friends to English men and *England*, when they are out an't, in the world, then they are. And for my part, I would a hundred thousand of 'hem were there, for wee are all one Countreymen now, yee know; and wee shoulde finde ten times more comfort of them there, then wee doe heere.

This is a copious amplification on Gertrude's apparently innocent question about her farthingale: "is this a right Scot? Does it clip close?" But the other offending passage is more puzzling: when the adventurers are cast up upon, yes, the same Isle of Dogs where Jonson earlier made shipwreck, an unnamed "First Gentleman" tells Sir Petronel Flash that he is not in France, chides him for drunkenness, and concludes: "Farewel, farewel, we wil not know you for shaming of you. I ken the man weel, hee's one of my thirty pound knights." Did the actor mimic King James's

[7]*H&S* I, 36.
[8]Everything that connects the play with the Gunpowder Plot will be found in B. N. De Luna, *Jonson's Romish Plot* (Oxford, 1967).

Scottish accent? "Most unlikely," say Herford and Simpson: "This was a sure way of inviting trouble. It need not be more than a sneer at Scottish knights." But then the play *did* invite trouble, serious trouble, so that the report was that the three playwrights "should then had their ears cutt & noses." And it is hard to imagine what other Scot would refer to new carpet knights as "my knights," though it is equally hard to imagine King James casually walking on the beach – unless to make it an act of lese-majesty for an audience to recognize the King, and thus to save the playwrights' skins, as indeed they were saved. *Eastward Ho*, by the way, was given at court in January of the year of *Bartholomew Fair*.[9]

There being no need to consider minor troubles over minor topicalities in *Epicoene* and *The Devil is an Ass*, we may end this chronicle, remembering Jonson's complaints, "They make a libel which he made a play," and "Application, is now, growne a trade with many"[10] – somewhat disingenuous remarks, surely, for it is Ben Jonson himself who provided occupation for politic pick-locks in his own time and a livelihood in ours. But it may be safe to observe that, like a great orator with a slight hesitation in his speech, Jonson was a moralist and satirist and complimentary poet about whom his audience could never rest pre-assured.

With ample classical and contemporary precedent Jonson throughout his life at once claimed the right of the poet to judge the times and disclaimed any intention of offence against particular persons, private or public. His poems, he asserts, are not cyphers, not libels, not busy with secret politics, and yet he complains that he is "given out dangerous," and that the age cannot endure reproof.[11] Jonson told Drummond that "he heth a minde to be a churchman, & so he might have favour to make one Sermon to the King, he careth not what yrafter sould befall him, for he would not flatter though he saw Death." If Vulcan had not consumed "ane apologie of a Play of his St Bartholomees

---

[9]*Eastward Ho* 3.3.40–48, 1.2.49, 4.1.173–78; *H&S* IX, 667.
[10]Another [prologue] to *Epicoene*, line 14; dedication to *Volpone*, line 65.
[11]*H&S* VIII, 25, 44, 58–59, 117, 175; see the eloquent passage in *Discoveries*, maintaining the satirist's innocence of libel and his serviceability to his prince, *H&S* VIII, 604–5; also 633, 643, 565–66, 594–95. The prologue and conclusion of *Cynthia's Revels* and other passages in the "comicall satyres" may also be recalled.

faire,"[12] we might have seen that in welcoming His Majesty to a fair he had begun to preach a lay sermon, without flattery.

II

"The King being set in expectation": this reminds us that the Great Hall is a hall of audience and that the King, even at a play, sits (to use one of his own favourite phrases) "in God's throne on earth."[13] Any occasion involving the King is to some degree a state occasion, but we must not make heavy going of this. King James was as well aware as anyone of the old formulary of the King's two bodies; and if he pressed divine right and royal prerogative so hard as to provoke dissent and to make problematical what should be presupposed, one has the impression that he did so in order that, once the matter was settled and out of the way, he could live the life of a hunting squire with an interest in statecraft and theological controversy. His lack of dignity was noticed and taken advantage of early in his reign. "Consider for pity's sake," writes Beaumont, the French ambassador, on 14 June, 1604, "what must be the state and condition of a prince, whom the preachers publicly from the pulpit assail, whom the comedians of the metropolis bring upon the stage, whose wife attends these representations in order to enjoy the laugh against her husband." Beaumont's evidence is confirmed by a letter of 28 March, 1605, from Samuel Calvert to Ralph Winwood, in which he writes that "the play[er]s do not forbear to represent upon their stage the whole course of the present time, not sparing either King, state, or religion, in so great absurdity, and with such liberty, that any would be afraid to hear them."[14] But there is another side to this. King James could not bear – and did not even theoretically wish – to be bound by continual ceremony and protocol, but "liked to surround his majesty with a kind of homely and innocent confusion," and in the later years of his reign appeared to relish a certain "playful

---

[12]*H&S* I, 141, 134.
[13]*H&S* VII, 399; Allardyce Nicoll, *Stuart Masques and the Renaissance Stage* (London, 1938), pp. 33–34; Joseph Quincy Adams, *Shakespearean Playhouses* (Boston, 1917), p. 389; King James I, *The Political Works*, C. H. McIlwain, ed. (Cambridge, Mass., 1918), 3 (introductory sonnet to *Basilikon Doron*); 54 (*Trew Law of Free Monarchies*); 110 (*A Premonition*).
[14]Chambers, I, 325.

impudence" (not unmixed with deference and affection) in those about him.[15]

Sir Walter Scott, who immersed himself in the lore of the time and whose character of King James is a masterpiece of fictional history, called him fidgety and rather naughtily observed that the Scottish Solomon was rather shy of wives and concubines.[16] By 1614 England and London and the court had had eleven years in which to observe James, and the King himself had twice in *Basilikon Doron* used this apposite comparison: "for Kings being publike persons, by reason of their office and authority, are as it were set (as it was said of old) upon a publike stage, in the sight of all people; where all the beholders eyes are attentively bent to looke and pry in the least circumstance of their secretest drifts. . . ."[17] There was by this time nothing very secret about the King's mind and tastes. His early interests in poetry and witchcraft were clearly on the wane, but he continued to occupy his mind with sacred and humane learning, so that the dedications to him of the Authorized Version and the *Advancement of Learning* were not empty flattery. Fundamentally a good-natured man, he wished all nations to be at peace with him and all his subjects to be tolerable. Hunting was his chief solace, but he delighted in entertainments, both plays and masques – not just their magnificence but their merriment. Two things especially vexed him, a small and a great, tobacco and puritanism. He thought of himself as more fatherly than he was; he was a better uncle to his favourites than father to his sons. Like an avuncular dominie, King James was well-known for taking a pedagogical and sentimental interest in likely-looking young men. Reference, direct or indirect, to any of these matters would be immediately perceptible to the court audience.

The Prologue we have heard. The Induction, with its references to the Hope Theatre (which doubled as a bear pit), and with its address by Stage-keeper and Book-holder to the two kinds of auditor in the public theatre, we may assume to have been omitted from the court performance, though some particular

---

[15]David Mathew, *James I* (London, 1967), p. 175; D. Harris Willson, *King James VI and I* (London, 1956), p. 385.
[16]*The Fortunes of Nigel*, ed. F. M. Link (Lincoln, Neb., 1965), pp. 56 ff., 318, 320 and n.30 (on the Scots dislike of pork), 360, 381.
[17]*Political Works*, p. 5, also p. 43.

friends and admirers of Ben may still have been chuckling a day after the event over the way he kindled and at the same time doused the expectation of "application" in the indenture:

> it is finally agreed by the foresaid hearers and spectators that they neither in themselves conceal, nor suffer by them to be concealed, any state-decipherer, or politic picklock of the scene, so solemnly ridiculous as to search out who was meant by the Ginger-bread-woman, who by the Hobby-horse-man, who by the Costermonger, nay, who by their wares; or that will pretend to affirm, on his own inspired ignorance, what Mirror for Magistrates is meant by the Justice, what great lady by the Pig-woman, what conceal'd statesman by the Seller of Mousetraps, and so of the rest. (Induction, 136–47)

Some members of the public audience may have recalled George Whetstone's *Mirror for Magistrates of Cyties* (1584), with its recommendation that city officials don disguise in order to spy out petty crime and bad business practices; court people would be more likely to recall the original collections of politic poems, which are primarily a mirror for the superior magistrate, or the supreme. But, in keeping with the fair and its decorum of indecorum, this promises to be in either case a fun-house mirror for magistrates.

The rest of my space must be given to a commentary on certain aspects of the play that would stand out, I believe, at its performance at court. Fortunately, *Bartholomew Fair* has been well served by its modern editors and critics, and so there will be no need to repeat, only to applaud, Richard Levin on its structure, Jonas Barish on its language, and Brian Parker on themes and staging, to mention only three.

Various characters at the outset of the play stand at the rim of the vortex and are drawn in. The Littlewits, harmless ninnies whose vapidity contributes one sense to the key word "vapours" and whose puppet-dramaturgy and longing for roast pig easily combine to take them and their party to the fair; two fortune-hunting young gentlemen; a silly youth named Bartholomew, his betrothed and his irascible tutor; a "stone Puritan" with voracious "reformed mouth" and a Puritan widow, a "devourer of alms" – all converge on the place. The romping travesty and *reductio ad absurdum* of Puritan sectaries (the enemy alike of

King and poet) Jonson may have beamed from the beginning at the court audience, and there is nothing to prevent John Aubrey from being correct when he says that "King James made him write against the Puritans, who began to be troublesome in his reign."[18]

This leaves for specially prepared and emphatic introduction in the second act one other visitor to the fair, "a wise justice of the peace, *meditant*," Adam Overdo. Looking like a sane man disguised as a madman, he assays his mind in soliloquy:

> Well, in Justice' name, and the King's, and for the Commonwealth! defy all the world, Adam Overdo, for a disguise, and all story; for thou hast fitted thyself, I swear: fain would I meet the Lynceus now, that eagle's eye, that piercing Epidaurian serpent (as my Quintus Horace calls him), that could discover a Justice of Peace (and lately of the Quorum) under this covering. They may have seen many a fool in the habit of a Justice; but never till now, a Justice in the habit of a fool. Thus we must do, though, that wake for the public good: and thus hath the wise magistrate done in all ages. There is a doing of right out of wrong, if the way be found. (2.1.1–12)

He goes gloriously on and on, recalling the precedent of a city magistrate who assumed a disguise for purposes of investigation, elaborating on it to ludicrous length[19] and, after citing the dangers of relying on the eyes and ears of agents,

> I, Adam Overdo, am resolv'd therefore to spare spy-money hereafter, and make mine own discoveries. Many are the yearly enormities of this Fair, in whose court of Pie-powders I have had the honour during three days sometimes to sit as judge. But this is the special day for detection of these foresaid enormities. Here is my black book for the purpose, this the cloud that hides me: under this cover I shall see, and not be seen. On, Junius Brutus. And as I began, so I'll end: in Justice' name, and the King's; and for the Commonwealth! (2.1.40–9)

Take a moment to collect our wits after this curious outburst. To any experienced playgoer the Justice would be recognizable as belonging on a bench of disguised magistrates, mysterious fig-

---

[18]John Aubrey, *Brief Lives*, ed. O. L. Dick (London, 1949), p. 178.
[19]*H&S* X, 185, on Sir Thomas Hayes; also Horsman's introduction, xxx.

ures moving "like power divine" through their plays, representing for the audience (though not for the persons on the stage) a clear embodiment of articulate judgment upon moral and political evils which ultimately, on throwing off their disguises, they exert sufficient power to amend. But what a disguised magistrate this is! All the others were high-minded dukes, reigning or deposed, or heirs to dukedoms – Marston's Malcontent and his Fawn, Sharpham's Fleer and Middleton's Phoenix come to mind, and of course Duke Vincentio in *Measure for Measure*. If King James and his court see Overdo as another of these (and his disguise is not much more outlandish than Malevole's or the Fawn's), they must immediately begin to subtract the non-resemblances and laugh at the incompatibilities. A judge of Pie-Powders is a minuscule, not a sovereign, magistrate and partakes only minimally of the sacrosanctity of the law. If we should find him at moments resembling King James, it will be His Majesty minus his majesty. The activities of disguised dukes in dramatic fiction, though essentially wish-fulfilment fantasies, were directed at bringing to light and correcting serious abuses in private and public morals; but Overdo descends in his godlike cloud (vapours again!) to find what everyone knows he will find, and attempt to correct what everyone knows cannot be corrected – enormities in a fair.

In a little over a year's time King James, speaking in the Star Chamber, was to commend his judges and justices:

> And this you shall finde, that even as a King, (let him be never so godly, wise, righteous, and just) yet if the subalterne Magistrates doe not their parts under him, the Kingdome must needs suffer: So let the Judges bee never so carefull and industrious, if the Justices of Peace under them, put not to their helping hands, vaine is all your labour: For they are the Kings eyes and eares in the country.[20]

Nevertheless, the question must arise, can Adam Overdo be a sensible man? The goofy disguise he dons, the absurdity of the venture, combined with the solemnity of the language, are sufficient answer. He could well live to profit by an ensuing passage in the same speech in which the King distinguishes two kinds of inadequate justices: "slowbellies" and "busybodies." Overdo

20*Political Works*, p. 339.

is a little of a slowbelly, since he fails to appear to preside at a
court whose whole purpose is summary justice, but he is the
very embusybodiment of the other, who "will have all men
dance after their pipe, and follow their greatnesse, or else will
not be content; . . . these proud spirits must know, that the
countrey is ordained to obey and follow God and the King, and
not them."[21] We remember Overdo's name and see that he belongs with Busy and Wasp. In his quest of enormities he is sure
to exceed his function and get above himself.

Having so introduced Overdo as to force the court audience
to a quick double-take – first promotion as a disguised magistrate, as partaking of the *regnum*, then rapid demotion as the
wisest fool in Smithfield – Jonson is in a remarkably secure position. The withers of King James are hardly to be wrung by the
antics of an Overdo, whatever Overdo may do or say: the very
idea is to be laughed out of court.

Let us follow Adam Overdo into the fair, being prepared to
find that he is himself a greater curiosity than any. For the
audience at the public performance the day before, the spectacle
of Smithfield on the stage would bring a shock of recognition:
the swirl, the noise, the stink, would be familiar to almost everyone, especially since Smithfield had been paved that very year
to make the footing less noxious. To the court audience, most
of whom would be unfamiliar with the place, the impression of
confusion must have been overwhelming: "there is in it so much
too much of everything," as Edmund Wilson complained.[22]

In the first act, amid the twitter of the Littlewits and the
modulated speech of the young gentlemen, the "loud and coarse"
noise of Busy and the foul speech of Wasp have the pungency of
a contained indecorum. But once we are in the Fair, the fat is in
the fire. Ursula and Trash and Leatherhead and the roaring
horse-courser raise a continual din which Busy and Wasp and
that "new roarer" Overdo as Mad Arthur of Bradley bring to the
threshold of pain. Characters group and pair in new combinations
and are attracted and repelled to the accompaniment of an ever-
present noise and stink that breaks down purposes and inhibi-

[21]*Political Works*, p. 340.
[22]Henry Morley, *Memoirs of Bartholomew Fair* (London, 1857), p. 114;
Edmund Wilson, "Morose Ben Jonson," in *The Triple Thinkers* (New York,
1948), p. 216.

tions. The throbbing air is laden with fumes of pork and tobacco and ale and, increasingly as noise and licence collapse into the "wild anarchy of drink," urine (the pervasive smell of which links *Bartholomew Fair* with *Finnegans Wake*). Because of the built-in animal-stink at the Hope, it might be appropriate for fresh pork to cover stale bear; tobacco too might as well be actual where there is a change of air; even ale. At court, better not: without such ventilation, all smells should be imaginary, especially in view of the King's known dislike of pork and tobacco.

The fair is a place of licence within a world of law: it combines maximum impurity with minimum danger. *Miasma* in its original sense of ritual impurity (there's vapours again) is inbreathed on a plane below moral approval or rejection, and such is the skill of the dramatist that the experience is not disagreeable, for a limited time in a limited place, though no one (except Cokes) is such a fool as to want to take up residence in the fair or spend all his substance on fairings.

It is against these noises and fumes that Adam Overdo fires his counterblast to tobacco. In the style of the proverbs of Solomon he addresses young Edgworth: "Thirst not after that frothy liquor, ale: for who knows, when he openeth the stopple, what may be in the bottle? Hath not a snail, a spider, yea, a newt been found there? Thirst not after it, youth; thirst not after it." (2.6.10–13) And having by this outcry got his and our attention, he goes on: "Neither do thou lust after that tawny weed, tobacco . . . Whose complexion is like the Indian's that vents it! . . . And who can tell if, before the gathering and making up thereof, the alligator hath not piss'd thereon?" (2.6.20–25) And so he builds up to his grand, noisy climax, denouncing "a custome lothsome to the eye, hatefull to the Nose, harmefull to the braine, daungerous to the Lungs, and in the blacke stinking fume thereof, neerest resembling the horrible Stigian smoke of the pit that is bottomelesse."[23] No, I beg your pardon, this is not Justice Overdo but King James's peroration to his pamphlet against the weed. Let us hear two further sentences from it. "But for these base sorts of corruption in Commonwealths, not onely the King, or any inferior Magistrate, but *Quidlibet è populo* may serve as

---

[23]*A Counterblaste to Tobacco* (London, 1604), D2.

Phisician, by discovering and impugning the error and by perswading reformation thereof." We see where Adam Overdo took his cue; and if any think the matter beneath the attention of a Justice of the Court of Pie-Powder, hear this extenuation: "If any think it a light Argument, so is it but a toy that is bestowed upon it. And since the Subject is but of Smoke, I thinke the fume of an idle braine, may serve for a sufficient battery against so fumous and feeble an enemy."[24]

Bartholomew Fair is described in the Induction as "a new sufficient play . . . merry, and as full of noise as sport: made to delight all, and to offend none; provided they have either the wit or the honesty to think well of themselves." (Induction 81–85) The King, to be sure, had opinions on the subject of tobacco[25] but not such as to overthrow his judgment or sense of fun. *Counterblaste* is a light-hearted book, and the King as auditor is not likely to become testy here, and so Jonson runs concurrently with tobacco a much more ticklish theme.

"What pity 'tis so civil a young man should haunt this debauch'd company!" (2.4.29–30) the Justice remarks on first seeing Edgworth, then stands aside while Edgworth reveals himself to us as the cutpurse Overdo had wrongly suspected Knockem of being. One of the Bartholomew-birds notices that Master Arthur of Bradley is melancholy here, nobody talks to him, and the Justice, alone in his meditations, says, "If I can, with this day's travel, and all my policy, but rescue this youth, here, out of the hands of the lewd man, and the strange woman, I will sit down at night, and say with my friend Ovid, *Jamque opus exegi, quod nec Jovis ira, nec ignis &c.*" (2.4.56–57, 60–64) The roaring oration against bottle-ale and tobacco ensues after Overdo in a fit of abstraction hears the infernal racket around Ursula's stall, and begins thus: "These are the fruits of bottle-ale and tobacco! the foam of the one and the fumes of the other! Stay, young man, and despise not the wisdom of these few hairs, that are grown grey in care of thee." (2.6.1–4) The oration ends with his being beaten by Wasp.

Humble enough, yet vain enough, to believe that all the events of the world are arranged for his education in wisdom and

---

[24]*Counterblaste*, A4 and A4v (italics reversed).
[25]So did Ben Jonson; see *Epicoene*, 4.1.60, *EMOH*, 3.423, and the egregious Bobadill.

service, Adam Overdo when next we see him resolves: "I will make no more orations, shall draw on these tragical conclusions. And I begin now to think that, by a spice of collateral justice, Adam Overdo deserv'd this beating. . . . To see what bad events may peep out o' the tail of good purposes!" (3.3.1–3, 13–14) While we are savouring that metaphor, he goes on: "The care I had of that civil young man I took fancy to this morning (and have not left it yet) drew me to that exhortation, which drew the company, indeed, which drew the cutpurse; which drew the money, which drew my brother Cokes his loss; which drew on Wasp's anger; which drew on my beating: a pretty gradation!" (3.3.14–20)

The Justice thereupon departs the stage long enough for our politic pick-lock to recall that the handsome and amiable George Villiers, a young gentleman of small fortune or prospects, had caught the eye of the King at Althorpe that summer; he might also know that Villiers was likely to receive his first court preferment (as he did within the month). Robert Carr, Earl of Somerset, who some years before had had the good fortune to arouse the King's solicitude by breaking his leg while hunting, was now clearly on the wane as favourite, though not to fall until the disclosure of the Overbury murder in 1615, that is, within a year of the present performance.[26]

But here is Adam Overdo again. "I cannot beget a project," he says, aside, and goes on both to confirm our application and confute it:

> I cannot beget a project, with all my political brain, yet; my project is how to fetch off this proper young man from his debauch'd company: I have followed him all the Fair over, and still I find him with this songster; and I begin shrewdly to suspect their familiarity; and the young man of a terrible taint, poetry! with which idle disease if he be infected, there's no hope, in a state-course. *Actum est* of him for a commonwealths-man, if he go to't in rhyme once. (3.5.1–9)

At this, King James as author of *Notes of a Prentice in the Divine Art of Poetry* is free to lead the audience in hearty laughter, the heartier when, during the singing of the ballad of

[26]See G. P. V. Akrigg, *Jacobean Pageant* (Cambridge, Mass., 1962), pp. 188–89.

the cutpurse to the tune of Paggington's Pound, the infatuated Justice says, "It doth discover enormity, I'll mark it more: I ha' not lik'd a paltry piece of poetry so well, a good while." (3.5.114–15) But we are free to think our own thoughts, though not of course to utter them. (One of Ben Jonson's thoughts is that "a Poet should detest a Ballet maker."[27]) Justice Overdo, one last time, says, "Now, for my other work, reducing the young man I have follow'd so long in love, from the brink of his bane to the centre of safety. Here, or in some such like vain place, I shall be sure to find him, I await the good time." (5.2.130–34) There we leave the busy Justice, meditant, in the posture of a sentimental fool.

A fool has been defined as "he who gets slapped."[28] In donning the shape of Mad Arthur of Bradley, Justice Overdo puts himself within the definition. Two observations of Jonas Barish are apposite here. "Jonson cannot, like the stoic he longs to be, remain indifferent to the vicissitudes of fortune. He cannot despise the acclaim or the scorn of others; he exults in approval and smarts painfully under criticism. He cannot cleanse himself of the petty passions he would like to disown." No Adam Overdo, he. Later, Barish refers to *Bartholomew Fair* as Jonson's "real praise of folly."[29]

It is, in one respect, a very Erasmian play. Overdo in fool's guise delivers a sort of continuous soliloquy and oration that is folly shot through with deviations into sense; so too Erasmus' figure argues that "to pretend to be a fool is sometimes the highest wisdom" and uses such plausible double-edged phrases as "if Folly is any judge." But the real affinity between Jonson and Erasmus I believe to be their rejection of Stoic *apatheia*. "Although that double-strength Stoic, Seneca, stoutly denies this [that the passions spur a man to wisdom and well doing], subtracting from the wise man any and every emotion, yet in doing so he leaves him no man at all but rather a new kind of god, or demiurgos, who never existed and will never emerge." So Folly speaks for Erasmus. "What's six kicks to a man who reads

[27]*H&S* I, 145.
[28]By St. John Chrysostom, quoted without reference by Enid Welsford, *The Fool: His Social and Literary History* (London, 1935), p. 314.
[29]Jonas A. Barish, *Ben Jonson and the Language of Prose Comedy* (Cambridge, Mass., 1960), pp. 87–88, 185.

Seneca?" – a good sharp question asked in *Epicoene*. When one of the King's obedient subjects goes to the stocks here, the same tone is used in comment: "What's here! A stoic i' the stocks? The fool is turn'd philosopher." (4.6.96–97)[30] This open jocularity prepares the way for a more hidden serious comment on the pride and impiety inherent in Stoic self-reliance. Trouble-all says, "I mark no name, but Adam Overdo; that is the name of names; he only is the sufficient magistrate." (4.6.145–46) He is mad to think Adam's is the saving name, or even the most high-minded magistrate all-sufficient, and yet such is Overdo's self-infatuation that he speaks of himself, shortly before he is properly humbled, in closely analogous terms: first when he says "neither is the hour of my severity yet come, to reveal myself, wherein, cloud-like, I will break out in rain and hail, lightning and thunder, upon the head of enormity" (5.2.3–6), as if he were Jove and Marcus Aurelius in one; and secondly when he gives the supposed Trouble-all a blank warrant and says, "Well, my conscience is much eas'd; I ha' done my part; though it doth him no good, yet Adam hath offer'd satisfaction! The sting is removed from hence." (5.2.126–28) The sting of sin is the law: King James at least among the auditory was theologian enough to know that, and that Adam is in no position to offer "satisfaction" or to raise himself by his own stoical bootstraps.

III

We turn as judging spectators to the censure of the Fair, to see whether Ben Jonson as the thinking man's dramatist has given us something to think about. Concentrated in one play we find antinomies of moral judgment such as have often been remarked on when *Volpone* and *The Alchemist*, with their so apparently opposite moral bearings and outcomes, are juxtaposed: in *Volpone* all is rigour and severity; in *The Alchemist* all is lenity and indulgence.[31]

Bartholomew Fair has been called a comedy of vapours. An

[30]Desiderius Erasmus, *The Praise of Folly*, ed. and tr. H. H. Hudson (Princeton, 1941), pp. 103, 53, 39. Also *Epicoene*, 4.5.265; Donaldson, chapter i, for the magistrate in the stocks; illustration in T. W. Craik, *Tudor Interlude* (Leicester, 1958), pp. 93–94.
[31]Widely discussed: see my essay, "The Venter Tripartite in *The Alchemist*," *Studies in English Literature*, VIII, 1968, 323–34.

imitation of vapours is hard to keep in focus, especially when one is temporarily incapacitated by breathing a sort of laughing gas; but we must make the effort. The sun, we know, draws up, or "exhales," two sorts of evaporations: the hot and dry, properly called "exhalations," which include thunder and lightning, comets, winds and earthquakes; and the wet and usually warm "vapours," from which derive clouds, rain, hail, snow, dew, frost, and mist or fog. These outward vapours in the macrocosm are matched by inward vapours in the microcosm whenever bilious humours are in "unnatural heat because of physiological disorder or immoderate passion. The vapours rise, cloud the brain, and produce madness,"[32] or psychological states "in no way inferior to madness," as the surrealists used to say in days of yore.

The close, humid dog-days of August are thus vaporous, and so are the stinks of pig and tobacco, ale and urine; the silly notions of the Littlewits are vaporous and so are the notions that are waved about in the air at Smithfield, whether they be toys of fancy or gilded fairings. Gross eating, especially of gassy victuals, produces vapours and the pressing necessity of giving them vent; a *bellum intestinum* breaks out, signalled by that kind of confused speech later to be called (with Jonsonian pithiness) "talking wet": people at the Fair never talk so wet as when using the word "vapours" or playing the game. Attorney-General Francis Bacon, who might well have been a member of the court audience, would find Jonson's meaning clear. "So whosoever shall entertain high and vaporous imaginations instead of a laborious and sober inquiry of truth, shall beget hopes and beliefs of strange and impossible shapes," he wrote in *The Advancement of Learning*; and again, "let him but read the fable of Ixion, and it will hold him from being vaporous or imaginative."[33] In both these instances, it will be noticed, vaporous imaginings are seen as the opposite of the *lumen siccum*, the dry light of reason, which Bacon derived ultimately from the aphorism of Heraclitus, "a dry soul is wisest and best."

[32]James E. Robinson, *"Bartholomew Fair*: Comedy of Vapors," *SEL*, I, 1961, 65–80 esp. 66; S. K. Heninger, Jr., *A Handbook of Renaissance Meteorology* (Durham, N.C.), pp. 37–38 (this otherwise very full and useful compendium does not mention vapours in this play); see also Barish, pp. 217–19.
[33]*The Advancement of Learning*, in *The Works*, edd. Spedding, Ellis, Heath, 1869, VI, 229, 102; see also 95 (*lumen siccum*), 384 ("things imaginative or in the air").

Vapours, ungoverned imaginations, quarrelling: the three are brought together by Jonson as the Smithfield Muses were to bring them together for Pope; and there is perhaps an element of confession in Jonson's art here. "He heth consumed a whole night in lying looking to his great toe, about which he hath seen tartars & turks Romans and Carthaginions feight in his imagination."[34] Fight. Think of how many quarrels there are in his plays and how much empty noise: "blow, blow, puff, puff, and all flies in *fumo*," says Volpone as Scoto of Mantua; *Epicoene* is all about noise; the machine explodes in *The Alchemist*, which opened in a quarrel; in *Bartholomew Fair* the form of the game of vapours self-destructs into the wild anarchy of drink, and the puppets' victory over Busy is vapid and noisy. And finally, by a trick of that false secondary power by which we multiply distinctions, Ben Jonson, the prime inventor and patentee of humour theory and lingo, overgoes his own "humours" with his "vapours" and supplies the modish with a word and a notion to bandy about with empty noise.

"How? How? Urs, vapours!" says Knockem to the dripping pig-woman: "Motion breed vapours?" (2.3.44). Another word is being played on here. Knockem by motion means exertion, but we are already sensitive to two other meanings: motion in the sense of inward stirring of carnal appetite – "profane motion" to Dame Purecraft, or "the fleshly motion of a pig," or (of Zeal-of-the-Land Busy) "ever in seditious motion"; and motion as puppet-show (1.5.147, 1.6.13, 1.3.135). What they have in common is a busy physicality obstinately recalcitrant to whatever is reposeful, graceful, of the spirit. "*Ill Arts* begin, where good end," Jonson complains. "The Puppets are seene now in despight of the Players"; and he boasts with savage irony that "my Fame, to his, not under-heares,/That guides the Motions, and directs the beares." For him such entertainments are crass deception: "*Imposture* is ever asham'd of the light," he writes in *Discoveries*, and continues immediately, "A *Puppet-play* must be shadow'd, and seene in the darke: For draw the Curtaine, *Et sordet gesticulatio*." So much for his opinion of puppet-plays in general; what he would say to *Hero and Leander* as modernized by Littlewit to make it more relevant, less elitist, may be surmised by this weighty conclusion:

[34]*H&S* I, 141.

"Wheresoever, manners, and fashions are corrupted, Language is. It imitates the publicke riot. The excesse of Feasts, and apparell, are the notes of a sick State; and the wantonnesse of language, of a sick mind."[35]

With these mechanical motions we may seem to have hit bottom and, although plays chosen for performance at court were not marked by any particular refinement of speech or manners, surely nothing quite so gross could ever have been shown there before. Yet it is well to be reminded that "this ludicrous and coarse spectacle has performed the two primary functions of Renaissance art. It has delighted its audience, and now in its confrontation with Busy it shows its power to educate and persuade."[36] To which must be added, in this royal presence, Leatherhead's extenuating plea: "Sir, I present nothing, but what is licens'd by authority." (5.5.14)

Jonson promised a merry play and delivered one. It is the quality of the merriment that demands adjudication. Can we emerge with mind unmuddied and lungs intact after witnessing such motions and breathing such vapours? "For a lying mouth is a stinking pit, and murthers with the contagion it venteth," and "*Truth* is mans proper good; and the onely *immortall* thing, was given to our mortality to use."[37] The Fair is foul, let's face it, and that is no mere Bartholomew-birds' play on words (fowl play in a foul play, to outdo Littlewit). Are indulgent spectators of the play then merely wallowing in that foulness? Are we being asked to acquiesce too easily in a "discrepancy between law and life," like a slowbelly justice? The moral anarchy of the play is epitomized (for Alfred Harbage) in the fact that, whereas the merry Justice Clement sets things right in the end, the serious Justice Overdo is "the most deranged character in a deranged world."[38]

[35]*H&S* VIII, 572, 582, 219, 570, 593.
[36]Joel H. Kaplan, "Dramatic and Moral Energy in Ben Jonson's *Bartholomew Fair*," *Renaissance Drama*, n.s. III, 1970, 154.
[37]*H&S* VIII, 580.
[38]Harry Levin, "An Introduction to Ben Jonson," in Jonas Barish, ed., *Ben Jonson* (Englewood Cliffs, N.J., 1963), p. 48; Alfred Harbage, *Shakespeare and the Rival Traditions* (New York, 1952), p. 284. The play has been taken as something of a moral holiday by Horsman, introduction xiii; Barish, 222, 225; John J. Enck, *Jonson and the Comic Truth* (Wisconsin, 1957), ch. X; Hussey, ix–x. This view is vigorously challenged by Alan C. Dessen, *Jonson's Moral Comedy* (Evanston, Ill., 1971), ch. V.

No more than at a performance of *King Lear* are the spectators at *Bartholomew Fair* required to sacrifice to a day's entertainment the truths by which they order their lives. The audience is enthralled by the spectacle of the Fair, diverted by its change and variety, pleasantly confused and relaxed for a time, but at no point seriously deluded; on the contrary, it is confirmed in virtually all its initial judgments of the moral weight and worth of the characters and their purposes. Only Purecraft and Quarlous decline in our estimation – Purecraft by self-revelation, Quarlous by a self-defining choice (though their names might have alerted us from the beginning). All the figures of authority are ridiculed, to be sure, but their authority is spurious and mischievous (Busy) or minimal (Wasp in the private, Overdo in the public sphere). The comedy is astringent and (in Edward Partridge's phrase) "derisive not comforting." As he observes elsewhere, "If one can take life on the terms of the dirt and greed and idiocy of the Fair, one can take it on any terms. Similarly, if one can take a play on the terms of the bathos and extravagance of the puppet-show, one can take plays on any terms. Both life and the theatre are rendered as mean as the comic spirit allows";[39] and it is the triumph of Jonson's art to make all this cohere and please the mind, not just tickle the risibilities. There is a stillness and sobriety at the heart of the play, something that is not carnal and addresses what is not carnal in us and makes of carnality a "spectacle of strangeness." How would the Fair at Smithfield look to a spiritual being? We know, from Wordsworth:

> From these sights
> Take one, an annual Festival, the Fair
> Holden where Martyrs suffer'd in past time,
> And named of Saint Bartholomew; there see
> A work that's finish'd to our hands, that lays,
> If any spectacle on earth can do,
> The whole creative powers of man asleep!

. . . .

[39]The opening sentence of this paragraph echoes Alfred Harbage, *As They Liked It* (New York, 1947), p. 117. The passages by Edward B. Partridge are from "Ben Jonson: The Makings of the Dramatist (1596–1602)," *Stratford-upon-Avon Studies*, 9 (London, 1966), 242–43; and the introduction to his edition, xv–xvi.

> Oh, blank confusion! and a type not false
> Of what the mighty City is itself
> To all except a Straggler here and there,
> To the whole Swarm of its inhabitants;
> An undistinguishable world to men,
> The slaves unrespited of low pursuits,
> Living amid the same perpetual flow
> Of trivial objects, melted and reduced
> To one identity, by differences
> That have no law, no meaning, and no end;
> Oppression under which even highest minds
> Must labour, whence the strongest are not free. . . .[40]

Of this vision Ben Jonson has some part, though blessed with a stronger stomach than Wordsworth and a better head for drinking.

The art of *Bartholomew Fair* is, of course, to the highest degree, that of comedy; but, having used the phrase "spectacle of strangeness,"[41] I should like to suggest that it combines with it something of another art that Jonson was concurrently bringing to its highest perfection (if indeed he was not the inventor of it), the art of the antimasque. Here I am making somewhat more literal a metaphor suggested by Professor Partridge: "His major comedies seem now like antimasques to the Renaissance masque of the Golden Age – grotesque violations of the exalted vision."[42]

I suggest that, at the end of the performance of *Bartholomew Fair* at court, the elements of the masque to balance its anti-masque-like character are not merely absent but conspicuous by their absence, to the point of being present in their absence. After the hours of romp and desecration, grotesquerie of appearance and language, there is no transformation scene. Nothing is celebrated as worthy of fame or honour. There is no magnificence or glory, no poetry (except the verse of the puppets, which is beneath the floor of the prose), no music (except Nightingale's ballad to cover a scene of crime and folly), no dance (except the

---

[40]*The Prelude*, ed. Ernest de Selincourt, second ed., revised by Helen Darbishire (Oxford, 1959), book VII, lines 675–80, 694–706 (version of 1805–6).
[41]*H&S* VII, 282, preface to the *Masque of Queens*. See John C. Meagher, *Method and Meaning in Jonson's Masques* (Notre Dame, Indiana, 1966), 52–54.
[42]Edward B. Partridge, *The Broken Compass* (London, 1958), p. 235.

choreographed swirl and eddy of the Fair), no strength of reason to dispell madness and feigned madness, no sweetness of love or beauty to take the curse off the ugliness and end the quarrelling, not even a manifestation of power by which the disguised magistrate effectively asserts his authority. The play's mountain belly and rocky face are too enormously swollen to admit of a mere token of a masque-like element such as, for instance, a wedding song or dance of Winwife and Grace. To actors and audience, all of whom (except the inconsequential Cokes) are fully sated, comes only a promise of further feasting and fairing at the house of Adam Overdo.

We must take a moment to consider Jonson's antimasques,[43] one before and one after *Bartholomew Fair*. *Love Restored* (1611/12) opens with a long informal colloquial speech of Masquerado apologizing for a hitch in the performance; it is comparable in tone to the Induction but is, like the Prologue, addressed to the King. "Though I dare not shew my face, I can speake truth, under a vizard. Good faith, and't please your Majestie, Your Masquers are all at a stand; I cannot thinke your Majestie wil see any shew to night at least worth your patience." A surly character disguised as Cupid then complains: "Thou, and thy like, thinke your selves authoris'd in this place, to all licence of surquedry. But you shall finde, custome hath not so grafted you here, but you may be rent up, and throwne out as unprofitable evils. I tell thee, I will have no more masquing; I will not buy a false, and fleeting delight so deare. . . ." Honest Robin Goodfellow, coming from the country to court, is indignant: "Slight, a fine trick! a piece of *Englands joy*, this. Are these your court-sports! . . . So many thornie difficulties as I have past, deserv'd the best masque: the whole shop of the *Revells*. . . ." But the pseudo-Cupid says, "Your rude good fellowship must seeke some other spheare for your admittie . . ." (other, that is, than performance at court). Robin then tells of trying to get in under the guise of various sorts of persons the door would be open to – a motions-man, an old tyre-woman, a musician, a

---

[43]Or "antick-masques" or "foyle or false-Masques" (*H&S* VII, 282, 638). "Contentious Musique," (213) and "praeposterous change, and gesticulation," (301) characterize antimasques. The passages from *Love Restored* are cited from *H&S* VII, 377–81. For the Christmas cut-purse, see Chambers, III, 387. The passages from *The Gypsies Metamorphosed*, *H&S* VII, 569, 574–75.

feather-maker of Blackfriars – "but," he says, "they all made as light of mee, as of my feathers; and wonder'd how I could be a *Puritane*, being of so vaine a vocation. I answer'd, We all are *masquers* sometimes: with which they knock'd *hypocrisie* o' the pate. . . ." Thereafter he sees a fine citizen's wife let in, and takes her shape, only to feel a blackguard's hand "groping of me as nimbly as the *Christmas* cut-purse. . . . I was glad to forgoe my forme, to be rid of his hot steeming affection, it so smelt o' the boyling-house." The pseudo-Cupid in a censorious vein attacks (as it were) enormities: "Away, idle spirit; and thou, the idle cause of his adventuring hither, vanish with him. 'Tis thou, that art not only the sower of vanities, in these high places, but the call of all other light follies to fall, and feed on them. I will endure thy prodigalities, nor riots no more; they are the ruine of states. . . ." But shortly he is exposed as neither the true Cupid, Love in Court, nor his brother anti-Cupid, the Love of Virtue, but spoil-sport Plutus the god of money, in despite of whom the rites proceed of Cupid in his chariot guarded by his masquers. The likeness of this in tone to *Bartholomew Fair* will be noticed, and in some details.

The masque we know best pleased the King was *The Gypsies Metamorphosed* (1621). The Gypsies, looking very outlandish, enter in two carts, one laden with children, the other with stolen poultry. After a dance, the Jackman promises a sort of fairing:

> Knacks we have that will delight you,
> Slights of hand that will invite you
> To indure our tawney faces,
> And not cause you *cut your laces*.

Then fortunes are told, the King's twice, the second one serious, the first this – perhaps the best indication we have (apart from Buckingham's letters) of the joshing tone King James could permit and enjoy on occasion:

> With you, lucky bird, I begin; lett me see,
> I aime at the best, and I trowe you are hee.
> Here's some luck alreadie, if I understand
> The grounds of my Art. Here's a Gentlemans hand.
> I'le kisse is for lucks sake, you should by this line
> Love a horse and a hound, but no part of a swine;

To hunt the brave stag, not so much for your food,
As the weale of your bodie, and the healthe of your blood.
Y'are a man of good meanes, and have territories store,
Both by sea and by land, and were borne, Sir, to more,
Which you, like a Lord and the Prince of your peace,
Content with your havings, despise to increase.
You are no greate wencher, I see by your table,
Although your *Mons Veneris* sayes you are able.
You live chaste and single, and have buried your wife,
And meane not to marrie by the line of your life.
Whence he that conjectures your qualitie, learnes
You'are an honest good man, and have care of your barnes.
Your *Mercuries* hill too a witt doth betoken,
Some booke craft you have, and are pretty well spoken.
But stay! in your *Jupiters Mount*, what's here!
A Kinge! a Monarch! what wonders appeare!
High! bountifull! just! a *Jove* for your parts!
A Master of men, and that raigne in their harts!

The Gypsies Metamorphosed, with its swirl of low-life, cony-catching, purse-taking impudency, its flood of demotic speech, its extravagant attack on tobacco, and its "applications" that it would be absurd to take offence at, is the likest to *Bartholomew Fair* among the masques, indeed among the works, of Ben Jonson.

IV

The Epilogue comes forward and speaks:

> Your Majesty hath seen the play, and you
> Can best allow it from your ear, and view.
> You know the scope of writers, and what store
> Of leave is given them, if they take no more,
> And turn it into licence: you can tell
> If we have us'd that leave you gave us, well:
> Or whether we to rage, or licence break,
> Or be profane, or make profane men speak?
> This is your power to judge, great sir, and not
> The envy of a few. Which if we have got,
> We value less what their dislike can bring,
> If it so happy be, t' have pleas'd the King.

His Majesty was made welcome to a fair, but he has seen a play; and a play is to be judged as a fair is not, and is to be judged by the one who is literally and metaphorically able to see and hear it best, who has the right and power to do so: "This is your power to judge, great sir."

It is certainly within King James's right and power to agree with the stage-keeper in addressing the playgoers the previous afternoon – "it is a very conceited scurvy one"; or, to move from small critics to great, to mistake the fun altogether, like Augustus in *Poetaster*. But if the King lasted out the play, he could hardly object to anything on looking back, and there is no point at which it would not have been absurd to rise and cry, "Give me some lights. Away!" The worst the playwright had to fear from the Scottish Solomon would be a canny recourse to the old verdict of "not proven" to the charge that there was "offence" in it: that is, "not guilty, but don't do it again." As for the court audience, some may have noticed "applications" shifting in and out of focus, but after the event it would be difficult to find words to state them even to themselves. Their representatives on the stage – Grace Wellborn and Winwife and Quarlous – do not constitute an ironic confederacy. Grace shows some reluctance to enter the Fair (as the court ladies well might), but endures it without defilement if without pleasure; the two young gentlemen communicate a spirit of gamesomeness; but none touches a sensitive point or precipitates an assessment of the action.

In what possible way could *Bartholomew Fair* make the spectator a wiser and better man, the King a wiser and better king? It cannot simply be an antimasque of anarchy, can it? One earnest, somewhat self-important character comes to realize the easy lesson that he is flesh and blood. But easy lessons are perhaps the hardest to teach so that they reach home. The child Ruskin stood on a sofa and preached, "people, be good," but that was not the end of his life's exertions. So, too, with such lessons as behave yourself and don't be a fool, or make the best of a bad job, or resign yourself to be the fool you are; so too with the realization that the fair is fun but an enormous waste of life if extended beyond leave to licence. There is quite enough to think about: the inefficacy of direct intervention against tolerable little enormities; that flesh and blood are subject to vapours; that intellect and spirit can see this but must allow for it; that the fleshly motions of fairgoers and Bartholomew-birds, the carnal and seditious motions of Puritan sectaries, the high-minded fidgets of the busybody Justice, the testy buzzing of Wasp, the juvenile hyperactivity of Cokes, and the mechanical jerks of the puppets – all busily seeking with a continual change – can be held in stasis only by a judicious spectator whose mind is in repose. These realizations have weight enough to make this a good all-sinners' play for All Saints' Day.

Masques, we know, made a specialty of cloud effects[44] ("cloud capp'd towers"), and iridescence (clear air taking on the nature of fire). Francis Bacon, in his essay "Of Masques and Triumphs," observes that "some sweet odours suddenly coming forth, without any drops falling, are, in such company as there is steam and heat, things of great pleasure and refreshment."[45] Such pleasure and refreshment are not written into the text Jonson prepared for court; instead, the gross vapours of the Fair, mixing water and earth with air, remain apparently undispelled. No, the presence of the court itself must, if it can, serve as its own masque to dispel this antimasque.[46] If you wish a more enduring monument than the Fair, look about you – at the Great Hall not the booths, at the King and Queen not Adam and his wife, at the perfumed and barbered courtiers not the visitors to the Fair. Surely that is sufficient transcendence; it would be almost treason to suggest otherwise.

If fully successful, the play can end in the happiest of transformation scenes, in which the King turns the sunlight of his countenance on playwright and players, and the vapours disperse. Or, to quote Bartholomaeus Anglicus, "when mist is all smitten with the beames of the Sunne, it falleth down & turneth again into the matter that it came of, and vanisheth . . . and so the air is purged."[47]

[44]Nicoll, pp. 161–67.
[45]*Works*, XII, 209–211.
[46]Donaldson, *The World Upside-Down*, p. 72, for whom the final appeal to the King has "something of the effect of the entry of the main masque after the anarchy of the antimasque."
[47]Bartholomaeus Anglicus, *De Proprietatibus Rerum*, fol. 163–163 v, tr. Trevisa, 1495, quoted by Heninger, *Handbook*, p. 62.

Things as They Are
and the World of Absolutes
in Jonson's Plays and Masques

EUGENE M. WAITH

Ben Jonson's attention to theatrical detail is everywhere apparent. Much more often than Shakespeare (though not as often as we sometimes wish), he describes precisely a piece of stage business: *"Edgworth gets up to him, and tickles him in the eare with a straw twice to draw his hand out of his pocket."*[1] Such stage directions seem to serve well a classical theory of comic mimesis which he often stated: no *"Tales,"* no *"Tempests,"* just "deedes, and language, such as men doe use" (*Bartholomew Fair*, Ind., l. 130; *Everyman in His Humour*, Prol. l. 21). Yet no one who knows Jonson would make the rash leap from the evidence of this concern with the precise rendering of everyday reality onstage to the conclusion that Jonson was what the late nineteenth century called a realist. Equally clear is a very different concern. Gabriele Jackson opens her study of *Vision and Judgment in Ben Jonson's Drama* (New Haven, 1968) with the sentence: "To read Jonsonian drama is to come immediately and repeatedly upon the distinction between things as they are and things as they should be and to witness over and over the ritual of converting the one into the other." As satirist and teacher Jonson must project in the theatre more than careful observation.

---

[1] *Bartholomew Fair*, III. v. 145 ff. All quotations from Jonson are taken from the Herford and Simpson edition, 11 vols. (Oxford, 1925–1952), referred to as H & S. I have silently altered "u/v" and "i/j" spellings in accordance with modern usage.

At times he seems to be pulled in opposite directions by the moral principles he asserts so strongly in the *Discoveries* and by a world which largely ignores them. It is not his departures from his principles that I shall discuss, however, but his ways of dramatizing the distinction of which Mrs. Jackson speaks, whether by emphasis on the world as we know it or on what he believes to be the underlying truths of existence. My topic is things as they are and the world of absolutes, as they are revealed in the conception and staging of certain plays and masques of the years 1616–1626. This was a crucial period for Jonson. In 1616 he published the first volume of his *Works* and received the pension which made him, in effect, the first poet laureate. In some twelve masques (the exact number depends on the strictness of one's definition) from *Mercury Vindicated* in January 1616 to *The Fortunate Isles* in January 1625, his last masque for the court of James I, he continued the success which had so much to do with his laureateship. In two plays, *The Devil is an Ass* in October or November, 1616, and *The Staple of News*, shortly after the coronation of Charles I, February 2, 1626, he began what most critics have considered the steep descent from his great success with *Bartholomew Fair*. The two plays and two masques, *The Vision of Delight* and *Time Vindicated*, will illustrate Jonson's treatment of things as they are and the world of absolutes during this period.

I think the difference between representing things as they are and as they should be is a real one, but there is no getting away from the fact that the distinction is slightly tricky, when it is seen in the light of seventeenth-century ideas of poetic mimesis. For example, in *Cynthia's Revels*, Jonson has Mercury say to Cupid, when they are planning to assume the roles of young boys, "let's . . . practise their language, and behaviours, and not with a dead imitation" (II. i. 5–7). "Jonson required of his actors a heightened reality," as Robert M. Wren comments.[2] "Heightened reality" suggests the elevation associated with epic and tragedy, as in Dryden's comment on "the nature of a serious play: this last is indeed the representation of Nature, but 'tis Nature wrought up to an higher pitch."[3] Yet comic acting is the subject of discussion

[2] "Ben Jonson as Producer," *ETJ*, 22 (1970), 286.
[3] "An Essay of Dramatic Poesy," in *Essays of John Dryden*, ed. W. P. Ker, 2 vols. (Oxford, 1900), I, 100.

in *Cynthia's Revels*, and the point is to achieve a *lively* imitation, to get at the essence of the assumed characters. Although in Renaissance poetics comedy is supposed to portray the more ordinary and less admirable sort of men, it is assumed that all poetic imitation should go beyond historical accuracy to suggest general or ideal truth. In one sense every poet imitates things as they should be. In fact, the standard comparison to painting is often used to encourage the poet to bring out the inner truth of his subject by means of highlights and shadows. As Chapman says: "it serves not a skilfull Painters turne, to draw the figure of a face onely to make knowne who it represents; but hee must lymn, give luster, shaddow, and heightening; which though ignorants will esteeme spic'd, and too curious, yet such as have the judiciall perspective, will see it hath, motion, spirit and life. . . ."[4] We move in such discussions by almost imperceptible stages from what we would call imitation to something which seems to us very different. And since the didactic purpose of poetry is never long neglected, we find that the ideal truth to be imitated has moral as well as ontological significance.

The representation of things as they potentially are or ought to be is thus a part of the task of representing things as they are in any genre, and the comic "mirror of custom" in the standard definition attributed to Cicero is not entirely different from the mirror Jonson refers to in his epistle "To Katherine, Lady Aubigny," when he declines to describe her outward beauty, which everyone can see:

> My mirror is more subtile, cleere, refin'd,
> And takes, and gives the beauties of the mind.
> (H. & S., VIII, 117, ll. 43–44)

It is not inconsistent with Jonson's acute awareness of generic distinctions that he has recourse to both kinds of mirror in his comedies and in his masques. In the period under consideration his combinations of the two mimetic modes are especially conspicuous. They succeed to varying degrees.

A vital part of such dramatic mimesis is its visual dimension. The continental "scenes and machines" imported by Inigo Jones

---

[4]Dedication to *Ovid's Banquet of Sense* in *The Poems of George Chapman*, ed. Phyllis B. Bartlett (New York, 1941), p. 49.

for staging at court could be used to create an exact image of the world the spectators knew, but in the early masques of Jonson and Jones they were used to portray such sights as the "ugly hell" and the turning House of Fame of *The Masque of Queens*. By astounding the spectators, such spectacular staging might lift their minds to the contemplation of an ideal, specifically the triumph of order and goodness which regularly concludes the Jonsonian masque. As Stephen Orgel shows in an important article,[5] the poetics of this sort of spectacle are basically those of heroic and panegyric.

The emblematic staging of the theatres lent itself to various genres. Capable of representing an indefinite number of places, simultaneously or successively, it could also, on occasion, create the illusion of a particular place, as it probably did in *Bartholomew Fair*, with booths for Ursula and Leatherhead very like actual fair booths, and, in the words of the Induction, "as stinking every whit" (ll. 159–60). Here would be a clear instance of the "mirror of custom." On a stage so hospitable to symbolism, however, the booths could readily take on further significance as representations of various hazards in a predatory world or, as R. B. Parker suggests, of heaven and hell.[6] Since the powerful illusion of place is not broken by these intimations of further significance, this system of staging seems especially appropriate for a play which emphasizes the necessity of accepting the world, however short it falls of the ideal.

In the next two plays the relationship between things as they are and the world of absolutes is worked out less happily – a failure which partly accounts for their inferiority to Jonson's best. *The Devil is an Ass* begins with a promising use of the conventions of the English theatre. The stage was that of Blackfriars, which in Richard Hosley's plausible reconstruction[7] was a rectangular space twenty-nine feet wide by eighteen and a half feet deep in front of three arches of a hall screen which was the tiring-house wall. Each of the arches could be an entrance. On the second level the space over the arches was divided into six

---

[5]"The Poetics of Spectacle," *New Literary History*, 2 (1971), 367–89.
[6]"The Themes and Staging of *Bartholomew Fair*," *University of Toronto Quarterly*, 39 (1970), 295.
[7]"A Reconstruction of the Second Blackfriars," *The Elizabethan Theatre*, ed. David Galloway, [I] (Toronto, 1970), pp. 74–88.

windows, behind which was an area that could be used for either actors or spectators. For the first scene, where Satan agrees against his better judgment to send the eager but foolish devil Pug to the earth, Gifford supposed that the audience would have seen a hell-mouth, or at least that Satan and Pug would appear through a trap.[8] Possibly so. Jonson's revival of the old-fashioned but still popular devil-play strongly suggests the conventions of medieval drama, but the hell-mouth would have to be taken off after this one brief scene, and there is nothing in the stage directions to indicate the use of a trap. Nor is anything of this sort required. At the end of the scene, before they leave the stage, Satan points out Fitz-Dottrell *"coming forth"* from his house; so by that time the scene is London. The location shifts while the characters remain onstage, or perhaps it is both hell and London, for the joke of the whole play is that London outdoes hell. The very indeterminacy of the setting is an asset.

Again, in later scenes of *The Devil is an Ass* the imagined location changes even though the characters do not leave the stage. Fitz-Dottrell, as we have seen, comes out of his house. Here he is accosted by Pug and, later, by Wittipol and Manly. These two remain onstage when Fitz-Dottrell goes to get his wife, but the entertaining wooing scene which follows seems to be indoors; for when it is over and Mrs. Fitz-Dottrell has been sent "Up to [her] Cabbin againe" (I. vi. 238), Pug is ordered to let Ingine "in," and Meercraft is said to be "without" (I. vii. 3, 7). Scene v of Act III begins in Fitz-Dottrell's house. At the end of the scene Meercraft and Pug start walking to Lady Tailbush's "hard by here / Over the way" (ll. 66–67). By the beginning of the next scene they are apparently outside her house, and at the end of that scene Meercraft sends Pug off to return to Fitz-Dottrell's house.

In one scene, for which Jonson gives exact directions, the facilities of the stage are used to reproduce with some care the exterior of two adjoining houses. From a speech of Mrs. Fitz-Dottrell's we know that Manly has a "chamber-window in *Lincolnes-Inne* there, / That opens to my gallery" (II. ii. 53–54). Wittipol later leans out of this window to talk to Mrs. Fitz-Dottrell in her window, and then, as one stage direction frankly

[8]*The Works of Ben Jonson*, ed. W. Gifford, 9 vols. (London, 1875), V, 7.

110

puts it, "*He growes more familiar in his Courtship, playes with her paps, kisseth her hands &c*" (II. vi. 71 ff). "This is indeed growing familiar!" says Gifford (V, 63). Another stage direction tells us "*This* Scene *is acted at two windo's as out of two contiguous buildings*" (ll. 37 ff).[9] The windows over the stage doors in Hosley's reconstruction would admirably serve the purposes of this scene, the point of which would be sharpened by the faithful rendering of the locale.

In the first half of the play Jonson's blend of fantasy with the depiction of the London of his time produces effective satire. Not only is Meercraft a more artful deceiver than little Pug, but his "projects" soar into a realm fully as fantastic as that inhabited by supernatural beings. But the untying of the plot is much less satisfactory than its knotting. Fitz-Dottrell, gull extraordinary, is rescued from the consequences of his folly in two unrelated stages. In the first of these Mrs. Fitz-Dottrell is so honest but also so steadfast in her virtue (despite her having allowed her admirer certain trifling liberties), that Wittipol, the would-be seducer, is moved to say: "Lady, I can love *goodnes* in you, more / Then I did *Beauty*" (IV. vi. 37–38). A few minutes later he frustrates one of Meercraft's principal schemes against Fitz-Dottrell, though in a way which does not altogether please the intended victim. To Mrs. Fitz-Dottrell Jonson holds up the "more subtile" mirror that "takes, and gives the beauties of the mind."

The scene of Wittipol's conversion is altogether surprising, especially because of its tone which, as J. B. Bamborough has remarked, "becomes very similar to that of eighteenth-century Sentimental Comedy."[10] In fact, one needn't go so far. There is a striking analogy to this scene in Southerne's *The Wives Excuse* (IV. i), where Mrs. Friendall's loyalty to a husband she does not love evokes Lovemore's admiration. In Jonson's play Mrs. Fitz-Dottrell's display of virtue is given further emphasis by Wittipol's friend Manly, who emerges from behind an arras (presumably hung over one of the doors) to say, "O friend! forsake not / The

---

[9]Irwin Smith, in whose reconstruction of the theatre some fifteen feet of "tarras" separate the two windows, is forced to suppose that Wittipol climbs out of Manly's window and crosses the tarras to Mrs. Fitz-Dottrell's window. He thinks that the stage direction was written after Jonson had forgotten how the scene was done at Blackfriars. See *Shakespeare's Blackfriars Playhouse* (New York, 1964), p. 385.

[10]*Ben Jonson* (London, 1970), p. 123.

brave occasion, vertue offers you, / To keepe you innocent . . ."
(ll. 28–30). He is a veritable guardian of the T. S. Eliot variety.
Such behaviour comes as a shock in a play seemingly devoted to
shaming the devil by showing that the average Englishman can
easily out-play him at his own game.

The final stage of the rescue of Fitz-Dottrell is achieved by
purely supernatural means. When Pug gives up his bumbling
efforts at corruption and is taken home by Satan and Iniquity,
there is a great bang and a cloud of sulphurous smoke, which are
reported to Fitz-Dottrell. It is the realization that he has employed a genuine devil as a servant which finally puts him out of
his humour and simultaneously turns him against Meercraft.

Despite Jonson's use of absolute evil in the person of Satan and
of an embodiment of goodness in Mrs. Fitz-Dottrell, *The Devil
is an Ass* has considerably less universal significance than
Bartholomew Fair. The nature of the joke is to reduce the importance of the supernatural agents of evil and to make one feel
that the human goodness of Mrs. Fitz-Dottrell is, alas, manifested
in an unworthy cause. The "intersection of the timeless with
time" does not quite come off, and only in occasional flashes
does the imitation of things as they are have the brilliant immediacy of *Bartholomew Fair* or *The Alchemist*.

Although *The Devil is an Ass* seems, from any point of view,
only moderately successful – a joke of modest proportions extended somewhat too far – it indicates clearly the direction in
which Jonson was to move in his next plays. In *The Staple of
News* characters in the familiar world are continually confronted
by representatives of the world of absolutes, recalling, to the
Oxford editors, "the characteristic themes of the Masque proper"
(H & S, II, 171). In the staging, again at Blackfriars, and later
at court, it is tempting to suppose that Jonson tried to recapture
the immediacy of *Bartholomew Fair* by again using booths,
though it is possible that the three doors at the Blackfriars could
have provided the necessary discovery spaces. The two *loca*
which might benefit the most from presentation in practicable
onstage structures are the staple and the house of Peniboy Senior.

After the Induction the prodigal Peniboy Junior enters, supposedly in his house, trying out a new pair of boots which the
shoemaker has just pulled on. Shortly he has to put his watch on
a table. No special structure is required here. The stage, with a

table already set on it, may easily represent an extension of his living quarters to which he may enter through one of the three doors – let us suppose the centre one. When others come to see him this door must represent the outside door to his house, or a door that leads both to the outside and to other parts of the house; for he tells us that the new staple of news is "Here in the house, almost on the same floore" (I. ii. 32), and when he and his friends leave the stage, probably by the same door, they are on their way to the staple.

At the opening of the fourth scene the Register and the Clerk are setting up the staple for the day, arranging desks, and setting forth a table, a carpet and a chair. The table is still there from the preceding scene, and the other furniture could be brought through one of the other doors, but it might be even more effective to draw back the curtains surrounding a booth placed in front of one of the doors – say the door at stage right – revealing the desk, carpet and chair. Soon Peniboy Junior and his party enter, probably through the centre door, which is now the outside door of the staple. With them come Cymbal and Fitton, as if taking them on a tour of the premises. "This is the outer roome," says Cymbal, "where my *Clerkes* sit . . . The *Examiner,* he sits private there, within . . ." (I. v. 2, 4). The door leading "within" is referred to later and might well be the right-hand door at the back of the booth. At the end of the fifth scene the staple operators excuse themselves and leave Peniboy Junior and his friend Peniboy Canter, who is his father in disguise. When they are joined by Picklock, the scheming lawyer, the location seems once more to be Peniboy Junior's house, which may be suggested by simply closing the staple booth. This way of staging the staple would not only be convenient and congruent with all the stage directions, but would enhance the symbolic significance of the staple by having it before our eyes, a constant presence even when not in use.

The other location which might have been a booth is the house of Peniboy Senior, the miserly uncle who is the exact antithesis of the young prodigal. Since he is the guardian of the Lady Pecunia, whom Cymbal would like to lure to the staple, there would be an obvious neatness in having Peniboy Senior's house a booth in front of the door at stage left, opposite the staple. More precisely, the booth in this case would be a room in his house. In the first scene of Act II the old man is talking to Pecunia, whom he asks to retire at the arrival of the herald, Pyed Mantle. In a stage direction preceding the fifth scene she and her ladies-in-waiting are said to be "*hid in the study*," and a later direction reads: "*The study is open'd where she sit[s] in state*" (ll. 44 ff), surrounded, apparently, by her ladies. Since such a discovery could most easily be accomplished by pulling the curtains of a booth, it is likely that Pecunia and her ladies retire *into* this booth in the first scene. Here we may note that Glynne Wickham gives the study and the shop, with actors already in them, as two of what he considers the relatively infrequent occasions on which booths may have been used.[11] The opening of the staple in Act I and the discovery of Pecunia in Act II exactly fit his specifications. Between Scene i and Scene v Pecunia is supposed to be "above" with her ladies, where Madrigal goes to visit her, presumably by going out the centre door, but there is nothing very troublesome about her supposed trips up and downstairs between retirement and discovery.

Both booths could be used effectively in later scenes. In Act III the action is again at the news "office," now called the "house of *fame*" (III. ii. 115), to which Peniboy Junior brings Pecunia. At the end of Scene iii Nathaniel tells Thomas to "Shut up the *Office*" (l. 54), and the curtains are closed for the last time.

Immediately after this business, action begins at Peniboy Senior's as he is surprised by the arrival of Broker, one of Pecunia's ladies. He might be discovered in his study by Broker "knocking" there after her entrance through the centre door. When he hears that she has brought Cymbal he asks for a chair, from which he tells Cymbal he is too ill to rise. Growing angry with Cymbal, he sends him packing with the words, "There lies your way, you see the doore" (III. iv. 76) – presumably the centre door once more.

Although the booth is not required, it would be useful for this scene, and almost essential for the final scene of the play, again at Peniboy Senior's, introduced by the stage direction, "*He is seene sitting at his Table with papers before him*" (V. iv). This scene is preceded by three at Peniboy Junior's, which may take place, like those of Act I, in the centre of the stage. In Scene iii

[11]*Early English Stages 1300–1660*, Vol. II, Pt. II (London and New York, 1972), 199.

Lickfinger startles Peniboy Junior and his father (whose identity has now been revealed) with the news that Peniboy Senior has gone mad, leaves all his doors open, and can be seen by passers-by sitting at a table like a judge, presiding at the trial of his two dogs. Obviously we must not see this little tableau at this moment. The scene ends with the characters deciding to go "thither," and probably going out the centre door. Then comes the stage direction just quoted, which seems to call for the curtains of the study-booth to be drawn, discovering Peniboy Senior and his dogs.

I have left out one *locus*, where the entire fourth act takes place – the Apollo Room at the Devil Tavern. The most literal realism would require this to be in the gallery over the stage, since, when Peniboy Senior is forced to leave, his nephew says "get you downe the staires" and later, "Downe with him" (IV. ii. 63, 81), but there are too many characters onstage for too long to make action in the cramped space of the gallery conceivable. What would do admirably for a bit of dalliance in *The Devil is an Ass* would not do at all for these crowded scenes. Almost certainly the whole stage except for the two closed booths at either side must have been used.

So far so good. Two *loca* of crucial and contrasting significance might be visually present as in *Bartholomew Fair*. But certain problems remain. In the first place, there is a chorus sitting onstage. Referring to Hosley's reconstruction, we may imagine the four gossips sitting, two on each side, in the "side-stage audience areas," but even if they were to the left and right, respectively, of the outermost of the stage doors, booths in front of those doors could not project far onto the stage without obstructing the view when closed. On the other hand, the alternative of discovery spaces behind the openings in the screen to represent the "outer room" of the staple and Peniboy Senior's study does not seem acceptable. I suggest that relatively shallow booths may have been used.

Next a much more interesting problem. In the opening scene of Act V Thom tells Peniboy Junior that the staple disappeared when they heard they had lost Pecunia – "quite dissolv'd!" "Shiver'd, as in an earthquake! heard you not / The cracke and ruines?" (ll. 39–41). How is this done? Its disappearance would be visually much more effective if the office were not a purely imaginary structure. Yet destruction corresponding to Thom's frantic description could only be achieved by Inigo Jones's scenes and machines: "not only the *Hagges* themselves, but they^r *Hell*, into w^{c}h they ranne, quite vanished; and the whole face of the *Scene* alterd . . ." (H & S, VII, 301). In fact it would seem that such staging is precisely what this incursion of the supernatural calls for. But obviously something much less exciting must happen. Perhaps during the fourth Intermean this booth is taken down as the gossips chat. If so, one other problem would be solved. In the second scene of Act V it is necessary for Thom to be concealed "behind the hangings" (1. 70). If there are booths in front of the left and right doors, only the centre opening remains visible, and on several occasions it is explicitly referred to as a door. Even in Act V Picklock has to enter through some door which cannot be behind the hangings where Thom is. There is no room for hangings between the doors or to the side of them. If the staple booth is gone by Act V, however, there can be hangings over the door at stage right where it was.

There are solutions, then – possibly quite simple ones – to the problem of the disappearing office, but, as I have already hinted, none that I can think of seems to me entirely congruent with Jonson's action. In *The Staple of News* the revelation of true value has a far more dramatic impact on the mutable world of appearances than in *The Devil is an Ass*. When Mistress Fitz-Dottrell proves virtuous, only a beginning has been made toward rescuing her husband from the clutches of Meercraft. Even when Fitz-Dottrell sees his situation more clearly, the most we can hope is that he will be less egregious. The change which occurs at the end of the fourth act of *The Staple of News* is so great that the entire last act has somewhat the quality of a coda. Good has already triumphed. When Peniboy Canter, at the close of the tavern scene, reveals himself as the father of the prodigal and takes charge of Pecunia, the young man is instantly reduced from riches to rags and, as his subsequent actions show, sees the light. The staple vanishes.

Jonson makes fun of the choral gossips for mistaking this episode for the catastrophe. Commentators have been quick to point out that it is in fact the catastasis or false resolution, since Picklock has one further scheme by which he hopes to defraud both father and son. But does this analysis adequately describe the situation? Technically, no doubt, it does, but Peniboy Junior's outwitting of Picklock in Act V is a direct consequence of his enlightenment at the end of Act IV, and the madness of the old miser is merely one final manifestation of his folly before he, too, repents of it.

Not only is Peniboy Canter's self-revelation the major turning point of the plot, but Jonson manages it so as to give it climactic importance in the thematic structure. The errors of prodigality and miserliness represented by Peniboy Junior and Peniboy Senior are, of course, instances of false valuation – failures to perceive the truth. The news business, with its sale of false rumours, is obviously devoted to obfuscation. Still other forms of false valuation are the malicious misrepresentations of the jeerers and the double-talk of the canters. In the tavern scenes one sort of falsity is piled on another up to the moment of revelation: jeering is followed by its polar opposite, extravagant praise, and then by a violent quarrel, which ends with the expulsion of Peniboy Senior. At this point the custodian of true value, ironically called Peniboy Canter, shows how each occupation represented there has its own form of cant to escape plain-speaking. Peniboy Junior, enchanted by the demonstration, decides to found a Canters' College. The build-up of folly to this pinnacle is symphonic. It is immediately succeeded by the deflation of each fool as Peniboy Canter, having revealed himself as no canter, proclaims the difference between these self-satisfied pretenders and true practitioners of the professions to which they belong. Taking Pecunia with him, he leaves, tossing his son the beggar's cloak in which he has been disguised.

Nothing that follows is so important as this moment. The lives of most of the principal characters are instantly transformed, and only Picklock and Peniboy Senior have to wait until the next act to feel the effects. It is for this reason, and not because of the presence of allegorical characters, that the play is so similar to a masque. And for this reason the traditional English staging, ingeniously effective as it may well have been for most of the play, seems unequal to the demands of Jonson's idea, which cries out for a visual transformation.

Some critics have suggested that Jonson's preoccupation with the masque in the ten years between *The Devil is an Ass* and *The Staple of News* was responsible for the weaknesses of the later play, but this does not seem to me quite the way to put it. Even *The Devil is an Ass*, as C. G. Thayer notes, shows something of the pattern of antimasque and masque,[12] and Jonson had been writing masques for years before *Bartholomew Fair*, which does not have this pattern. It seems rather that in the years following *Bartholomew Fair* he again felt more strongly the urge to counter-poise his imitation of the familiar with an imitation of the ideal, as he had earlier done in the comical satires and, with questionable success, in *Volpone*. In the masques of this period one may observe a corresponding change. As foils for the ideal order created by the idealized James I, Jonson and Jones first devised such chaotic visions as the "ugly hell" of *The Masque of Queens*, the "fallen House of Chivalry" of *Prince Henry's Barriers*, and the wild "satiricall scene" of *Oberon*; but *Mercury Vindicated* of 1616 "undertakes something quite new to masques," as Stephen Orgel says,[13] by opening in *"a laboratory, or Alchymists workehouse,"* the sort of scene from the everyday world which one might expect in Jonsonian comedy. If, that is, Jonson is moved to portray more of the ideal in *The Devil is an Ass* and *The Staple of News*, he is moved to portray more of the familiar in some of the masques during these same years.

The problem of representing the intersection of the two realms and the interactions of their inhabitants presents itself in very different terms in the masque as opposed to comedy. The distinctions between the two systems of staging have already been mentioned, and it may be worth while to recall the equally well-known distinctions between the conditions of performance and the relationships of the audience to the performance. Though Jonson often breaks the theatrical frame of his plays by direct address to the audience and even by representing members of the audience onstage, as in *The Staple of News*, there can never be in the theatre that special relationship brought about by the participation of members of the court as masquers and by the descents from the platform to the floor of the hall for dancing with the spectators and ceremonial visits to the state. The ritual by which the courtly audience is transformed, in Orgel's words, "into the idealized world of the poet's vision" (*Complete Mas-*

[12]*Ben Jonson: Studies in the Plays* (Norman, Okla., 1963), p. 160.
[13]*Ben Jonson: The Complete Masques*, ed. Stephen Orgel (New Haven and London, 1969), p. 33.

ques, p. 2) constitutes a special way in which the ideal penetrates the here and now.

Several of the masques of the last ten years of the reign follow the lead of *Mercury Vindicated* in the relative faithfulness of their portrayal of things as they are. *The Vision of Delight* has "A Street in perspective of faire building." *Pleasure Reconciled to Virtue* returns to older conventions by opening on Mt. Atlas, but in the revised form of this opening Atlas is changed to Snowdon "for the honour of *Wales*," bringing the antimasque considerably closer to home. In *News from the New World*, *Neptune's Triumph*, and *The Fortunate Isles* the location of the opening is simply the banqueting hall itself, though in *Neptune's Triumph* two pillars dedicated to Neptune are visible. *Pan's Anniversary*, like *Pleasure Reconciled to Virtue*, opens with a more remote scene, a pastoral altar. Of the remaining masques performed at Whitehall, *The Masque of Augurs* opens in "The Court Buttry-hatch" and *Time Vindicated* before "a prospective of Whitehall" (H & S, X, 649).

For the sake of completeness I should mention the two Jonsonian masques of this period not given at court, *Lovers Made Men*, which opened on a triumphal arch, and that greatest of successes, *The Gypsies Metamorphosed*, in which the scene throughout was whichever of the three halls in which it was performed. I do not take *Christmas his Masque* or *The Masque of Owls* to be proper masques.

It is essential to a discussion of the scenic portrayal of things as they are in these masques to make one broad distinction. Those masques which begin in the hall where the spectators are assembled rely partially or wholly on conventions of staging which preceded the innovations of Inigo Jones, conventions similar to those of the theatres. In the portrayal of the "*Alchymists workehouse*" or the "Street in perspective," however, the resources of the new staging are used to create a convincing illusion of the familiar locale. It is this sort of use of painted scenery which constitutes the presentational novelty in the Jonsonian masques of this period.

In the familiar setting of these opening scenes, however staged, were performed not only antimasques but what Herford and Simpson appropriately term "comic inductions" (II, 316), some of which, as is well known, correspond closely to scenes in the comedies. The most striking examples are the re-use in *The Staple of News* of the satire on newspapers in *News from the New World* and of the conceit of a cook who is a poet in *Neptune's Triumph*. What Orgel says of the antimasque applies, as I believe he intended, to the comic induction as well: "Structurally, the function of the Jonsonian antimasque was to set up a world of particularity, which was organically related, and at the same time in contrast, to the symbolic world of the masque. In other words, the antimasque set up a problem for which the masque was a solution."[14]

Two masques, *The Vision of Delight* of 1617 and *Time Vindicated* of 1623, provide unusually interesting examples of how Jonson and Jones set up and solved such problems. If *The Devil is an Ass* and *The Staple of News* may be seen as plays in which appeal was also made to a symbolic world to solve the problems that had been posed, it may be possible to compare the solutions in those plays with the ones found in these masques.

No design for "A Street in perspective of faire building," discovered at the opening of *The Vision of Delight*, has been identified, but one may imagine something of the order of the street through which one sees "London Afar Off" in *Britannia Triumphans*[15] – a somewhat idealized version of the sort of city street which any of the spectators might know. It was probably less grand than the massive "Great City" that Jones designed later for *Salmacida Spolia* (Strong, No. 102), or his Serlian "Tragic Scene" done for some unidentified play (No. 106). From afar off Delight "Is seene to come . . . accompanied with *Grace, Love, Harmonie, Revell, Sport, Laughter.* WONDER *following.*" Though she presents the first antimasque, Delight is not the sort of figure found in the comic inductions. Instead, she is the spirit of enjoyment, determined, like a very high-class cruise director, to make everyone have a good time, and specifically, since the masque is being given in January, to lead them to imagine that spring has arrived. In her first words about turning "every sort / O' the pleasures of the Spring, / to the graces of a Court" are anticipated the transformations that will be brought about by

---

[14]*The Jonsonian Masque* (Cambridge, Mass., 1965), p. 93.
[15]*Festival Designs by Inigo Jones: An Exhibition of Drawings . . .* , catalogue by Roy Strong (International Exhibitions Foundation, 1967–68), Nos. 76, 77.

altering the point of view. Delight speaks her encouraging words in the latest of musical fashions, the *"stylo recitativo"* of Italian opera, almost unknown in England at this time. At the end of her brief opening lines the first antimasque is danced by grotesque *commedia dell' arte* figures.

While it would be futile to search for any significance beyond entertainment in this little show, there is more to what follows, an appeal to Night "to help the vision of DELIGHT" (l. 31). A stage direction reads: *"Here the Night rises, and tooke her Chariot bespangled with starres."* As Delight continues her invocation, Night and Moon rise and hover above the street scene, symbolizing that combination of "adherence to the truth of nature" and the "modifying colors of imagination" which Coleridge was to see in the "sudden charm which accidents of light and shade, which moon-light or sun-set diffused over a known and familiar landscape."[16] Urged to delight the spectators with *"Phantomes,"* Night now sings a song (following Delight's recitative), in which she summons Phant'sie. Immediately a cloud begins to cover the "Street in perspective" – one of Inigo Jones's machines, from which Phant'sie emerges to give a doggerel description of various "Phantasmes" or dreams which might please the audience. Orgel shows in his notes how this "verbal antimasque," as he calls it, is made up of a tissue of references to gluttony, lechery, sloth, and a world turned upside down by perversions of nature (*Complete Masques,* pp. 486–88). In a second antimasque proper (if that is not a contradiction in terms) these imaginary creatures dance, but they are banished again by Phant'sie, who then presents Peace, the "gold-hair'd *Houre*," descending in another machine. Simultaneously the cloud-scene changes to the *"Bower of* Zephyrus," as Peace addresses Delight and her attendants, who have been onstage since the beginning. Following Delight and Phant'sie, Peace in her turn promises many pleasures, specifically those of the spring "to warme your blood" (l. 134). The choir of attendants answers:

> We see, we heare, we feele, we taste,
> we smell the change in every flowre,
> we onely wish that all could last,
> and be as new still as the houre. (ll. 136–39)

[16]*Biographia Literaria*, ed. J. Shawcross, 2 vols. (Oxford, 1907), II, 5.

Wonder expresses her particular admiration of the bower, which seems to be a miraculous cross between art and nature. Is this vision as illusory as the dance of the "Phantasmes"? It is a vision controlled by Peace but still presented by Phant'sie, who makes the definitive comment on Wonder's speech: "How better then they are, are all things made / by WONDER!" (ll. 167–68).

These words provide a key for the interpretation of the entire masque and of other Jonsonian works of this period. Things as they are can be made to seem worse or better by altering the way they are seen – altering the mirror in which they are reflected. No reflection is totally and absolutely truthful, and yet perception of the truth is aided by the distortions of Phant'sie. Only through wonder, or admiration, can the approximation of the ideal in the actual be seen.

Wonder continues to exclaim after the Bower opens *"to a loud musicke,"* revealing the masquers as the *"glories of the Spring"* (l. 171). The ultimate cause of this perfection of nature, as Phant'sie points out, is the king on his state, "Whose presence maketh this perpetuall *Spring"* (l. 202). The masque has reached the traditional moment of transformation, in which the ideal and actual blend.[17] Then, following the main masque and the revels, Aurora replaces Night and Moon, who descend, and the choir of Delight's attendants dance *"their going off."*

Unpretentious as this masque is, it is an unusually persuasive rendition of the ideal vision in the midst of things as they are. The transition from one world to another is made smooth by the continual presence of Delight as a presenter and by her relationship to the other presenters, Night, Phant'sie, Peace and Wonder, each of whom offers a slightly different way of looking at things. The scenic effects, at times symbolic, at times illusionistic, perfectly support the poetic contrivance.

In *Time Vindicated* the familiar scene is re-created verbally with more particularity than in *The Vision of Delight*. As in the earlier masque, a character who belongs to the main masque appears at the very beginning and aids in the presentation of the antimasque. Fame in *Time Vindicated*, however, is more sharply contrasted than is Delight with the characters in the first section

---

[17]Orgel writes: "for Jonson, one of the most compelling aspects of Jones's theater was the way it could make the stage's illusion merge with the court's reality . . ." (*Complete Masques*, p. 32).

of the masque, a conceited satirist and his ignorant admirers. Fame comes as an emissary from Time to announce a "great spectacle he meanes, to night, / To'exhibite" (ll. 39–40), but is immediately surrounded by three foolish people called "*the Curious, the* Ey'd, *the* Ear'd, *and the* Nos'd," who, like the customers at the staple of news, are eager for gossip and rumour, the dirtier and the more sensational the better. "I have it here," says Nose, "here, strong, the sweat of it, / And the confusion (which I love) I nose it, / It tickles mee" (ll. 57–59). Thoroughly immersed in the times (as opposed to absolute time), he and his friends are not only curious – "Wee only hunt for novelty, not truth" (l. 259) – but eager to do as they please, censure as they please, and revel in the anarchy of Saturnalian licence. Their hero, and the figure most exactly opposed to Fame is Chronomastix, the scourging satirist, who was immediately recognized as a cruel caricature of George Wither. The portrayal of things as they are is decidedly topical. The first antimasque is danced by the Curious and certain other supporters of Chronomastix, who "adore" him and bear him out in triumph – perhaps, since he is a satyr-satirist, in the manner of a "triumph of Silenus." When the Curious return to plague Fame again, she brings on an antimasque of tumblers and jugglers, led by the "*Cat and fiddle*," who finally drive the Curious away and thus bring the comic section of the masque to an end.

The exact scenic arrangements for *Time Vindicated* constitute somewhat of a puzzle, though we know from Sir John Astley's account in the Revels Office-book that the scene "was three tymes changed during the tyme of the masque: where in the first that was discovered was a prospective of Whitehall, with the Banqueting House; the second was the Masquers in a cloud; and the third a forrest" (H & S, X, 649). Jonson's references to the scenery in the published text are so slight that it is difficult to be sure how these scenic effects were coordinated with speeches and actions. It is surprising to find that the comic induction and the antimasques were performed in front of Jones's view of his new Banqueting House, in which the masque was being performed. In the dialogue it is clear that Time's spectacle is awaited in "This roome" (l. 62). Perhaps this discrepancy should not worry us, however. Wither and his Curious friends are, after all, outside the hall, and to an audience familiar with the stage conventions of the popular theatre it might not be troublesome to suppose that the location was both outside and inside. What is more important is the great accuracy of Jones's depiction of the Banqueting House, with its improvised exterior wooden staircase, in the drawing discovered only a few years ago. The sense of a particular place is very strong. As John Harris points out, the fictitious trees on either side suggest tree-wings, and the building may have been painted on shutters that could be drawn aside,[18] though we have no positive proof of the use of shutters in England until a few years later.

If a shutter-and-groove system was used, the Banqueting House must have been relatively close to the front of the stage in order to provide for the subsequent discovery. Astley tells us it was a cloud with the masquers. The stage direction is "Loud Musique. *To which the whole Scene opens, where* Saturne *sitting with* Venus *is discover'd above, and certain* Votaries *comming forth below, which are the* Chorus" (ll. 271–274). The set is divided vertically, then, and the cloud containing the masquers is visible, though not as yet the masquers. Fame, who is on the lower level with the Votaries, says that Venus has found "certaine glories of the *Time*" detained by Hecate "Within yond' dark-nesse" (ll. 279–81) – that is, behind some dark cloud-pieces, which will presently be pulled aside. Since the masquers are later given time to "descend," it seems likely that the machine in which they are seated is poised at the upper level with Saturn and Venus when the first discovery is made.

The vertical division of the stage, though in no way novel, is especially appropriate at this point in *Time Vindicated*, for the contrast between the gods and the characters of the comic in-duction differs from the contrast between these same characters and Fame. It is as if the earlier hostility had been elevated to the level of essential oppositions. Saturn, as Chronos, is a more absolute opposite to the time-scourger, Chronomastix, than is Fame, while Venus, as Love, is more absolutely opposed than Fame to the ill nature of Chronomastix and the Curious. The stage provides an iconic equivalent of the translation of the argument to this level.

[18]"A Prospect of Whitehall by Inigo Jones," *The Burlington Magazine*, 109 (1967), 89–90; reproduction, p. 54.

The basic pattern of contrasts is strikingly similar to that of *The Masque of Queens*, but one cannot observe the similarity without becoming aware of how differently the contrasts are handled. Instead of witches dancing in an "ugly hell," a foolish satirist and his stupid friends disport themselves near Whitehall. They are routed, not magically by the sound of loud music, but ignominiously by tumblers and jugglers. If the enemies of fame are more ordinary, the representatives of true worth are even more exalted than Heroic Virtue, Fama Bona, and the great queens who triumph over the witches. Yet their connection with the world of Whitehall is in a way more real. In *The Masque of Queens* King James is, of course, apostrophized as the patron of true fame, just as in *Time Vindicated* he is said to be responsible for the return of the Saturnian Age of Gold,[19] but in the fable of the earlier masque the chief link to the court is in the identity of the principal masquer, Belanna, or Queen Anne, whereas in *Time Vindicated* not only is Prince Charles a masquer, but Venus and Saturn have brought him and his companions, the "glories of the Time," to display their virtues in the service of the court.

After some brief speeches by Venus, Saturn and their Votaries, the dark cloud parts, and the masquers are discovered. As they descend to the stage the Votaries say *"These, these must sure some wonders bee!"* (1. 311), and Venus and Saturn "passe away" from their lofty posts. Following the first dance they reappear, presumably on the main stage, where, in response to their Votaries' request, they summon Cupid and Sport. After the main dance of the masquers these two step forward to address the masquers, the king, the lords and the ladies in a rather familiar, jesting style, *"To breed delight,"* as the Votaries say, *"and a desire / Of being delighted, in the nobler sort"* (ll. 347–48). In plainer terms, they are encouraging the masquers to dance with the ladies and thus begin the revels. This is the first task of these "glories of the *Time.*"

When the revels are finished, however, further tasks are enumerated in the sort of final scene which is found in several late masques. The cloudscape, which has presumably remained during

---

[19]See the good discussion of this theme in *Time Vindicated* by W. Todd Furniss in "Ben Jonson's Masques," *Three Studies in the Renaissance: Sidney, Jonson, Milton* (New Haven, 1958), pp. 109–19.

the main masque, now gives way to a wood, out of which Hippolitus comes as Diana "descends" to him, probably in a machine. She defends herself to her devotee against the accusation made by Venus that she had selfishly kept the "glories of the *Time*" out of circulation, so to speak, for her own pleasure. To Saturn, Venus and their Votaries, who have all appeared once more, she explains that in her grove she merely trained them in riding and hunting (dearly loved by King James) "*To make them fitter so to serve the* Time" (l. 495). Now they will hunt, not men, but vices, thus making practical use of the virtues which she has taught them in retirement from the world. Things will be made better than they are by these "wonders."

In the contrivance of this masque there is a neat circularity: we move from Whitehall, beset by ignorance and malice, to the clouds, where Love and Time are watching over it, back to the court itself, and to the wood where, like Achilles, the heroes who will defend the court against ignorance and malice have been trained. *Time Vindicated* is, if anything, an even more satisfying artistic whole than *The Vision of Delight*.

Neither of these masques is so ambitious an undertaking as *The Devil is an Ass* or *The Staple of News*, although, to a surprising extent, they share with the plays the preoccupation with ways of introducing the world of absolutes into the familiar world. The conventions of the new court entertainment opened some ways which were not available to the writer of comedy for the theatres, and in his plays Jonson seemed to suffer from this handicap. Only in the form against which he was soon to expostulate so bitterly did he achieve a seemingly effortless blend. If the masques are, finally, no more than elegant *jeux d'esprit*, one must admit that the game here is exceedingly well played.

The Revenge on Charis

S. P. ZITNER

In a recent brief but comprehensive survey of Jonson's works, the plays are discussed in over one hundred pages, the non-dramatic verse in a mere eighteen. If lyric is the wine of language, we might well alter Prince Hal's astonishment at Falstaff's tavern bill: "O monstrous! but one halfpenny-worth of sack to this intolerable deal of bread." In scholarship and criticism, the concern with Jonson's non-dramatic poetry suggests an intimate boutique operating in one corner of a vast department store. Explanations for this circumstance of want in plenty are not hard to find. After all, the non-dramatic verse occupies only one volume of the Herford-Simpson edition; the plays and masques five.[1] The inevitable contrast with the plays of Shakespeare churns up a considerable Jonsonian by-product of that industry, while the lyrics – for all the talk of the Tribe of Ben – remain, as Bamborough suggests, "largely independent of fashions and schools"[2] to which they might be interestingly attached to point morals or adorn tales. Further, it is far easier to discuss dramatic than lyric writing, especially lyric that aims at "pure and neate language . . . plaine and customary,"[3] rather than at providing the clenches, strong lines, opulence and paradoxy that obscure Donne in explication. Finally, these qualities in Jonsonian lyric, its precision, its lucidity, its economy – in a word its transparency – have repelled critics for whom poetry is in the first place language that, as Coleridge put it, "calls atten-

[1]The Herford-Simpson *Ben Jonson* (1925–1953), 11 vols., is employed throughout and cited in parentheses. The text of the Charis poems appears in VIII, 131–42, the commentary on them in XI, 49 ff.
[2]J. B. Bamborough, *Ben Jonson* (London, 1970), p. 151.
[3]*Discoveries, 1870* (VIII, 620); Jonson here paraphrases Quintillian.

tion to itself." For Eliot, Jonson's poetry is often superficial, lacking "a network of tentacular roots reaching down to the deepest terrors and desires."[4] It is no wonder that the classic study of Jonson's language is a study of his prose.[5] The dramatic critic flushes sources, humours, ethical problems, topical allusions, and triumphs of staging and construction from a thicket. The critic of Jonson's non-dramatic verse eyes a plain, well-tended lawn where only a few modest flowers of rhetoric blow, and stands wondering what to say.

But both the dramatic and the non-dramatic writing are products of one sensibility. Though we have yet to elaborate the sorts of connections critics find, say, between "The Rape of Lucrece" and Shakespearian tragedy, Jonsonian lyric insinuates itself into Jonsonian drama, and the satiric bent or the conservatism of the plays into the poems. Jonson would hardly have accepted Webbe's dichotomy between the dramatist who seeks to "stirre both the eyes and eares of [his] beholders" and the poet who seeks to "satisfy the exact judgements of learned men in their studies."[6] Indeed, Jonson conspicuously fails Webbe's test for distinguishing between the two, since what he desired "to be liked of on stages" he also wanted to "bee regestered in libraries" as works, much to the amusement of some of his contemporaries.

My purpose here is to contribute to the resolution of what sometimes seems a false double image of Jonson, by showing how he re-worked along analogous lines the same materials in both a dramatic and a lyric context. But primarily I am concerned with the meaning of a particular stretch of material in its lyric context, because it is wrought into high art. Moreover, I am concerned with this material in its lyric context, because the poem I want to treat has recently come under attack – mistakenly I think – as exemplary of Jonson's supposed defects as a lyric poet.

Readers of Jonson's sequence, "A Celebration of Charis," will recall the revenge promised by the rejected, aging lover in the last lines of its third poem. What follows will consider how the argument of the fourth poem, "Her Triumph," makes that

---

[4]T. S. Eliot, *Essays on Elizabethan Drama* (New York, 1956), p. 76.
[5]Jonas Barish, *Ben Jonson and the Language of Prose Comedy* (Cambridge, Mass., 1960).
[6]Quoted in Bamborough, *Ben Jonson*, p. 9.

promise good. With single exceptions in each case, critics have not taken seriously either the threat of the third lyric or the argument of the fourth.

"Her Triumph" is generally recognized as one of the great successes of the seventeenth-century lyric, often anthologized, often praised: the best illustration of "the complex delicacy of Jonson's metrical technique,"[7] a sympathetic embodiment of "the finest traditions of the mode" of Elizabethan love poetry,[8] a union of classical, neoplatonic, and native elements, and even, according to Quiller-Couch,[9] an anticipation of "the best manner of Robert Browning."

His near-contemporaries (and Jonson himself) would have joined at least in the praise. Suckling parodied the last stanza in a lute-song for the fourth act of *The Sad One* (1659); Carew rang changes on it, and Jonson himself employed the second and third stanzas in *The Devil is an Ass* (II, 6).[10]

To understand its significance in the Charis sequence, it is useful to examine the dramatic context Jonson gave the poem in *The Devil is an Ass.* The Herford-Simpson commentary tells us that the Charis poems "have the romantic note which characterized Wittipol's wooing in that scene of the play" (XI, 49). Yet this seems to me inaccurate. Before the song, Wittipol and Mistress Fitz-Dotterel are (so Wittipol believes) alone and unobserved in Manly's chambers (VI, 201 ff). Wittipol makes his suit, celebrating "these sister-swelling breasts," "this brave promontory," "this valley," "these crispèd groves," and other landmarks of the female topography mapped in Donne's "Elegie XIX" and Carew's "A Rapture." But the "romantic" effect of the song is undone in three ways. First, the language (as so often in Jonson), conveys both a mode of apprehension and a conviction of the inadequacy of that mode. Toward the end of the erotic sequence, Jonson betrays Wittipol into professing a desire to play with Mistress Fitz-Dotterel's "smooth, round,/And well-torn'd [in this context, machine-made] chin, as with the *Billyard* ball." Jonson picks up this ludicrous analogy once again, in the

[7]J. W. Trimpi, *Ben Jonson's Poems* (Stanford, 1962), p. 233.
[8]P. M. Cubeta, " 'A Celebration of Charis': An Evaluation of Jonsonian Poetic Strategy," *ELH*, 25 (1958), 169.
[9]Quoted in Herford-Simpson, XI, 49.
[10]These imitations are reprinted in Herford-Simpson, XI, 50.

ninth lyric of "A Celebration of Charis." It is employed there as
a simile for the cheek of the ideal man, "wanton wise," described
by Charis in "Her owne Dictamen." Second, the warmth of
Wittipol's erotic fancy is undone by its removal from the comfortable realm of metaphor. The stage directions read: "He
growes more familiar in his Courtship, playes with her paps,
kisseth her hands, &c." The mode – and mood – of the Donne and
Carew poems depends on their operation in the picturesque
distance of language only. This "unmetaphoring" of the genre, to
use Rosalie Colie's word, must have been riotous rather than
romantic onstage. Finally, there is the plot context itself. All the
time the seduction has been going on, Wittipol, who has slipped
into speaking of himself as "Love [who] hath the honour to
approach/ These sister-swelling brests," has been under observation by none other than Fitz-Dotterel himself, who appears at
his wife's back as the song ends. Threats follow, and in a rage
Fitz-Dotterel strikes his wife. Such is the comic context into
which Jonson inserted the ardent sweetness of "Have you seene
but a bright Lillie grow." For Jonson, this is a familiar game;
one recalls that "Come, my Celia" is sung my Volpone.

The importance of Jonson's use of the two stanzas from "Her
Triumph" in *The Devil is an Ass* lies in what it tells us of his
sense of contexts and their role in colouring language, sometimes
through irony, sometimes through a less easily defined shifting to
and fro of alternative moods and meanings.

It would seem proper, then, to begin a consideration of "Her
Triumph" with a close look at the poem which precedes it, and
with the idea that it may, as does the part of it sung by Wittipol,
convey something more and other than what appears dominant
in the poem viewed in isolation.

The third lyric in "A Celebration of Charis" is entitled "What
hee suffered." It treats the "scornes" and "hurt" of the rejected
aging lover, the degrading terms on which Charis allows reconciliation, and the lover's further wounding both by Cupid and
by Charis' repentance. But, the poem concludes,

> the Pittie comes too late.
> Looser-like, now, all my wreake
> Is, that I have leave to speake,
> And in either Prose, or Song,
> To revenge me with my Tongue,

> Which how Dexterously I doe,
> Heare and make Example too.

I am unaware that anyone has taken these lines seriously in print except for Cubeta, who "cannot help querying whether his [Jonson's] real scheme of revenge is not to seduce her love through the medium of poetry," in this case the famous lyric which follows. Yet this is not revenge, but salary and hire. And Cubeta himself senses the logical problem in a threat of revenge followed by this "most idealized, rapturous portrait."[11]

One of the characteristics of Jonson's lyric verse is that while it has a Senecan conversational parsimony, it has, unlike much of his dramatic writing, little of the jolt and intellectual discontinuity of actual conversation. Jonson's objection to rhyme is specifically that it "expresseth but by fits / True conceipt / Spoyling Senses of their Treasure, / Cosening Judgement. . . ." Jonson as poet has a continual care for the syntax of discourse, a respect for the *series iuncturaque* (the "order and connection" of Horace's *Ars Poetica*), which prevent obscurity. He wrote his first drafts in prose and willingly consigned "strong lines" to the fire. This should warrant our looking for a closer connection between "What hee suffered" and "Her Triumph," and make us pause over the loose connection between the second and last stanzas of the latter poem.

The second stanza of "Her Triumph" ends with an evocation of Charis' face, in which "alone there triumphs to the life / All the Gaine, all the Good, of the Elements strife." Then follows the remarkable third stanza beginning: "Have you seen but a bright Lillie grow." The ardent specificity of this last stanza answers so well to the triumph the poem's title proposes, that it is easy to neglect looseness in argument. In most anthologies, as in the Herford-Simpson commentary, the last line of the second stanza goes unglossed. The only sustained attempt to deal with it, so far as I have been able to discover, is Trimpi's. He finds in the poem a primary indebtedness to "Neoplatonic commentary [rather] than to classical models."[12] Trimpi claims that the light from Charis' eyes is "easily associated with the divine light emanating from God, which is responsible for the harmonious

---

[11]Cubeta, " 'A Celebration of Charis.' "
[12]Trimpi, *Ben Jonson's Poems*, 210 ff.

proportion of parts that is called beautiful." This proportion in turn, Trimpi continues, depends on the balance of the four elements which, according to Ficino, results in a body resembling the heavens in its harmony. Such a view of the lines connects with Trimpi's main argument that Jonson seriously employed neoplatonic ideas throughout the Charis sequence.

An alternative view would, I think, base itself less on a complex neoplatonic interpretation of the strife of the elements and the light from Charis' eyes, than on a recurring, emphatic strain in the language of the third stanza, and on the need to connect these stanzas more closely by some syntax of argument, and then to connect the whole of the "Triumph" with the promise of revenge. The strife of the elements, in short, may refer to earthly mutability and variety rather than to celestial harmony; the light of Charis' eyes may be a commonplace of the Renaissance theory of vision; and the language of the poem may slyly convey the promised revenge as well as the promised triumph.

That the elements were in continual contest was a commonplace as early as Hesiod. The struggle was localized outside historical time, as in Ovid (*Metamorphoses* I) or Plato (*Timaeus* 32), where it was mitigated by the intervention of celestial love. In the obligatory English version, the twelfth stanza of Spenser's *Hymne in Honour of Love*, whose language Jonson seems to have had in mind, Love first "severs" primal Chaos into its elements, then reconciles their "contrary forces" with "loved meanes" and "Adamantine chaines." The result is that

> in every living wight
> They mix themselves, and shew their kindly light,

"kindly" here of course meaning "natural." Inside historical time, the elements also contended, as they do in Shakespeare's sonnet LXIV, with the result that the elements both alter form and interchange. Again, the *locus classicus* of Renaissance citation of these alterations is Ovid, specifically in Pythagoras's speech in *Metamorphoses* XV. If this strife of the elements beyond and within historic time received a neoplatonic interpretation, it was also interpreted in other ways. Nor, given the confusions in terminology and the syncretism of Renaissance thought, were the

132

alternatives always clearly distinguished or consistently held. Spenser in the *Mutabilitie Cantos* and Shakespeare in the sonnets were not the only poets to rail at mutability and yet delight in the bitter-sweetness of earthly variety.

It is hardly likely that Jonson would have joined Marlowe's Tamburlaine in discovering either gain or good in that "warring of the elements within our breasts for regiment" that prompted men to have "aspiring minds." Yet a completely acceptable meaning for the gain and good of the elemental strife in Charis is the obvious and homely one: transience, with its momentary beauties.

Whether this is the meaning that ought to be seen in the line depends in part on how well it accords with the rest of the poem. For all the apostrophe of the opening stanza, and the swan and dove that are Venus's traditional iconographic trappings, for all Cupid's belief in a later poem that Charis is his mother, and even Charis' name (in the *Iliad* Charis is the wife of Hephaestus), Jonson's heroine is at least as much an earthly as a celestial Venus. As "Her Triumph" progresses, off-notes sound in the Ovidian material concentrated in the first stanza. There is a playful and possibly trivializing literalness in the first lines of stanza two:

> Doe but looke on her eyes, they doe light
> All that Loves world compriseth.

Given Renaissance theories of vision, one may suspect mere conventionality or even self-centredness here, as well as a complimentary platonic attribution of illumination. But when one comes to

> Doe but marke, her forehead's smoother
> Then words that sooth her,

the negative possibilities begin to peep out more definitely. Smooth words and soothing ones hardly win Jonson's approbation. There is a creaturely limitation in a forehead which takes on the form of what flatters it.

Let us be quite literal. Jonson's ideas about smoothness in diction can be traced in two related passages, one in the *Discoveries*, the other in the *News from the New World Discovered in the Moon.* In the fifth note under the rubric *Ingeniorum discrimina,* Jonson remarks:

> Others there are, that have no composition at all; but a kind of tuneing, and riming fall, in what they write. It runs and slides, and onely makes a sound. Womens-Poets they are call'd, as you have womens-Taylors.
>
> They write a verse, as smooth, as soft, as creame,
> In which there is no torrent, nor scarce streame.
>
> You may sound these wits, and find the depth of them with your middle finger. They are *Creame-bowle,* or but puddle deepe.
>
> (VIII, 585)

News from the New World (1621) amplifies this notebook material, as the Herford-Simpson Commentary (XI, 235) points out. There the difference between a "Man's Poet" and a "Woman's Poet" is again at issue, the same (unidentified) couplet is quoted, and the same invidious comparisons made. "Your Womans Poet must flow, and stroak the eare" (VII, 518). Jonson is probably thinking of Daniel and Campion, whose creamy word-palette he evidently disliked. Part of the revenge strategy in "Her Triumph" was second nature to the literary moralist; Jonson often exploited the verbal trappings of attitudes he objected to in order to demonstrate that they grew out of false estimates of experience.

But there is another sort of revenge. Behind what has been called the "romantic" flush of the third stanza, for all its celebrated concreteness, there is an insistence on the transitoriness of the beautiful. We are asked to attend not so much to the lily as to the lily growing, and "before rude hands have touch'd it." We are asked to observe not the snow, but its fall, and *that* before it has been discoloured in the partial melting that makes for its softness. The parallel construction of the first four lines insists on these points. Elsewhere the insistence on catching the excellence of the sensuous in flight is less obvious but present nevertheless. The perfume is that of the briar, but in the bud only, and of spikenard even as it is being consumed by flame. The transitory quality of the other materials is perhaps less simply presented. But to feel the wool of the beaver or the down of the swan is to experience these things already altered from their living states. Beavers – if I may introduce what is now called "Canadian content" into this discussion – are notoriously elusive and naturally unwilling to give up their wool, and live swans often ferocious. Both the wool and the down are so placed that one must well nigh kill the beasts to get at them.

The subtlety of Jonson's revenge – his insistence that Charis is as vulnerable to time as the old lover she rejects, that indeed her freshness and his wrinkles are equally accidents of temporality and change – is Jonson's own. But the general form of the revenge is traditional. Hugh Richmond, in *The School of Love*, shows how the Stuart lyric poets transmuted classical themes and attitudes, among them the theme of the rejected lover's revenge by way of allusion to the effects of time on the proud beloved. Yet in his own discussion of the concluding stanza of "Her Triumph," Richmond sees only "the parallelism and cumulative sequence of Martial," an effort that "reads, without pedantry, like an attempt at formal definition." For Richmond, in short, the stanza is illustrative only of the superiority of control in Jonsonian syntactical and rhetorical patterns over those of Martial. "What is new in Stuart verse," he concludes some pages later, "is not the so-called metaphysical imagery, which pervades nearly all Renaissance lyricism, but the power to discipline any image to a logically or rhythmically significant end."[13] Indeed he treats the last stanza of "Her Triumph" almost as an Arnoldian touchstone of this power. But the logically significant end of the lyric is precisely what one has to recover by examining the content of its cumulative parallels.

Behind the concreteness of the third stanza there is a persistent concern with the momentary, the eclipsing. This prepares for the final line of the poem, "O so white! O so soft! O so sweet is she!" The summary description of Charis refers us again to the transience of lovely things in nature.

This view of the language of the last stanza can answer the questions raised earlier about its construction as argument and about its relation to the revenge promised in the poem immediately before "Her Triumph." A strict punctuator might, if this reading of Jonson's language is correct, place a colon after

[13]Hugh Richmond, *The School of Love* (Princeton, 1964), pp. 131, 134–35.

"strife" in the second stanza. All the gain and good of the strife of the elements, a transitory Nature with the lovely fragility the idea implies, is embodied in what follows. Thus the third stanza becomes a set of instances which illustrate, clarify, and affirm what we are to see triumphing "to the life" in the face of Charis: namely, the accidents of Time. Further, in the implications of the poet's treatment of his materials, one can see the most delicate and dexterous of promised revenges, a revenge especially appropriate to one who "now write[s] fiftie years" and accordingly has been rejected. The revenge is a reminder of the transience that makes physical beauty a triumph; and it is dexterous because Jonson does not merely rattle the skull of *memento mori* or insist on the sourness of new grapes.

At least two sorts of objections might be raised here, one to this interpretation of Jonson's rhetoric, the other to the interpretation of his ideas. These objections are related. Is not the last stanza of "Her Triumph," one might ask, rather like the last of Lovel's song from Act IV of *The Newe Inne*?

> It was a beauty that I saw
> So pure, so perfect, as the frame
> Of all the universe was lame,
> To that one figure, could I draw,
> Or give least line of it a law!
>
> A skeine of silke, without a knot!
> A faire march made without a halt!
> A curious forme without a fault!
> A printed booke without a blot!
> All beauty, and without a spot! (VI, 468–69)

One might argue that the rhetoric of the last stanza of "Her Triumph" is, like this, simply an attempt to define an excellence by comparison and contrast. Yet there are several differences. Lovel is "the compleat gentleman," or at least on his way to becoming one. Not so the imagined speaker of the Charis poems, who has promised us a dexterous revenge. But there is a less arguable difference between the materials of Lovel's song and those of "Her Triumph." Lovel's song is almost all abstraction, and where not, it certainly lacks the sensuous immediacy of Jonson's lily, snow and briar-bud. We may perhaps congratulate ourselves on the ameliorations that have made silk less subject to ravelling, infantry less dependent on long rest periods, and books somewhat freer of errors in printing. Yet the difference of immediacy between the stanzas comes less from improved technology than from the objects evoked for comparison, especially "march," "form" and "book" (is "blot" an ink smudge or a metaphor for error?) These are in a realm of discourse far more removed than lilies, fur and honey from the physical lady. And this is proper to beauty conceived so abstractly. Yet the crucial difference between Lovel's song and "Her Triumph" lies in the logical strategy behind their comparisons. In Lovel's song, beauty is depicted through qualities impossible or extremely unlikely of actualization. But Charis' beauty is compared with qualities in everyday experience, something which the language insists on in the almost gross "smutch'd" and "bag." This difference between the not-ever-to-be-realized and the soon-realized-soon-lost defines the rhetoric and the thought of the two poems. In the third stanza of "Her Triumph," the sensuous immediacy is present so we can feel its transitoriness. In Lovel's song, the impossibility or near-impossibility of perfection in temporal things is the platonic proof of the speaker's inability to give the least line of supernal beauty a law. The law which governs Charis' beauty is implicit in the overthrow of the objects which resemble it.

This leads again to the question of Jonson's neoplatonic ideas, and to the possible objection that the last line of stanza two of "Her Triumph" ought to be connected with other passages in Jonson's work which treat the myth of the emergence of Love from Chaos in neoplatonic terms. In an essay on "Ben Jonson's Lyric Poetry," R. S. Walker invited comparison of the "warm lush meadow of actual experience" in Keats with the "cool, paved terrace" of the mind erected in such lines as Jonson's

> So love emergent, out of Chaos brought
> The world to light,
> And gently moving on the waters wrought
> All formes to sight.

"Instead of springing from the contemplation of variety and diversity in man and nature," Walker concludes, Jonson's "beauty belongs to the apprehension of their underlying symmetry. It is the harmony and finish of the scheme of things which is beautiful to Ben Jonson, and not any incidental development in nature. . . ."[14]

Jonson was of course familiar with the neoplatonic armament of ideas and epithets. To describe excellences, he employs allusions to law and harmony, and metaphors of arrest and closure, especially the circle, that "perfect'st figure." This image of the perfect he employs with almost compulsive frequency in everything from the "summ'd circle" of the grotesque infant of Saguntum to the "ring of Vertues" about that touching figure, Lady Jane Pawlet.

More than once, as Walker argues, Jonson takes up the creation myth and elemental strife. In *Hymenaei*, a fruitful marriage of King and Queen is evidence of the power of union:

> . . . how well it binds
> The fighting *seedes of things*,
> Winnes *natures, sexes, minds*,
> And ev'rie discord in true musique brings. (VII, 212)

Thus not only are the Four Elements, but also the Four Humours and the Four Affections controlled by Reason. Again, in *The Masque of Beauty*, the idea of Love emerging from Chaos is taken up in song:

> So beautie on the waters stood,
> When *Love* had sever'd earth, from flood!
> So when he parted ayre, from fire,
> He did with concord all inspire! (VII, 191)

The masque concludes with Januarius's declaration that beauty is "Now made peculiar, to this place, alone" and the Chorus echoes that "Th' *Elysian* fields are here" in England. The whole is designed as elaborate court compliment, and it hardly demands that we accept as Jonson's settled belief that "Beautie, at large, brake forth, and conquer'd men," especially Englishmen.

This sort of platonizing that one finds in the masques is wholly appropriate to the high degree of abstraction and idealization in

---

[14]R. S. Walker, "Ben Jonson's Lyric Poetry," *Criterion* 13 (1933–34), 436–37.

the genre. But one cannot transport it without qualification to the mixed mode of realism, satire and lyricized idealism that makes the Charis sequence so interesting, even in some ways so uncharacteristic, of Jonson. One must be reluctant to deny the author of *The Newe Inne* (which has some shrewd hits at platonism misused), the perceptiveness and intellectual flexibility of a rival poet who could write both "The Ecstasy" and "Love's Alchemy." Whoever finds underlying order must also find overlying confusion. In the masque *Pleasure Reconciled to Virtue*, Daedalus puts in its most charitable form one of the main motifs of Jonsonian comedy and satire: that

> . . . all actions of mankind
> Are but a Laborinth, or maze. (VII, 488)

Yet the surface of life can include for Jonson not only the barbarities, but the "sweet neglect" that strikes the heart, and the physical delights ordered but not made abstract by the "proportion" of Penshurst and its mode of life. In the ode "To the Immortall Memorie, and Friendship of that Noble Paire, Sir Lucius Cary, and Sir H. Morison," Jonson writes that

> A Lillie of a Day,
> Is fairer farre, in May,
> Although it fall, and die that night;
> It was the Plant, and flowre of light.
> In small proportions, we just beauties see:
> And in short measures, life may perfect bee. (VIII, 245)

The lines are redolent of the transience of human perfections and suggest how easily, as in Wordsworth, a sense of supernal "platonic" patterns can tip in the direction of a recognition that attainable human excellences are, as Elegie XL of *Under-wood* puts it, "a bitter-sweet." All this is by way of suggesting perhaps the obvious; that a platonizing esthetic will not preclude a rather simpler and more accessible awareness and a homage to the passing manyness. But in any case, one has to weigh the "realistic" element in the Charis sequence, the promise of revenge, and the precise effect of the rhetoric of the third stanza.

Yet platonizing elements do play a role in the poem which, as Frost said of all poems, is entitled to everything in it. Both the

platonizing idealism of Lovel and the realistic sensualism of
Beaufort in *The Newe Inne* were attitudes available to Jonson,
as were their doctrinal antecedents in Castiglione, who thought
both Bembo and his opponent worthy of a voice in the great
conversations. The platonic motifs of the opening stanza, and the
echoes of *Phaedrus* 250 in the lines

> such a grace
> Sheds it selfe through the face,

are undeniable, as are other platonizing motifs elsewhere in the
Charis sequence. But the particular poignance of "Her Triumph"
lies in the manner in which these ideas are linked with their
reductive and realistic opposites. Jonson could see the physical
world as hieroglyphic. Yet in "Her Triumph" he can suggest the
supernal meanings and tell us also that the meanings are not the
emblems themselves which, having a life of their own, must also
have a death.

The puzzle of the date of composition of the lyrics that make
up "A Celebration of Charis" is probably insoluble. The Herford-
Simpson notes (XI, 49) argue that the first poem in the sequence,
which mentions the poet's age at "fiftie yeares," is suspiciously
general and, in any case, may be an Horatian echo. *Under-wood*,
in which the Charis poems appear, was not printed until three
years after Jonson's death, and there are not many clues to their
order of composition. *The Devil is an Ass* dates from 1616. It is
perhaps best to argue, then, that until he assembled the Charis
poems in their final order, Jonson was experimenting with various
contexts which would enrich the significance of several lyric
fragments or whole poems. If this is allowed, then the use of two
stanzas of "Her Triumph" in *The Devil is an Ass* would become
part of a movement in the direction of the meaning we have
argued for, rather than a lucky appropriation of part of an
already finished poem. In short, the first stanza of "Her Triumph"
might well have been written after the second and third, inte-
grating them into the Charis sequence and further exploiting the
irony that underlies their use in the situation of Wittipol and
Mistress Fitz-Dotterel. In *The Devil is an Ass*, a wildly comic
meaning is thrust on the sensuality of the stanzas. In "Her
Triumph," Jonson's ironic moral sense is still in control, but its

insights are more subtle, more deeply and ruefully present, even as the stanzas are allowed a less encumbered exhibition of their excellence in the erotic mode. The nature of the triumph, rather than the contrivance of theatrical circumstance, leads to a defeat.

Finally there is something to be said about the implications of this view of "Her Triumph" for our understanding of Jonson's entire lyric achievement. In his discussion of Jonson as lyric poet, Principal Bamborough argues that "One significant characteristic of Jonson's verse is that it often draws its strength from objects rather than giving strength to them." He goes on to quote the stanza we have been discussing and concludes: "There is no question of the effectiveness of this, but it depends on reminding us of the actual physical qualities of the objects mentioned, and then transferring the sense-traces thus evoked to the idea of the mistress; Jonson does not, through his language, *convey* the sensual impressions to us, or modify them in any way."[15] One can accept almost all of this save the very end. To miss the irony of the stanza is to miss Jonson's art; it is not – in the language of Jonson's own caution to his readers – to use him well, "that is, to understand."

Jonson is notoriously, in Eliot's phrase, "a poet of the surface" of life, in his plays a collector of the chicaneries and the jargon that express "the fury of men's gullets and their groins." Against these the disciplined clarity and concreteness of his lyric diction are both antidote and defence. Yet not all surfaces are alike. The specificity of descriptive detail in a relatively early poem like "To Penshurst" is different in kind from the specificity of the later "Her Triumph." There is, of course, a difference of genre, a difference of theme, a difference of context. Yet in "Penshurst" there is a significant recurrence of the unadornedly enumerative as in

> Thy sheepe, thy bullocks, kine, and calves
> doe feed. (VIII, 94)

And the epithets employed there can be formalized and remote in a way that hovers too near the mishaps of the eighteenth century, as in "the purpled pheasant," "the painted partrich,"

---

[15]Bamborough, *Ben Jonson*, p. 163.

141

"The blushing apricot, and woolly peach." In the final stanza of "Her Triumph" the restraint proceeding from a central moral vision is also present, but the language relents enough to allow pathos to the sensual surface of things. And this occurs without a weakening, even with a clarification, of the moral strength, because now both reader and writer have a greater awareness of its cost. I suppose that one of the things I have been trying to say is that we will do the non-dramatic Jonson and our understanding of him less good by trying to supply him with elaborate, hidden sub-texts, neoplatonic or otherwise, or lamenting his lack of them, than by looking for what is perhaps more difficult to see – the artifice of the apparent.

Jonson's Large and Unique
View of Life

E. B. PARTRIDGE

"Dryden lacked what his master Jonson possessed, a large and
unique view of life; he lacked insight; he lacked profundity."[1]
So wrote T. S. Eliot fifty years ago in that magisterial way of his.
We don't talk much any more, thank heaven, about what Dryden
lacked, not after all we have discovered about how much he has
to say and how consummately he says it. But we can still talk
confidently, I trust, about what Jonson possessed, though I had
better begin by making two admissions about his reputation, past
and present. One is that not everyone would agree with Eliot
even today. Alfred Harbage, for instance, thinking that satire
offers only a minority report on human nature and that Jonson
wrote satire only for a coterie, would apparently deny his view
of life largeness, though he might grant it uniqueness – of a
repellent kind.[2] Even J. B. Bamborough, who has done much for
Jonsonian studies, wondered in 1959 whether Jonson was a minor
genius or only a man of great talent, and still felt in 1970 that he
lacked the uniqueness of vision Shakespeare had.[3] The other
admission is that for part of the eighteenth and most of the nineteenth centuries many readers and critics considered Jonson's
view narrow or obscure or laboured or coarse – to choose some
of the quieter terms of dismissal. As late as the 1890s Bernard
Shaw thought him a "brutish pedant."[4] Only a little before Shaw,

[1]*Selected Essays, 1917–1932* (New York, 1934), p. 274.
[2]*Shakespeare and the Rival Traditions* (New York, 1952).
[3]*Ben Jonson* (London, 1959); *Ben Jonson* (London, 1970).
[4]*Our Theatre in the Nineties* (London, 1932), II, 183.

Tennyson said, "I can't read Ben Jonson, especially his comedies. To me he appears to move in a wide sea of glue" – a superb image, which suggests that not all great poets are shocked into recognition of each other's worth.[5] A few years after Shaw's remark, Maurice Castelain concluded, after nine hundred pages of commentary on all of Jonson's work, that he was a mediocre poet except in his satire.[6]

While I am admitting things, I'd better make a confession too. I must confess that I use this loose term, "view of life," as though I knew what Eliot meant by it. I don't. But nothing so vulgar as ignorance is going to keep me from using it as though I knew. For my purposes here I take a man's "view of life" to mean his particular way of considering human existence on this earth: something more carefully thought out than casual opinions; something less systematic than a coherently worked out philosophy. Henry James may be referring to this loose sense of the term when he writes that, "The great question as to a poet or a novelist is, How does he feel about life? What, in the last analysis, is his philosophy? When vigorous writers have reached maturity, we are at liberty to look in their works for some expression of a total view of the world they have been so actively observing. This is the most interesting thing their works offer us. Details are interesting in proportion as they contribute to make it clear."[7] "In their works," James says. An artist's view of life is expressed quintessentially, though not exclusively, of course, in his deliberate acts of creation and judgment. As you will see, I shall deal with, but not confine myself to, what Jonson wrote. I shall also be concerned with what he made of himself and with all that he did as a man of letters.

Could I quickly remind you how great Jonson was once thought to be, by referring to John Oldham's ode, "Upon the works of Ben Johnson Written in 1678"? In this poem Oldham, the young friend of Dryden, echoes what other poets and critics had been saying about Jonson for over seventy years. To Oldham, Jonson was "the mighty Founder of our stage," the lawgiver and god-like creator, the wise, judicious, and all-seeing artist who brought order and harmony to the "Anarchy of Wit."

[5]*Alfred Lord Tennyson: A Memoir by his Son* (New York, 1899), II, 73.
[6]*Ben Jonson, L'Homme et L'Œuvre* (Paris, 1907).
[7]*French Poets and Novelists* (London, 1884), p. 243.

Nature, and Art together met, and joyn'd,
Made up the Character of thy great Mind[8]

which, star-like, gave great light and exerted immense influence.
Most surprising of all is Oldham's praise of Jonson's knowledge
of human nature and his characterization of it, two aspects of
his artistry in which later critics were to find him especially
weak. So great was his knowledge of "human kind" and so faithfully did the images appear in the mirror of his art that he
seemed "the universal vast Idea of Mankind." Greater than such
a Platonic Adam it seems impossible to go, but Oldham ventures
to compare Jonson and his poetry with the "Almighty Poet" who
had of old designed the "World's fair poem." After this Tenerif
of praise it is all downhill, both in Oldham's poem and with
Jonson's reputation. Even with advocates like Congreve, Pope,
Fielding, Coleridge, Gifford and Dickens, Jonson became in time
Meredith's excogitator of the comic, Tennyson's glue-maker,
Shaw's brutish pedant, Eliot's appalling figure of a poet praised
for virtues least likely to attract, and Harry Levin's "greatest
unread English author." In short, the great mind had shrunk; the
view of life, once thought so large and so unique, had lost its
spaciousness if not its uniqueness.

What happened? I once had a wonderfully simple notion of
what happened to the reputation of Jonson. It went like this:
Jonson, the handsome son of a clergyman, cheerfully joined his
stepfather as an apprentice bricklayer, was discovered singing at
his work (or was it reciting the verses of Homer?) by a famous
teacher, Camden (or was it the lawyer, John Hoskyns?), who
arranged for free tuition at Westminster and was willing to send
the bright young lad to university; but Benjamin, too easy-going
for college, joined the army and served in Europe, where, quite
by accident, he killed an enemy in single combat, returned home
a war hero, wandered into acting, then into writing plays (thinking, no doubt, that if a country boy like Shakespeare could do it,
why couldn't he, city-bred and Westminster-educated?). So he
did, and prospered, giving up acting to write full time and
gradually working his way even into court circles where he became the favourite of Queen Anne and various duchesses. All

---

[8]C. H. Herford and Percy and Evelyn Simpson, *Ben Jonson* (Oxford, 1925–
1952), XI, 540. Hereafter, H & S.

went well with him: most people liked him, even his opponents in a make-believe war of words about the turn of the century. Oh, there were difficulties now and then: he accidentally killed an actor (if a dramatist can ever be said to kill an actor accidentally), and went to prison from which his sweet old mother was ready to spring him by pretending to poison him; and he landed in prison twice more because of some thin-skinned figures at court. And there was trouble with that impossible little bounder, Inigo Jones. But, all in all, up to 1618 a splendidly successful life. Then he made one dreadful error which undermined his reputation forever after: he went to Scotland. While there, he had the bad luck to run into an absolutely humourless man, one Drummond, laird of Hawthornden. Jonson's error – and it made him unconsciously act the master-fool he liked his chief characters to act – was that he decided, just for laughs, to act the part of the carping critic, the self-loving poet, the Genius. In other words, he acted the part of lusty, sack-drinking, self-centred "Ben Jonson" for the provincial Scotsman whom G. M. Matthews later called a "marooned Elizabethan." So he filled the ears of his witless host with all sorts of stale gossip about Queen Elizabeth's membrane and Overbury's designs on the Countess of Rutland, and cut and jabbed at his fellow writers, boasted about his practical jokes and sexual adventures, laughed derisively at everyone and got ingloriously drunk and endlessly praised his own genius. Did he know that Drummond could not quite understand self-mockery and sardonic wit, and certainly did not like malicious gossip? Was he aware that his host was recording, with remorseless fidelity, even his most off-hand remarks? He may have known both and relished the situation all the more for knowing. At any rate, these conversations set for all time, so I thought, the picture of Jonson as envious, self-loving, and small-minded.

Now there is one tiny thing wrong with this simple story: it is not true. He could never have been handsome, wall-eyed as he was from birth, mountain-bellied and rocky-faced as he became later in life. Nor could he have been entirely happy, I imagine, about his mother's moving down the social scale in marrying a bricklayer after being a lady as a minister's wife. He could scarcely be thought of as a peace-loving man even in an age we complacently think of as more rowdy than our own. Besides,

Drummond was no fool, though not heavily encumbered with a sense of humour. And then there is the little fact that Drummond's notes on the conversations were not published until 1711, and even then only in an abridged form, the full text not being made accessible to the general public until Cunningham's revision of Gifford's edition in 1875 – too late to form the dominant image of Jonson during the seventeenth and eighteenth centuries.

But there is at least one thing right about my fanciful picture of Jonson: he *was* acting a part much of the time at Hawthornden, as Ralph Walker suggested some years ago, and his remarks have to be interpreted in terms of the sardonic mask he had on.[9] It was a mask that he had on so often after he became established, and perhaps before, that it nearly became his face. James Howell described a supper, given presumably after the visit to Scotland but before his paralytic stroke in 1628, during which Jonson began to "engrosse all the discourse, to vapour extreamely of himselfe, and by vilifying others to magnifie his owne *muse*."[10]

This self-magnification may have been one of his less pleasant ways of coping with the special problem any ambitious and self-conscious writer would have had early in the seventeenth century. If, as we now like to say, a writer's first task is to invent himself, Jonson lived at a time when, surrounded by men of great genius, a writer had a lot of inventing to do just to get himself noticed. A man of minor talent would have been content to be a gentleman poet or one of Henslowe's hacks; but not Jonson. He wanted to be the great writer of his age – poet, dramatist, critic, classical scholar, masque writer for the court, Jonsonus Arbiter of England. In short, the exemplary man of letters. The "Ben Jonson" he invented to help him become that man of letters may have been his greatest single creation. His "best piece of poetry" may not have been his son, but his self. For he imposed himself on his age in a way that no one else quite did and at a time when the competition was more formidable than it was ever again to be. Could even Jonson have fashioned a more ironic fate than the one he found himself in – or, more precisely, the one we find him in? To write plays – when Shakespeare did? To write occasional poems for a circle that

[9]*Ben Jonson's Timber, or Discoveries*, ed. Ralph S. Walker (Syracuse, N.Y., 1953), pp. 125–28.
[10]H & S, XI, 420.

Donne moved in and wrote for? To be a critic – just after Sidney? To conceive of the heroic life – in the shadow of Spenser? To be concerned with the "advancement of Letters" – when there was a high government official who could write *The Advancement of Learning* and a *Novum Organum*? One could argue that Jonson did not know how good the competition really was. But his own praise of all these writers, except Spenser, makes clear that he did know. Surely the man who wrote that extraordinary poem for the 1623 Folio had known for a long time how great "the applause! delight! the wonder" of his stage was. Is there any greater just praise of Shakespeare than Jonson's? Furthermore, he saw that Donne was "the first poet in the world in some things": again, a remarkably judicious criticism, both for its main point and its shrewd qualification. Sidney he pairs with Hooker as "great Masters of wit, and language; and in whom all vigour of Invention and strength of judgement met."[11] He thought Bacon not only the most persuasive speaker of his age, but "one of the greatest men, and most worthy of admiration, that had beene in many Ages."[12] Only Spenser is not given his proper due by Jonson, though in a late poem he did refer to "*Spenser's* noble booke" and, in *The Golden Age Restored*, he brings Spenser in with Chaucer, Gower and Lydgate to help Pallas restore justice.[13]

That such competition did not silence him is in itself a superb achievement. Just to keep on writing when there is someone around who can write *Hamlet* takes nerve. True, it may have been precisely the greatness of Shakespeare and Donne and Sidney and Bacon, and precisely their kinds of greatness, which forced Jonson into the peculiar expression of his own genius. Faced with the fact of Shakespeare, what does one do? One can try competing, as Jonson may have done when, in his early years, he collaborated with Dekker and Chettle, or when he wrote *The Case is Altered* all alone. But competition with someone who could write *A Midsummer Night's Dream* and *Romeo and Juliet* within months of each other might be pretty stiff. Still, imagine a poet who could write *The Sad Shepherd*, perhaps late in life, and yet who had not written in that vein many times before! Was he trying to avoid any comparison with the author of *As*

[11]*Ibid.*, VIII, 591.
[12]*Ibid.*, 591–92.
[13]*Ibid.*, VII, 425.

You Like It? If you have as friend and judge "the first poet in the world in some things," you set about doing other things than he does. You do what Jonson soon did: you find your own voice, create your own worlds, become your own unique self.

Or selves. Which prompts the question: who *is* Ben Jonson? His life alone suggests a variety of answers. He worked with his hands, as few gentlemen then did, and remained close enough to this ungentle life to obtain the freedom of the Company of Tylers and Bricklayers in 1598, an action which ought to make one hesitate to accuse him of being a social climber. He fought as a common soldier, killed a man both on and off the battle-field, brawled on occasion and boasted of his aggressiveness. As actor, playwright, poet, writer of masques and entertainments he lived at the centre of England's literary and theatrical life for over thirty years. As a scholar, he was the friend of John Selden, Sir Robert Cotton and William Camden. Young as he was in 1605, he was already prominent enough as a Catholic to be used by Salisbury during the Gunpowder Plot to negotiate with the conspirators. He may even have been, if C. J. Sisson's speculation about his being at Gresham College is right, one of us, a Professor of Rhetoric. He wrote nearly everything, even a grammar, and most of what he wrote is still worth reading and re-reading. He was an arbiter of literary matters so authoritative that, when he died, he received the unusual tribute, not accorded any other English writer in his age, of a memorial volume of poems. John Danby has drawn our attention to the career of Jonson the outsider, who invaded the field of "greatest persons" and made his way by his pen, thereby giving to such later artists as Dryden and Pope a sense of security and independence they might not otherwise have had.[14] His career, then, involved the city, the court, the Inns of Court, the Company of Tylers and Bricklayers, the great houses, the universities, and the various theatres of London and the country. The uniqueness of this career comes from the singular fact that only in the last, the theatres, was he there, strictly speaking, by his vocation. (I am aware that G. E. Bentley has denied him even this professional status, claiming that, since his livelihood did not depend on writing plays, he was not a professional dramatist.[15] A fine distinction.) Every-

[14]*Poets on Fortune's Hill* (London, 1952), pp. 42–45.
[15]*The Profession of Dramatist in Shakespeare's Time, 1590–1642* (Princeton, N.J., 1971), pp. 30–32.

where else he had to make his way by his wits alone. He did not belong to the court by birth or title, as Sidney and Beaumont did. He never lived at the Inns of Court, as Bacon and Donne did. He visited Wilton House and Penshurst, but never lived in anything one-tenth so grand. If he went to university at all, he stayed long enough to use up what little money he had. Yet by his wits, his will-power, and his incorrigible egotism he became the first great professional man of letters England had produced – a *Johannes factotum* of letters in a way that Shakespeare never was nor, I suppose, wanted to be. Of course, we have to remember that he may have seemed less remarkable in an age in which the Lord Chancellor was a lawyer-philosopher-scientist, and the Dean of St. Paul's was a poet-preacher-diplomat. Still, even in an age of polymaths, Jonson stood out.

But variety of life and virtuosity of roles, though they may suggest a large view of life, do not necessarily produce it. If they did, then sailors, foreign correspondents, actors, and other vagrants might be especially noted for their comprehensive vision and perceptive insight. A large view of life comes as much from inside as from outside: we receive but what we give, and in our life alone does nature live. Jonson gave to his life, as to his wit and the works of his wit, a direction, a control and a searching study that he meant to be exemplary. He shaped his career and his writings with a deliberateness that aroused jibes for its self-conscious effort and with a courage that helped him endure these jibes as well as unpopularity, poverty and neglect. The twentieth century is now happily re-discovering in what ways he set examples for his age and for any age perceptive enough to listen to him.

I should now like to deal with several exemplary Jonsons in order to emphasize special aspects of what Ivor Winters calls his "dramatic and heroic" view of life. Winters calls it dramatic apparently because Jonson "deals with problems of conduct arising from relationships between one human being and another," and heroic because some of these relationships involve "tragic or other difficulties."[16] In concentrating on this dramatic and heroic view of life I shall have to slight several of his other great achievements. For instance, his voice in *Discoveries*, that

[16]"The 16th Century Lyric in England: a Critical and Historical Reinterpretation," *Poetry*, LIV (April, 1939), 42–43.

commanding voice which shows how thoroughly he has possessed the ideas of others and made an original treatise of what might have been merely a commonplace book. There are other Jonsons I shall have to ignore: the tender father who mourns a son and a daughter with touching reticence, the lover who wittily celebrates Charis or asks a lady delicately, passionately, to drink to him only with her eyes, and the devout believer who quietly confesses his sin to "Good and great God." There is the pastoral poet of *The Sad Shepherd* and the poet of the great house who pictures a right true society in "To Penshurst." Not to deal with these Jonsons is to narrow lamentably the largeness of his view. But no help. One can't say everything.

I'd like nothing more than to start with the most familiar Jonson, the comic dramatist; but I think I shall not, in part because I have elsewhere written at some length, though, alas, one-sidedly about him, and in part because wiser heads than mine have already spoken to you about his comedies. Instead, I shall turn to a Jonson now too often neglected, though once highly praised, Jonson the empiricist. The first time this Jonson was noticed he was not exactly praised, I must admit. In fact, he was jibed at in *The Return from Parnassus* (c. 1601) as "a meere Empyrick, one that getts what he hath by observation, and makes onely nature privy to what he endites, so slow an Inventor, that he were better betake himselfe to his old trade of Bricklaying."[17] Though we may see this as part praise of a writer who creates his world from empirical observation and sets down nothing that he cannot find a counterpart of in the natural world, we ought to remember that the Renaissance, which did not have our interest in day-by-day behaviour, would not have considered such empiricism particularly praiseworthy. Besides, the Parnassus writers suggest that Jonson made plays, as he laid bricks, one detail fitted in with another, and none invented by him, but picked up from around him. This jibe lost some of its sting as Bacon, Hobbes, and the growing interest in the "new science" made a reliance on observation and experience more respectable than it would have been in the still largely scholastic atmosphere of Cambridge University when the Parnassus plays were written. By the time Oldham wrote, Jonson was being praised for the way

[17]*The Three Parnassus Plays (1598–1601)*, ed. J. B. Leishman (London, 1949), p. 244.

his "strict Observation" had surveyed human nature so compre-
hensively and accurately. Nearly a hundred years after Oldham
this praise had been conventionalized into the pat couplets of
Charles Churchill:

> The book of man he [Jonson] read with nicest art,
> And ransack'd all the secrets of the heart;
> Exerted Penetration's utmost force,
> And trac'd each passion to its proper source[18]

"Jonson the empiricist" is stretching things a bit, of course,
though L. J. Potts thought him a "Baconian through and
through."[19] Even if he is not strictly an empiricist, his reliance on
observation, his respect for experience, his "faith in things" need
emphasizing. His "faith in things" – what does that curious phrase
mean? What is he getting at when, in praising Camden, he
exclaims:

> What name, what skill, what faith hast thou in things!
> What sight in searching the most antique springs!
> What weight and what authority in thy speech![20]

A helpful comment on these lines is a passage in *Discoveries*
where, drawing on John Hoskyns's *Directions for Speech and
Style*, he writes that "the conceits of the mind are Pictures of
things, and the tongue is the Interpreter of those Pictures. The
order of God's creatures in themselves is not only admirable, and
glorious, but eloquent; Then he who could apprehend the consequence of things in their truth, and utter his apprehensions as
truly, were the best Writer, or Speaker."[21] In both passages, I
gather, "things" do not necessarily or even primarily mean
material objects, as they often do with us, but deeds, events,
facts, whatever is done, experience. If this is so, then the thing
which is pictured when the mind conceives of anything may be
a situation or an object or a complex chain of events, past or
present. The tongue (or pen, I suppose) interprets these pictures

---

[18]*The Poetical Works of Charles Churchill*, ed. Douglas Grant (Oxford,
1956), p. 11.
[19]"Ben Jonson and the Seventeenth Century," *Essays and Studies . . . for
the English Association*. New Series, 2 (1949), 13.
[20]H & S, VIII, 31.
[21]*Ibid.*, 628.

– that is, translates the mental images into verbal signs. The best writer is one who conceives these pictures most faithfully, understands the consequence of the things pictured most thoroughly, and expresses what he understands most truthfully. "Faith in things," then, can carry one or both of these meanings. First, a man who has "faith in things" has put his trust not in imagination, which can mislead him, or in abstract ideas, which may be out of touch with reality; he has put his trust in the actual circumstances of life, past as well as present, or in what is now being done, or what was once done and is recorded as having been done. In short, he has put his faith in facts, or, more precisely, in facts as understood by man. Second, a man demonstrates his "faith in things" when he has faithfully conceived the full consequence of things and truthfully writes and speaks of what he conceives in his mind. So "faith in things" can also mean an accuracy in understanding and passing on the sense of words – sense which is "wrought out of experience, the knowledge of humane life, and actions, or of the liberall Arts."[22] The first kind of faith is a habit of attention; the second, a mode of understanding and rendering.

An extraordinary example of Jonson's own double "faith in things" and his own apprehension of the consequence of things in their truth is his use of historical facts in his tragedies. He conceived of tragedy as a historian might if the historian were willing to mix fable with fact. "Grave historie," as he wrote in explaining the frontispiece of Raleigh's *History of the World*, "Raising the World to good and evill fame, / Doth vindicate it to eternitie."[23] History vindicates the world by rescuing the past from death and oblivion and by disentangling the true from the false. Just so, in his tragedies, Jonson set about to vindicate to eternity two exemplary periods of Roman history. The shaping principle of form in both *Sejanus* and *Catiline* is the tragic fall of a corrupt state. Back of both of them is the image of an ideal state which Arruntius and Cicero evoke for us, but which we see only retrospectively. *Sejanus* dramatically renders what happens when Augustan Rome has declined into the perverted Tiberian state; *Catiline*, when the corruption of the Roman Republic is seen in the image of Catiline's conspiracy. The focus of the

[22]*Ibid.*, 621.
[23]*Ibid.*, 175.

tragedy is on the state itself rather than on any "hero," and the emotional power comes from the scale of the fall which ensues – a whole country, a long cultural tradition, a civilization. Jonson's models for grave and majestic renderings of the decline and fall of actual civilizations may have been Thucydides's *Peloponnesian War* and the *Annals of Tacitus*. One can only speculate on what he would have thought of Gibbon's history, especially with its ironic villain, Christianity.

In these tragedies Jonson sought "truth of argument" on the supposition that what has actually happened has a power to move one which no invented detail could possibly have. Facts – incorrigible, recalcitrant little facts – have a power of conviction exactly because they exist. The plot of Renaissance tragedy, as J. V. Cunningham puts it in explaining the theory of Donatus which Jonson accepted, "is commonly historical and true, not feigned . . . it is not merely realistic as distinguished from being fanciful; it has rather the compelling absoluteness of accomplished fact. Hence its effect will be accompanied by the recognition that things could not be otherwise, since this is how in fact they were."[24] What actually happened, then, according to this theory of tragedy, moves one deeply exactly because it happened, and happened not in the private world of one's imagination, but in the public world of history itself. Besides, what actually happened happens still: the reverberations of an historical fact are potentially endless in that it unsettles everything forever. The past perpetually creates the present; so we'd better get the past straight in our minds. Anyone can tell a lie about the past, and most people do daily. Only a few can do what everyone should try to do: discover the truth and publish it.

Though Jonson seems an unlikely Nietzschean, he might have agreed with Nietzsche's praise of Thucydides as one who wills not to gull himself, but to see reason in reality – "not in 'reason,' still less in 'morality.'" Thucydides was to Nietzsche "the great sun, the revelation of that strong, severe, hard factuality which was instinctive with the older Hellenes. In the end it is *courage* in the face of reality which distinguishes a man like Thucydides from Plato: Plato is a coward before reality, consequently he flees into the ideal. Thucydides has control of himself, conse-

[24]*Tradition and Poetic Structure* (Denver, Col., 1960), pp. 167–68.

154

quently he also maintains control of things."[25] I doubt that Jonson thought Plato a coward before reality though he certainly felt that one must maintain control of things. But how? His answer is strong and simple: "*I know* no disease of the *Soule,* but *Ignorance;* not of the Arts, and Sciences, but of it selfe: Yet relating to those, it is a pernicious *evill:* the darkner of mans life: the disturber of his *Reason,* and common Confounder of *Truth:*" In short, one must *know.* "Knowledge is the action of the *Soule;* and is perfect without the *senses,* as having the seeds of all *Science,* and *Vertue* in its selfe." To which he was empiricist enough to add immediately, "but not without the service of the *senses:* by those Organs, the *Soule workes:*"[26] Jonson, we gather, never fled into the ideal. He saw that, since "*Reason* is a weapon with two edges . . . and takes in errors into her, by the same conduits she doth Truths," one who cares about the truth will constantly distinguish the true from the false and make clear which is which for all to see. Jonson cared enough about the truth, not merely to maintain his control over things by mastering the facts of two periods of Roman history, but also to demonstrate how true his knowledge of things in at least one of them was. So he added to *Sejanus* those unforgivable notes on his sources, just as Eliot did for *The Waste Land.*

Jonson believed, then, that a scrupulous use of fact can make the death of a civilization a moving spectacle. Perhaps the spectacle will only move those capable of an act of historical imagination somewhat like that needed to write these tragedies. If we can rise to the height of his great argument by such an imaginative act, we may be able to feel something of the grandeur of at least *Sejanus,* which Jonas Barish and G. R. Hibbard (to name only two of several critics) have recovered for us.[27] Though we may finally feel that not even *Sejanus* and still less *Catiline* move us as most of Shakespeare's tragedies move us, perhaps because we are now more deeply touched by psychological truth than by historical accuracy, yet we should not fail to see how comprehensive his view of the past was and

[25]"Twilight of the Idols," *The Portable Nietzsche,* ed. Walter Kaufmann (New York, 1967), pp. 558–59.
[26]H & S, VIII, 588.
[27]*Sejanus,* ed. Jonas Barish (New Haven, Conn., 1966). G. R. Hibbard, "Goodness and Greatness: an Essay on the Tragedies of Ben Jonson and George Chapman," *Renaissance and Modern Studies,* 11 (1968), 5–54.

"what skill, what faith" he had in things. Actually, in an age like ours when we are so resolutely trying to find out what happened in our blood-soaked past and what is happening in our awful present – the age of Artaud, Brecht, Hochmuth, Peter Weiss, and *ciné vérité* – these tragedies might prove to be more moving than they are now thought to be. Certainly they should have more readers than they obviously have. And more productions: why Peter Brook has not given *Sejanus* one of his heartless productions I don't know. Jonson got to the twentieth-century theatre of cruelty, in both his comedies and his tragedies, before any other English dramatist did, and we have cruelly paid him back for his early arrival.

Jonson's reverence for "strong, severe, hard factuality" explains much about his art and the view of life that it expresses. This reverence should help us to understand better the next two exemplary Jonsons I should like to speak about: the celebrator of heroes and the castigator of rascals and fools. The two are closely connected, celebration and castigation being opposite but related reactions of a poet whose secure sense of values requires him to satirize those who fail to live up to the honourable life led by those he admires. Sometimes the satiric and the heroic are in continuous engagement, as in the "Epistle to Sir Edward Sacville," where "proud, hard, or ingratefull Men" and "Dwarfes of Honour" are contrasted with generous and honourable men of fortitude and virtue. Other times, as in "An Epistle to a Friend, to perswade him to the Warres," Jonson starts out derisively and remains so for most of the poem, only to yield in the last twenty lines to a plain exposition of the virtuous actions expected of good men. Still other times, as in his *Epigrammes*, he arranges the separate poems of celebration and castigation so that they comment on each other, placing, for example, an epigram satirizing would-be men of affairs in "The New Crie" between epigrams praising two genuine statesmen, the valiant Sir Horace Vere and the virtuous Sir John Radcliffe. Throughout his work runs the dialectic of the heroic virtues – truth, honour, fortitude, judgment – and the ridiculous follies and vices – imposture, a worship of opinion, and non-sense. The antimasque which he developed as counterpoint in his mature masques constitutes one of the richest expressions of this dialectic of the heroic and the false or mock heroic.

Underlying both the praise and the satire is a judicious sense of the way things are and a pious faith in human life as good men live it. Those who are too stupid to understand common-sense – fools, in a word – are ridiculous by nature. Those who are sharp enough to know the truth, but impious enough to use their knowledge for their own selfish ends – rogues and impostors, in short – are ridiculous because they affect another and an evil nature. When Jonson commented on Bacon's three distempers in learning, he described the third as "deceit, or the likeness of truth: Imposture held up by credulity," which W. A. Armstrong has called a fair summary of Jonsonian comedy.[28]

Jonson the castigator of imposture and credulity has been so long known and so thoroughly discussed that we are nearly blind to any other Jonson. He developed the art of sinking so brilliantly that we have nearly forgotten his sense of the sublime and his celebration of the heroic in masques, odes and epigrams. When we do study this celebration, we discover that, as we might expect, he drew heavily on such classical heroes as the Greek and Roman gods and semi-divine figures like Perseus, especially in his metaphorical language and as central characters in some masques. He partly ignored the medieval inheritance, not using saints and martyrs, but finding knights and personified abstractions useful both for genuine heroic effect and as mockery of false heroism. Most original of all was his creation of his own heroes of the active and the contemplative life, one of whom, as I have already said, is "Ben Jonson."

Part of the great work of recovering this celebrative Jonson has been done by the scholars who have opened up to us the significance of the Jonsonian masque – most recently, Stephen Orgel and John Meagher – and have helped us understand why a major writer would devote over twenty years at the height of his creative life to the composition of what used to be dismissed as a costume ball with scenery and lyrics. I should like to make only one point about his masques, because it reinforces what I have been saying about his tragedies. Often, though not always, Jonson did for his masques what he did for *Sejanus*: he annotated them. And for a similar reason, which he states in his autograph dedication of *The Masque of Queenes*: "The same

28"Ben Jonson and Jacobean Stagecraft," *Jacobean Theatre*, ed. J. R. Brown and Bernard Harris (London, 1960), p. 59.

zeale," he writes to Queen Anne about his annotations, "that studied to make this Invention worthy of yor Majestyes Name, hath since bene carefull to give it life, and authority." I do not know which is the more astounding claim – that his annotations give "life" to the invented fable, or "authority." Yet each is quite characteristic of the man. (He annotated, not so heavily as in *The Masque of Queenes*, five other masques, and always, one gathers, for the reasons given here.) The fable will have an authority it might not otherwise have if he can retrieve "the particular *authorities* . . . to these things, wch I writt out of fullnesse, and memory of my former readings." So he goes to ancient, medieval and contemporary sources to justify the actions which he invented and the properties which Inigo Jones devised – sources whose riches he had converted to his own aesthetic use in composing the masque in the first place. Jonson the empiricist is being empirical, but drawing on the past experience of others as he received it. Thus when Ate, Dame of the Hags, enters, Jonson has this annotation: "I present her barefooted, & her frock tuckd, to make her seeme more expedite; by *Horace* his authority." And then he adds the line in Horace's eighth satire describing Canidia. Or when Perseus, who represents Heroic Virtue, enters to disperse the witches, Jonson notes that he is "armed, as I have him describ'd out of *Hesiod*."[29] A detail in an imaginative work is authenticated, then, by a "fact": that is, by a use of it in actual history, literary as well as social and political. In fables that Jonson invents he can draw legitimately on what previous poets have invented because their inventions have entered history where they have been examined by thousands of intelligent people and either dismissed as fraudulent or foolish, or accepted as authentic or reasonable. So "authority" is given to a work of art when its details have been "justified." "Life" presumably comes in more fully, at least to those of "excellent understanding," because these details, having been experienced time and time again in man's long cultural history, have become images charged with special significance. Jonson apparently felt that what was once alive is never quite dead, especially if it has been given artistic form. When he remembers the death of the young Sir Henry Morison, he sees that the length of things is vanity unless the things be "vindicated to eternity."

[29]H & S, VII, 279, 286, 302.

Life doth her great actions spell,
By what was done and wrought
In season, and so brought
To light: her measures are, how well
Each syllab'e answer'd, and was form'd, how faire;
These make the lines of life, and that's her ayre.

Once anything – man, deed, object – obeys the "Holy laws of nature and societie" which govern man's life and which are suggested here to be proportion, harmony, season, and measure, the truth of its doing so never changes, though the man dies or the deed is forgotten or the object is destroyed. "The deed and the doer," as Thoreau reminds us, "together make ever one sober fact."[30] Whatever was, is. Or "is" if it be remembered. And precisely here is the great function of the poet, as Perseus in *The Masque of Queenes* makes clear when he declares that the columns of the House of Fame are "Men-making *Poets*" and the heroes so made.

But Jonson celebrates something more than the King in his court. He told Drummond that he was working on a Heroölogia of the worthies of England, and, in his "Epistle to Elizabeth, Countess of Rutland," he refers to a celebration of the ladies of Great Britain. This celebration was apparently never finished, and the Heroölogia was destroyed in the fire of 1622. A double pity, but perhaps not so much a loss as one might at first think, because Jonson celebrated his own heroes and heroines of England most of his adult life in his epigrams, epistles, and odes to living and recently dead Englishmen. When Jonson, the self-appointed critic of his own age, sought for his heroes, he turned not simply to literature and English and classical history, as Shakespeare usually did, or to legend and the matter of Britain, as Spenser did, though, as I said before, he could draw on all these sources when he needed to in his tragedies, his masques, and a sequence like "A Celebration of Charis." He was most original in finding his heroes in his own time and his own country. Of the one hundred and thirty-three epigrams he published in the Folio as his *Epigrammes: Book I*, over fifty refer to or are addressed to specific people. Five of the fifteen longer

[30]"A Week on the Concord and Merrimack Rivers," *The Writings of Henry David Thoreau* (Boston, 1906), p. 333.

poems in *The Forrest* are either epistles written to, or odes written about, contemporaries. Forty-five of the ninety poems in *The Under-wood* deal with people whom Jonson knew or knew about. To be sure, not all of these contemporary figures are treated as exemplars of heroic virtues. Inigo Jones is not, for one. But, in general, if Jonson names a person, he praises him. When he castigates folly and vice, he castigates types, though for particular characteristics he may have drawn on actual unnamed people.

The heroes he celebrates include the great statesmen, courtiers and soldiers – King James, Salisbury, Lord Ellesmere, Bacon, Pembroke, Lucius Cary – as well as those aristocratic ladies who patronized poetry and learning or conspicuously exemplified virtue. All of this is to be expected and is right. He never forgot that kings and lord chancellors were greater than even the greatest of other men in the immediate scheme of things. But Jonson celebrates over and over again a hero new to his age, new perhaps to English history. This new hero appears, quietly, in the epigram to Sir Henry Savile:

> Although to write be lesser then to doo,
> It is the next deede, and a great one too.

Jonson does not go so far as to say that writing is more important than protecting his country or running its affairs any more than Sidney before or Milton after him did. He is still ages away from the transfiguration of the artist which was to come with Romantic criticism; but he does see the heroic endeavour involved in being a writer, and he opens himself to the charges, which he got, of being pompous and self-indulgent in talking so grandiloquently about writing poetry. First of all, we had better understand all that he means by being a writer. He means something more than being enraptured or divinely mad in the old Platonic way. He does mean *that*, to be sure. And he can be just as taken with the image of the Orphic poet as any other Renaissance writer. Thus he tells Sidney's daughter, the Countess of Rutland, that "It is the *Muse*, alone, can raise to heaven," and that "onely *Poets*, rapt with rage divine," made Achilles and Hercules famous.[31]

---

[31]H & S, VII, 114–15.

But, rapt as he may be with this image, he thinks writing means more than divine rage, as we can see in his different, but not irreconcilable comments on Shakespeare in the *Discoveries* and in the Folio poem. Some time before 1623 Shakespeare became his great example of the poet as creator who was at least the peer of the greatest classical playwrights. Yet, great as he was, he was not faultless. Jonson drily records in *Discoveries* telling the players that Shakespeare should have blotted a thousand lines – surely a sensible remark unless one is no longer "this side idolatry." "His wit was in his owne power; would the rule of it had beene so too."[32] For the Folio poem, the splendid heroic poem about England's, if not the world's greatest dramatist, Jonson shifted the emphasis from what Shakespeare had not blotted or from what he should have done, to what he must have done if he had written a play like *Lear*. He

> Who casts to write a living line, must sweat,
> (Such as thine are) and strike the second heat
> Upon the *Muses* anvile: turne the same,
> (And himselfe with it) that he thinkes to frame;
> Or, for the lawrell, he may gaine a scorne,
> For a good *Poet's* made, as well as borne.

So, however great his natural endowment, Shakespeare must have made himself to some extent. This act of self-creation is one that Jonson emphasizes as a critic and exemplifies as a writer. Indeed, he is, as he wanted to be, the best instance in his age of a man who made himself a poet. Perhaps the best proof of this is his revision of *Every Man in His Humour*.

Evidences of rewriting, whether in manuscript or in variant published versions, are so frequent in modern literature that scholars who alone could not write a single line of decent poetry find themselves extraordinarily creative when helping Yeats or Eliot write the poem that finally was written. This privilege is usually denied to students of literature written before 1700, with the result that their *poésie manquée* has to be pieced together from the patches of bad Shakespearean quartos, Milton's punctuation and a stray manuscript of Sir Thomas Wyatt. Rarely can one look over the shoulder of a Renaissance poet as he revises

---

[32]*Ibid.*, 583–84.

his whole work, passage by passage, line by line, and have the ineffable pleasure of agreeing with a great poet's deletion of an inexact word or choice of a more intense image. But, rare as it is, the pleasure still exists. And Jonson gives it to us. What an extraordinary act of judgment and re-creation is his revision of the Quarto *Every Man in His Humour* for its inclusion in the *Workes*! It would be hard to find a more illuminating example of a great Renaissance poet at the painful business of turning and true-filing his lines and striking a second heat upon the Muse's anvil. He excises the abstract, clarifies the obscure, compresses the sprawling, slashes away the irrelevant, however beautiful it is (such as the eulogy to poetry in the final scene), tightens the syntax and, all the time, with judicious care, works to achieve that "propriety of speech" which Pepys was to find so remarkable fifty years later, and, as Joseph Bryant, Jonas Barish, and J. W. Lever have shown, to reshape his play to produce the comic effect he wanted. No wonder his fellow poets admired Jonson as the age's finest judge. The man who could look with so cold an eye at his first version of a play and fashion it anew into the folio version was a shrewd critic exactly where it is hardest to be critical – with one's own successful writing. If J. M. Nosworthy is right about Shakespeare's being his own careful reviser, especially in his later plays, one would like to know how much he and Jonson taught each other about that difficult art.[33] Would that Shakespeare had left as exemplary an act of revision as the two versions of *Every Man in His Humour*!

By the "writer," then, Jonson meant Apollonian reviser as well as Dionysiac poet. And he meant still more. When he told Savile that writing is the next deed to doing, he was not addressing a fellow poet or dramatist or even a critic. Savile was one of England's most learned scholars, translator of Tacitus (to whose *Histories* he had added a section of his own on Nero and Galba), and later editor of Chrysostom and founder of chairs of geometry and astronomy at Oxford. Whoever uses "his pen [to] write the things, the causes, and the men," as a translator, historian and editor like Savile did, is doing an heroic deed next only to those of the great leaders in the world of action. So by "writer" Jonson meant not merely poets – Shakespeare, Donne, Sidney – but also

[33]*Shakespeare's Occasional Plays: Their Origin and Transmission* (London, 1965), pp. 217–24.

antiquarians like Camden, historians and jurists like Selden, translators like Clement Edmonds and Thomas May, and editors like Sir Henry Savile – or Ben Jonson.

Which brings us to the 1616 Folio, surely one of the significant events in English culture. It is a remarkably self-conscious, courageous, and exhausting piece of work, one of the great exemplary acts of the seventeenth century, because it is one of the first instances (and it may be the greatest early instance) we know of in England when a practising man of letters collected, edited and saw through the press works of his he thought acceptable for publication. It may have been the first time that plays, masques and poems were so combined and treated so carefully. The care with which Jonson edited his works impresses one even when one sees that exhaustion or impatience or in-attention left its mark here and there. Jonson showed his fellow poets and dramatists how a serious artist concerned about civilization should act. That he prints his poetry is not the main thing – Spenser and lesser poets had done that. More important is that he revised what he considered defective (both *Every Man* plays), refused to publish what he wanted rejected (*The Case is Altered*), disowned what was not entirely his (*Eastward Ho*), and rationalized his critical theories in the various prologues to the plays when he felt they needed rationalizing. So far as drama goes, the great redeeming act is that he associated plays, which were then often thought to be ephemeral, with epigrams, devotional and occasional poems, which were respectable enough so that even gentlemen could publish them. In a fine recent article on Jonson's career, David Kay argues convincingly that, when Jonson published his works in 1616, and especially when he placed his revised version of *Every Man in His Humour* at the beginning of the Folio, he was continuing to "interpret himself to his age as a writer whose individual works formed a unified corpus animated by his conception of the poet's function."[34] I think this is quite true, and I wish that I had time to say something about the unity of the 1616 Folio, but, not having the time, I can only urge a reading of Mr. Kay's excellent discussion.

So Jonson discovered a new hero for his age: the writer himself, the man who sits down at a desk and puts one word after

[34]"The Shaping of Ben Jonson's Career: a Reexamination of Facts and Problems," *Modern Philology*, 67 (February, 1970), 236.

another to create a virtual world out of his daily experience and his remembrance of the past. Shakespeare had found in Prospero a hero who was stage manager and playwright, as well as magus and mystic, but, complex as he is, Prospero would not have been to Jonson all that the writer should be, remaining too much the demonic creator. Jonson saw the complex heroism of the writer more clearly than any one in his age, and he lived it and wrote about it. He invented that magnificently centred self so well described by Thomas Greene, in order to embody this hero and to carry out the exemplary deeds of writing, revising and editing.[35] The writer, the reviser, the editor as hero – how close, how courageously close, Jonson was willing to come to bathos in an age that had not yet dignified the writer except as frenzied poet! Yet he was willing to risk sinking because he had a rare sense of the value of human culture, the dangers it was open to, and the courage, honesty, judgment and faith that were needed to protect it from its enemies, however great or numerous they might be. It would be a long time before any Englishman could say, as Ruskin said in 1860, that "the market may have its martyrdoms as well as the pulpit; and trade its heroisms, as well as war," though Puritan merchants, even in Jonson's day, were moving toward an heroic sense of commercial enterprise.[36] Yet Jonson would have claimed that the great deed of writing required a grasp of facts, a devotion to duty, and a fortitude only less heroic than those of the active heroes of military and political life.

Fortitude, devotion to duty, a grasp of facts are central to the view of life of Jonson's Christian Stoic, though they are not alone · at the centre. In his odes and epistles he states his ethical beliefs with a forthrightness that, in an age like ours, which prizes indirection and ambiguity, leaves many unmoved, or even a bit put off. Jonson is direct and plain in these poems for at least two reasons I can think of. One is that, having spent so much time with the objective and therefore relatively impersonal form of drama, he may have felt that he needed to say unequivocally what he believed in. The other and more probable reason is that his strong mind naturally worked toward massively simple

[35]"Ben Jonson and the Centered Self," *Studies in English Literature, 1500–1900*, X (Spring, 1970), 325–48.
[36]*The Works of John Ruskin*, ed. E. T. Cook and Alexander Wedderburn (London, 1905), XVII, 39.

affirmations. To him, one gathers, there is a country of truth – the eternally true principles of life and the universe and man's history – which can be discovered by patient study, careful judgment, and sceptical understanding. "In action, there is nothing new, / More, then to varie what our elders knew."[37] Universal, objective and unalterable laws order what we call "reality," and rational investigation can discover these laws. So sure is he that the standards of ethics and aesthetics naturally depend on these intelligible laws that he seems but a step away from the enlightened world of the *philosophes*; but it is a giant step, because he allows room for the saving grace of God in a way that they usually do not. There seems to have been no great quarrel between the Hebraic and the Hellenic sides of his nature, perhaps because he took his "good and great God" so much on faith, and remained so largely what Heine called a "Hellene" in his love of life, his pride in his own self-development, and his interest in the realistic. So far as one can see, he had no difficulty in reconciling the Bible as a sourcebook of systematic theology with those other treasures of eternally true propositions, the works of the poets, the critics, and the philosophers of ancient Greece and Rome. That there might be irreconcilable contradictions in what these scriptural writings, Christian and pagan, say, apparently did not bother him. That they were themselves subject to change – indeed, that all things are in vast processes of change – scarcely occurred to him, even though his motto, *tanquam explorator*, implies a world constantly unfolding. His *Discoveries* are re-discoveries of a land explored long ago. "For *Truth* and *Goodnesse* are plaine, and open: but Imposture is ever asham'd of the light."[38] It all sounds so simple, but the remarkable thing about Jonson's country of truth is that, though one can draw a map of it with deceptive ease, one cannot travel in it for long without discovering how closely connected everything is. Raymond Southall has recently pointed out that "art" to Jonson was finally the art of living in that he conceived of life and art as governed by the same standards – standards such as "measure" and "proportion."[39] Quite true. I should only add that the arts of living and of creating usually meant to Jonson all that later ages

[37]H & S, VIII, 72.
[38]*Ibid.*, 570.
[39]"Understanding Jonson," *Essays in Criticism*, XXII (Jan., 1972), 83–91.

separated out into morality, manners, poetics, philosophy and piety. When Jonson speaks of any one of these apparently separable aspects of life, he often means several of the others at the same time. Thus, generosity in the giver and gratitude in the receiver are at once moral, social and religious in their implications. The virtues he emphasizes – temperance, measure, diligence, decorum, judgment, grace, honour, honesty, valour, friendship, love, reverence for one's betters, consideration for those weaker – each may be simultaneously a social grace, a great moral value, the mark of a "right generous mind," and the emblem of a pious life. For him, as for Burke, a stain is like a wound. Manliness is a son of piety. A parasite stinks. Speech is the audible sign of a spiritual grace – or gracelessness. Certain values, like decorum, honour, judgment and "faith in things," are especially resonant in Jonson's world. A good example of such resonance is his "Epistle to John Selden," which may be as much an idealized self-portrait as a picture of Selden. A passage from it will allow Jonson to have, as he would want, the last word about his view of life: a view that is large because he searched for the truth deep in the past, studied intently much of his present, and richly converted to his own use a good deal of what he had observed; a view that is unique because he created an absolutely individual self who had his own "peculiar Notion of the Times," gave him heroic deeds to do, and found for him an unmistakable voice. Here is that voice and one side of that self:

> Stand forth my Object, then, you that have beene
> Ever at home; yet, have all Countries seene:
> And like a Compasse keeping one foot still
> Upon your Center, doe your Circle fill
> Of generall knowledge; watch'd men, manners too,
> Heard what times past have said, seene what ours doe:
> Which Grace shall I make love to first? your skill,
> Or faith in things? or is't your wealth and will
> T[o] 'instruct and teach? or your unweary'd paine
> Of Gathering? Bountie' in pouring out againe?
> What fables have you vext! what truth redeem'd!
> Antiquities search'd! Opinions dis-esteem'd!
> Impostures branded! and Authorities urg'd!
> What blots and errours, have you watch'd and purg'd
> Records, and Authors of! how rectified
> Times, manners, customes! Innovations spide!

Nothing but the round
Large claspe of Nature, such a wit can bound.
Monarch in Letters! 'Mongst thy Titles showne
Of others honours, thus, enjoy thine owne.

The Contributors

WILLIAM BLISSETT, Professor of English, University College, University of Toronto. Editor of *University of Toronto Quarterly*, author of numerous articles on Renaissance poetry and drama.

J. W. LEVER, Professor of English, Simon Fraser University. Author of *The Elizabethan Love Sonnet, The Tragedy of State* and numerous articles; editor of the New Arden *Measure for Measure* and of the New Penguin *The Rape of Lucrece*.

J. M. NOSWORTHY, Reader in English, University College of Wales, Aberystwyth. Author of *Shakespeare's Occasional Plays* and of numerous articles on Shakespeare and Elizabethan Drama; editor of the New Arden *Cymbeline* and of the New Penguin *Measure for Measure*.

E. B. PARTRIDGE, Professor of English, Tulane University. Author of *The Broken Compass* and numerous articles; editor of *Epicoene* in the Yale Ben Jonson.

S. SCHOENBAUM, Professor of English, Northwestern University. Author of *Thomas Middleton's Tragedies, Internal Evidence and Elizabethan Dramatic Authorship, Shakespeare's Lives* and numerous articles; editor of *Research Opportunities in Renaissance Drama*.

T. J. B. SPENCER, Professor of English Language and Literature and Director of the Shakespeare Institute, University of Birmingham. Author of *Fair Greece Sad Relic* and numerous articles. Editor of *Modern Language Review*, general Editor of the New Penguin Shakespeare.

EUGENE M. WAITH, Professor of English, Yale University. Author of *The Pattern of Tragicomedy in Beaumont and Fletcher, The Herculean Hero, The Dramatic Moment, Ideas of Gre ness* and numerous articles; editor of *Bartholomew Fair* in the Yale Ben Jonson.

S. P. ZITNER, Professor of English, Trinity College, University of Toronto. Author of numerous articles on Renaissance poetry, poetics and drama.

Index

Accius (Attius), Lucius, 34-35
Actors: "Ambros," 73-75; "Barot" (Barret, John), 73-79; Bedowe, Ellis, 58, 59, 74; Beeland, Ambrose, 58, 59, 74, 75; Bird, Theophilus, 76; Burbage, Richard, 39; Cartwright, William, 75; Cherrington, Will, 76; Clark, Hugh, 76; "Ellis," 58, 59, 73, 74; Fenn, Ezekiel, 76; Guest, Ellis, 59, 74; Jordan, Thomas, 58-60, 72, 74-78; Loveday, Thomas, 75; Lovel, Thomas, 75; Matchit, Ambrose, 75-76, 78; Morris, Mathias, 73-75; "Noble," 74; Sands, Thomas, 74-75, 77; Williams, Walter, 75; Worth, Ellis, 58-59, 74
Adams, Joseph Quincy, 85
Akrigg, G. P. V.: *Jacobean Pageant*, 93
Anne (of Denmark), Queen to James I, 82, 125, 145, 158
Aristophanes, 36
Aristotle, 42, 56
Armstrong, W. A., 157
Arnold, Matthew, xi
Artaud, Antonin, 156
Astley, Sir John, 123, 124
Aubrey, John: *Brief Lives*, 88
Auden, W. H., 10

Bacon, Sir Francis, ix, 150, 151, 157, 160; *The Advancement of Learning*, 86, 96, 148; *Novum Organum*, 148; "Of Masques and Triumphs," 105
Bamborough, J. B., 111, 127, 128, 141, 143
Barish, Jonas A., 87, 94, 98, 128, 155, 162; *Ben Jonson and the Language of Prose Comedy*, xii, 9
Bartholomaeus Anglicus, 105
Basse, William, 32, 33
Beaumont, Comte de (French ambassador), 85
Beaumont, Francis, 33, 150; *The Faithful Friends*, 65
Belleforest, François de, 43
Benson, Sir Frank, 51
Bentley, G. E.: *The Swan of Avon and the Bricklayer of Westminster*, 22; *The Jacobean and Caroline Stage*, 59, 60, 74, 75; *The Profession of Dramatist in Shakespeare's Time*, 149
Blissett, William, xiii
Blount, Edward, 25
Boas, F. S.: *Introduction to Stuart Drama*, 14, 18
Boccaccio, Giovanni, 56
Bradley, A. C., 51
Brecht, Bertolt, 156
Britannia Triumphans (by William Davenant), 120
Brome, Richard: *Five New Plays*, 30
Brook, Peter, 156
Browning, Robert, 129
Bryant, Joseph, 162
Burke, Edmund, 166
Byron, George Gordon Noel, Lord, 40

Calvert, Samuel, 85
Camden, William, 145, 149, 152, 163
Campion, Thomas, 134
Carew, Thomas, 129, 130
Carradine, John, 16
Cary, Lucius, Viscount Falkland, 160

Castelain, Maurice, 144
Castiglione, Baldassare, 140
Chapman, George, 26, 108; *The Widow's Tears*, 65
Charles I, King of England, 107; as prince, 125
Chaucer, Geoffrey, 33, 148
Chettle, Henry, 148
Chetwood, W. R., 4
Churchill, Charles, 152
Cicero, Marcus Tullius, 31, 108
Cinthio, Giraldi, 56
Coleridge, Samuel Taylor, 8, 40, 55, 121, 127, 145
Colie, Rosalie, 130
Congreve, William, 145
Coryate, Thomas: *Coryats Crudities*, 24
Cotton, Sir Robert, 149
Craik, T. W., 20
Crane, Ralph, 27
Cubeta, P. M., 129, 131
Cunningham, J. V., 154

Daborne, Robert: *The Poor Man's Comfort*, 74
Danby, John, 149
Daniel, Samuel, 134
De Luna, B. N., 83
Dekker, Thomas, 8, 72, 148; *The Welsh Ambassador*, 65, 73
Denores, Giasone di, 56
Dessen, Alan: *Jonson's Moral Comedy*, 9, 98
Dickens, Charles, 145
Donaldson, Ian, 8, 10: *The World Upside-Down*, 81, 105
Donne, John, 28, 127, 148, 150, 162; "The Ecstasy," 139; "Elegie XIX," 129, 130; "Love's Alchemy," 139
Dramatic companies: Admiral's Men, 12; Chamberlain's Men, 13; Children of the Chapel, 13; King's Men, 39, 59, 75; King's Revels, 59, 74, 75, 77, 78; Lady Elizabeth's Men, 12; National Theatre Company, 7; Queen Henrietta's Players, 59, 77; Royal Shakespeare Company, 21; Stratford Festival Theatre Company, 7
Drayton, Michael, 28, 29
Drummond, William of

Hawthorden, 19, 23, 28, 29, 36, 82, 84, 146-47, 159
Dryden, John, x, 39, 107, 143, 144, 149; "A Discourse concerning the Original and Progress of Satire," 29, 30

Edmonds, Clement, 163
Egerton, Sir Thomas, Lord Ellesmere, 160
Eliot, T. S., x-xiv, 9, 10, 112, 128, 141, 143, 144, 145, 155, 161
Elizabeth I, Queen of England, 82, 146
Ellesmere, Lord. *See* Egerton, Sir Thomas
Empson, William, 6
Enck, John J.: *Jonson and the Comic Truth*, 5-6, 98
Erasmus, Desiderius, 93
Euripides, 34

Ferrer, José, 17
Ficino, Marsilio, 132
Field, Nathan, 28
Fielding, Henry, 145
Fletcher, John, 39; *Two Noble Kinsmen*, 73
Friar Bacon (John of Bordeaux), 58
Frost, Robert, 139
Furniss, W. Todd, 125

Galba, Emperor of Rome, 162
Galloway, David, 22
Geoffrey of Monmouth, 65-66
Gibbon, Edward, 154
Gifford, William, x, 3, 110, 111, 145, 147
Glapthorne, Henry: *The Lady Mother*, 73, 77
Gourlay, J. J., 58-60, 72, 78
Gower, John, 148
Gray, Thomas, 40
Greene, Thomas, 164
Greg, Sir Walter, 58, 59, 60, 72-75

Harbage, Alfred, 12, 98, 99, 143; *Shakespeare and the Rival Traditions*, 11
Hardy, J. Duffus, 72
Harris, John, 124
Hathaway, Anne, 46
Hazlitt, William, 8

Index

Hebel, J. W., 28, 29
Heine, Heinrich, 165
Henslowe, Philip, 12, 147
Heraclitus, 96
Herford, C. H., and Simpson, P.,
    2, 5, 10, 14, 15, 18, 84, 119,
    127, 129, 131, 134, 140
Hesiod, 132, 158
Heywood, John: The Four P's, 20
Heywood, Thomas, 8
Hibbard, G. R., 155
Hobbes, Thomas, 151
Hodgson, William, 39
Holland, Hugh: Pancharis, 38
Homer, 28, 145; The Iliad, 133
Hooker, Richard, 148
Horace, 28, 30, 33, 34, 38, 140,
    158; Ars Poetica, 131
Hoskyns, John, 145; Directions for
    Speech and Style, 152
Hosley, Richard, 109, 111, 115
Howell, James, 147

Isle of Dogs, The, 82

Jackson, Gabriele: Vision and
    Judgment in Ben Jonson's
    Drama, 106-107
Jaggard, Isaac, 25
James, Henry, 144
James I, King of England, xiii, 25,
    38, 81, 83-85, 89-91, 95, 102,
    104, 107, 118, 125, 126, 160;
    Basilikon Doron, 86; Counter-
    blaste to Tobacco, 92; Notes of
    a Prentice in the Divine Art of
    Poetry, 93
Jenkins, Harold, 44
John of Bordeaux, 58, 72
Johnson, Dr. Samuel, 27, 28, 40,
    43, 55
Jones, Inigo, 108, 109, 116, 118,
    119, 120, 121, 123, 124, 125,
    146, 158, 160
Jonson, Ben, ix-xv, 1-40, 63, 64,
    80-167; Works (1616), 25-27,
    107, 162, 163; Works (1640),
    27; Plays: The Alchemist, 2, 3,
    7, 11, 12, 18-21, 95, 97, 112;
    Bartholomew Fair, ix, xiii, 7,
    12, 80-105, 106, 107, 109, 112,
    115, 118; The Case is Altered,
    8, 148, 163; Catiline, 83, 153,
    154, 155; Cynthia's Revels, 12,

13, 82, 107, 108; The Devil is
    an Ass, xiii, 84, 107, 109, 110,
    112, 115-18, 120, 126, 129, 140;
    Eastward Ho, 83, 84, 163;
    Epicoene, 13, 21, 84, 92, 94-5,
    97; Every Man in His Humour,
    5, 10, 64, 106, 161-63; Every
    Man Out of His Humour, 11-13,
    163; The New Inn, 8, 11-12,
    136-37, 139, 140; Poetaster, 8,
    11, 12, 83, 104; The Sad
    Shepherd, 148, 151; Sejanus, 8,
    12, 64, 82, 153, 155-57; The
    Staple of News, xiii, 107,
    108-18, 120, 126; Volpone, 6,
    9, 11-18, 21, 64, 84, 95, 97,
    118; Masques and Entertain-
    ments: The Masque of Augurs,
    119; The Masque of Beauty,
    138; Christmas his Masque, 119;
    The Fortunate Isles, 107, 119;
    The Golden Age Restored, 148;
    The Gypsies Metamorphosed,
    xiii, 101-103, 119; Hymenaei,
    138; Love Restored, xiii, 101;
    Lovers Made Men, 119;
    Mercury Vindicated, 107, 118,
    119; Neptune's Triumph, 119,
    120; News from the New World,
    119, 120, 133-34; The Masque
    of Oberon, 118; The Masque of
    Owls, 119; Pan's Anniversary,
    119; Pleasure Reconciled to
    Virtue, 119, 139; Prince Henry's
    Barriers, 118; The Masque of
    Queens, 100, 109, 118, 125,
    157-59; Time Vindicated, xiii,
    107, 119, 120, 122-26; The
    Vision of Delight, xiii, 107, 119,
    120-22, 126; Poems:
    Epigrammes, 156, 159: "To
    William Camden" (XIV), 152;
    "To John Donne" (XXII), 28;
    "To Fine Grand" (LXXIII),
    24; "The New Crie" (XCII),
    156; "To Sir Henrie Savile"
    (XCV), 160; "To John Donne"
    (XCVI), 29; The Forrest, 160:
    "To Penshurst" (II), 141, 150;
    "Epistle to Elizabeth, Countess
    of Rutland" (XII), 159;
    "Epistle to Katherine, Lady
    Aubigny" (XIII), 108; The
    Underwood, 24, 139, 160: "A

Hymne to God the Father" (I. 2), 151; "A Celebration of Charis" (II), 128-142, 159; "Epistle to Sir Edward Sacvile" (XIII), 156; "Epistle to John Selden" (XIV), 166; "An Epistle to a Friend, to perswade him to the Warres" (XV), 156; "Ode to Himself" (XXIII), 12; "To the immortal memorie, and friendship of that noble paire, Sir Lucius Cary, and Sir H. Morison" (LXX), 139; *Ungathered Verse*: "Ode allegorike" (VI), 38; "To the memory of my beloved, the Author Mr. William Shakespeare: and what he hath left us" (XXVI), 22-40, 148, 161; "The Vision of Ben Jonson, on the Muses of his Friend M. Drayton" (XXX), 29; **Prose:** *Timber: or, Discoveries*, 10, 11, 13, 37, 97, 107, 133-34, 150-51, 152, 161, 165. **Lost Works:** *Heroölogia*, 159; *Richard Crookbacke*, 12
Jonsonus Virbius, 27
Jordan, Thomas, 58-60, 72-74, 78: *Money is an Ass*, 75-78; *Poetical Varieties*, 76. See also Actors
Joyce, James, 12; *Finnegan's Wake*, 91
Juvenal, 30

Kaplan, Joel H., 98
Kay, David, 163
Keats, John, xiv, 40, 137
Knights, L. C., 14, 18; *Drama and Society in the Age of Jonson*, xi
Kyd, Thomas, 34, 43, 56; *The Spanish Tragedy*, 12, 33, 55, 64

Lamb, Charles: *Specimens of English Dramatic Poets*, 8
Lawrence, D. H., 14
Lever, J. W., xv, 162
Levin, Harry, 9, 98, 145
Levin, Richard, 87
Lucan, 28, 30
Lydgate, John, 148
Lyly, John, 33, 34

Manheim, Michael, 66
Marcus Aurelius, 95
Mares, F. H., 2, 3, 6, 18, 21
Marlowe, Christopher, 34; *Tamburlaine*, 33, 133; *Edward II*, 66; *Hero and Leander*, 97
Marston, John, 82, 89; *The Malcontent*, 65
Martial, 25, 35, 135
Mathew, David, 86
Matthews, G. M., 146
May, Thomas, 163
Meagher, John C., 100, 157
Mennis, Sir John, 3
Meredith, George, 145
Middleton, Thomas: *A Trick to Catch the Old One*, 64; *Michaelmas Term*, 65; *The Phoenix*, 89
Milton, John, 160, 161
Montgomery, Philip Herbert, Earl of, 25
Morison, Sir Henry, 158
Morley, Henry, 90
Muir, Kenneth, 24
Musgrove, S., 22

Nero, Emperor of Rome, 162
Newdigate, B. H.: *Michael Drayton and his Circle*, 29
Nicoll, Allardyce, 85, 105
Nietzsche, Friedrich, 154
Nobody and Somebody, 65-66
Nosworthy, J. M., xv, 162

Oldham, John, 144-45, 151-52
Orgel, Stephen, 9, 109, 118, 120, 121, 122, 157
Orton, Joe, 18
Overbury, Sir Thomas, 146
Ovid, 28, 33, 108, 132

Pacuvius, 34, 35
Parker, R. B., 87, 109
Partridge, E. B., 99; *The Broken Compass*, xii, xiv, 9, 19, 100
Pawlet, Lady Jane, 138
Pembroke, William Herbert, Earl of, 25, 160
Pepys, Samuel, 162
Percy, Thomas, 73
Percy, William, 73
Petronius Arbiter, 30
Pindar, 38

Plato, 154-55; *Phaedrus*, 140; *Timaeus*, 132
Plautus, 28, 36
Pope, Alexander, 30, 97, 145, 149
Potts, L. J., 22, 152
Putney, Rufus, 6

Quiller-Couch, Sir Arthur, 129
Quintilian, 35

Radcliffe, Sir John, 156
Raleigh, Sir Walter: *History of the World*, 153
Renwick, W. L., 58, 60, 72
Return from Parnassus, The, 151
Reynolds, Henry, 28
Richards, Nathanael: *Messalina*, 74, 75, 77, 78
Richmond, Hugh: *The School of Love*, 135
Robinson, James E., 96
Robison, Jeannie: "On Editing Jonson," 2
Rochester, John Wilmot, Earl of, 29, 30
Rowley, William: *A Match at Midnight*, 65
Ruskin, John, 104, 164
Rutland, Elizabeth Sidney, Countess of, 146, 159, 160

Sackville, Charles, Earl of Dorset, 29, 30
Salisbury, Sir Robert Cecil, Earl of, 149, 160
Salmacida Spolia (by William Davenant), 120
Savile, Sir Henry, 160, 162, 163
Schoenbaum, Samuel, xiv, 22, 24, 40
Scott, Sir Walter: *The Fortunes of Nigel*, 86
Selden, John, 149, 163, 166
Seneca, Lucius Annaeus, 28, 30, 34, 35, 94, 95
Shakespeare, William, ix, x, xii, xiv, 5, 10, 12, 14, 22, 23, 26, 27, 28, 30, 31-40, 63, 69, 106, 127, 133, 143, 145, 147, 148, 150, 155, 159, 161, 162, 164; First Folio, xii, 24, 26, 32, 48, 148, 161; *AYL*, 148-49; *Cym.*, 53; *Ham.*, xv, 24, 26, 41-56, 64, 148; *1H4*, 127; *2H4*, 27; *JC*, 7,

56; *John*, 66; *Lear*, 6, 14, 42, 99, 161; *Mac.*, 14, 64; *MM.*, 27, 89; *MND.*, 148; *Oth.*, 27, 42; *Rape of Lucrece*, 128; *R2*, 64, 66; *Rom.*, 42, 43, 56, 148; *Sonnets*, 132, 133; *Tmp.*, 26, 27, 164; *Tim.*, 42; *Tit.*, 55; *Troi.*, 26
Shaw, George Bernard, 143, 145
Shelley, Percy Bysshe, 40
Sidney, Sir Philip, 148, 150, 160, 162
Simpson, Percy. See Herford, C. H.
Sir Thomas More, 72
Sisson, C. J., 149
Skolimowski, Jerzy: *Deep End*, 18
Smith, David Nichol, 23, 30
Smith, G. Gregory, x, xi
Smith, Gordon Ross, 1
Smith, Irwin, 111
Smith, James, 3
Sophocles: *Antigone*, 56
Southall, Raymond, 165
Southerne, Thomas: *The Wives Excuse*, 111
Spence, Joseph, 30
Spencer, Hazelton, 24
Spencer, T. J. B., x, xii
Spenser, Edmund, 32, 33, 65, 148, 159, 163; "Hymne in Honour of Love," 132; "Mutabilitie Cantos," 133
Steele, M. S., 82
Stutfield, George, 74
Subject's Precedent, The. See *The Wasp*
Suckling, Sir John: *The Sad One*, 129
Swinburne, Algernon Charles, 8

Tacitus: *Annals*, 154; *Histories*, 162
Tawney, R. H., xi
Tennyson, Alfred, Lord, 40, 144, 145
Terence, 36
Thayer, C. G., 118
Theatres: Aldwych, 7; Blackfriars, 109, 112; Fortune, 75; Hope, ix, 12, 81, 86, 91; National Theatre, 7; Stratford Festival Theatre, 7
Theocritus, 28
Thoreau, H. D., 159
Thucydides: *Peloponnesian War*, 154

Trimpi, J. W., 129, 131, 132
Tudor, Owen, 38
Two Noble Kinsmen, The (by Shakespeare and Fletcher), 73
Tyrtaeus, 28

Vaughan, Henry, 39
Vere, Sir Horace, 156
Villiers, George, Duke of Buckingham, 67, 68
Virgil, 28, 35

Waith, Eugene M., xiii, 80
Walker, R. S., 137, 138, 147
Wasp, The, xv, 57-79
Webbe, William, 128
Webster, John, 8
Weiss, Peter, 156
Welsford, Enid, 94
Welsh Embassador, The (by Dekker), 73
Whetstone, George: *Mirror for Magistrates of Cyties*, 87

Whitgift, John, Archbishop of Canterbury, 5
Wickham, Glynne: *Early English Stages*, 114
Willson, D. Harris, 86
Wilson, Edmund, 6, 90
Wilson, F. P., 20
Wilson, John Dover, 22, 44, 47, 49, 51, 52
Winters, Ivor, 150
Winwood, Ralph, 85
Wither, George, 123
Woodstock (Thomas of Woodstock), 64, 66
Wordsworth, William, 40, 139; *The Prelude*, 99-100
Wren, Robert M., 107
Wyatt, Sir Thomas, 161

Yeats, William Butler, 10, 161

Zitner, S. P., xiii